STUDY GUIDE AND PROBLEMS

to accompany

Lipsey, Sparks, and Steiner

ECONOMICS, Second Edition

Study Guide and Problems
to accompany

Lipsey, Sparks, and Steiner

Economics

Second Edition

Douglas A. L. Auld
University of Guelph

E. Kenneth Grant
University of Guelph

Dascomb R. Forbush
Clarkson College of Technology

Dorothy F. Forbush

HARPER & ROW, PUBLISHERS
New York, Hagerstown, San Francisco, London

Study Guide and Problems to accompany Lipsey, Sparks, and Steiner, ECONOMICS,
Second Edition

Copyright © 1973, 1976 by Harper & Row, Publishers, Inc.

Standard Book Number: 06-044052-X

Contents

To the Student   ix

1   The Relevance of Economics   1
      Problem: Expenditure for the Environment   5

2   Economics as a Social Science   7
      Problem: The Normative Versus the Positive   9

3   The Methods of Economics   11
      Problem 1: Scattered Income and Time Series Plots   15
      Problem 2: The Spending Versus the Income Plot   16

4   An Overview of the Economy   18

5   Demand, Supply, and Price   21
      Problem 1: The Changing Appetites of Canadians   25
      Problem: Effects of Imported Wine on Canadian Sales   27
      Problem 3: Arabs Raise Prices   27

6   Elasticity of Demand and Supply   28
      Problem 1: Raising the Rates on Water   34
      Problem 2: Raising the University Tuition Rates   34

7   Price Controls and the Agricultural Problem   35
      Problem 1: Canadian Wheat Supplies   40
      Problem 2: The Federal Beef Subsidy   41
      Problem 3: The Fluid Milk Subsidy

8   Household Consumption Behavior   43
      Problem 1: Changes in Family Consumption Patterns   49
      Problem 2: The Switch to Bread   49

9   Measuring Demand   51
      Problem: Identifying a Demand Relationship Between Sales and
             Advertising   54

10   The Firm, Production, and Cost   56
      Problem 1: Diamond's for Rent   60
      Problem 2: Stocks and Bonds   61

11   Cost and Supply in the Short Run   63
      Problem: The Rising Cost of Driving an Automobile   70

12   Cost and Supply in the Long Run   71

13   The Very Long Run: Progress and Pollution   78
         Problem 1: The Economics of Pollution   83
         Problem 2: The Noisy Factory   85

14   Pricing in Competitive Markets   86
         Problem: Competition in World Markets   91

15   Pricing in Monopoly Markets   92
         Problem: The Northern Doctor   97

16   Industrial Organization and Theories of Imperfect Competition   99
         Problem 1: Setting the Price of Fuel Oil   104
         Problem 2: Cooperation in the Pulp and Paper Industry?   105

17   Price Theory in Action   106
         Problem: Why Prices Fall   109

18   Monopoly Versus Competition: Implications About Performance and Policy   110
         Problem 1: The Cost of a Free Press   113
         Problem 2: Evidence Before the Restrictive Trade Practices Commission   114

19   Who Runs the Firm and for What Ends?   118
         Problem: The Nonrefillable Container   121

20   The Distribution of National Income   123
         Problem: Lorenz Curves and Income Distributions   129

21   Labor Unions, Collective Bargaining, and the Determination of Wages   131
         Problem: Two Cases on Minimum Wages   135

22   Interest and the Return on Capital   137
         Problem: Cash Bonuses on Canada Savings Bonds (CSB)   143

23   Inequality, Mobility, and Poverty
         Problem 1: The Trend of Distributive Shares in Canada   146
         Problem 2: The Incidence of Poverty According to Occupations in Canada   148

24   The Price System: Market Success and Market Failure   149

25   Public Finance and Public Expenditure: Tools of Microeconomic Policy   152
         Problem: The Property Tax in Ontario   157

26   National Income   158
         Problem: National Income Accounting: Expenditure or Income Approach?   163

27   What Determines National Income?   164
         Problem: The Determination of Equilibrium Income   169

28   Changes in National Income   173
         Problem: Multipliers and Withdrawals   178

29   More on Consumption   180
         Problem: Regional Consumption Functions   183

30   Fluctuations in National Income: Business Cycles and Investment   185
         Problem: Potential Versus Actual GNP   190

31 Theories and Tools of Fiscal Policy   192
        Problem: The Full-Employment Budget Surplus and Canadian Fiscal Policy   197

32 Fiscal Policy in Action   199
        Problem 1: Was the 1965 Tax Cut Inflationary?   101
        Problem 2: A Turning Point in Fiscal Policy   202

33 The Nature and History of Money   203
        Problem: Olympic Coins   206

34 The Importance of Money   207
        Problem: Canada's Income Velocity of Money   211

35 The Banking System and Money Supply   213
        Problem: Pennies from Heaven   218

36 Monetary Policy   220
        Problem: The Effectiveness of Monetary Policy   225

37 Exchange Rates   228
        Problem: Mr. Coyne and the Exchange Rate   234

38 The Gains from Trade   236
        Problem: Breaking Through the Production-Possibilities Frontier
                with Trade   239

39 Tariffs   243
        Problem: Dumping and Requests for Additional Excise Taxes   246

40 International Economic Experience   247
        Problem: Recycling OPEC Dollars   251

41 Stabilization Policy: Tools and Objectives   253
        Problem: Inflation and the Nominal Rate of Interst   255

42 Conflicts of Policy in Developed Countries   258
        Problem 1: Canadian Productivity and Wages   265
        Problem 2: Policies for Price Stability   265

43 Growth in Developed Economies   267
        Problem: POT Equals Pollution   270

44 Growth and the Underdeveloped Economies   272
        Problem: Production Possibilities, Efficiency, and Growth   276

45 Comparative Economic Systems   278
        Problem: Comparison of the United States and the Soviet Union   282

Answers to Multiple-Choice Questions and Exercises   283

To the Student

This book is intended to do two things: to help you study and review independently the basic material in Lipsey, Sparks, and Steiner, *Economics*, Second Edition, and second, to deepen and extend your understanding of economic analysis through the use of problems, many of which use the case approach. These functions complement the approach to economics used in the text, which stresses the need for testing hypotheses against empirical data. You will find the checklists, review questions, and self-testing devices useful in your studying. We hope that you will be challenged and intrigued by such problems as "Sale of Imported Wines," "Positive Thinking About a Negative Income Tax," and "Was the 1965 Tax Cut Inflationary?" If you are discouraged at times by graphical analysis and numerical relationships, you should recognize that the graphs are useful visual aids to understanding economic relationships and that quantitative measurement is essential for testing economic theories.

Each chapter in the *Study Guide and Problems* corresponds to a chapter in the text and is divided into four basic sections. The checklist of terms in each chapter is a reminder of the important terms used in the text. You should learn definitions of terms not by memorizing them but by understanding them through reviewing their meaning in the context of the textbook itself.

The second section of each chapter, the review questions, should not be tackled prematurely. You should not use the review questions as a short cut or bypass to learning from the text; if you have to take frequent looks at the answers supplied, you are not ready. The degree of ease with which you travel through this section will indicate to you how well you have comprehended the contents of the chapter. These questions are of two types—choosing the correct answer from among two or three supplied, and filling in blanks. In general, the questions follow a train of reasoning designed to clarify as well as to review the material.

Specific details and facts not covered in the review questions may show up in the section of multiple-choice questions, along with a rephrasing of material already touched upon. When you answer these questions, avoid the temptation to leap at the first answer that seems plausible. For each question there is one best answer, and you should you should be able to explain why any other answer is not so satisfactory as the one that you have chosen.

Probably the greatest reinforcement to learning this subject is to be found in the exercises, in which you are usually asked to demonstrate numerically or graphically the sense of what has been expressed verbally.

One or more problems conclude each chapter. Usually in case form, they are intended to enhance your understanding of economic analysis by providing empirical data and illustrations of economic behavior. If the problem is to serve as a basis for class discussion, you will find space beneath the questions to jot major points that you might make in class. You can follow this same procedure for an independent assignment on which you might be tested.

Do not be discouraged if you have difficulties with certain problems. Some are quite challenging for a beginning economics student, and full understanding of the points involved is expected only after a subsequent class discussion or lecture; make your questions on them as explicit as possible. The answers to the problems at the end of the

Study Guide are in no way exhaustive. What we have tried to do is to highlight the main issues surrounding the problem.

Acknowledgements

We would like to express our gratitude to our colleagues at the University of Guelph who assisted with the preparation of the Second Edition through their comments and criticisms on the First Edition.

STUDY GUIDE AND PROBLEMS

to accompany

Lipsey, Sparks, and Steiner

ECONOMICS, Second Edition

Chapter One
The Relevance
of Economics

CHECKLIST | Make certain that you understand the following concepts: factors of production; production; consumption; scarcity; opportunity cost; production-possibility boundary; resource allocation.

REVIEW QUESTIONS

1. The central problem of economics is that resources are _____ *scarce* _____ but human wants seem to be _____ *unlimited* _____ .

2. It is therefore (possible/impossible) to satisfy all wants, and, when faced with several alternative wants to fill or commodities to produce, we have to make a _____ *choice* _____ .

3. If one alternative is chosen, another must be sacrificed; this sacrifice is called the _____ *opportunity cost* _____ of the alternative chosen.

4. The process of assigning scarce resources to the production of commodities is called _____ *resource allocation* _____ .

5. Scarcity, opportunity cost and the necessity for choice are illustrated in a diagram called a _____ *production-possibility boundary* _____ .

6. On this graph, the *boundary* line shows _____ *attainable combination of goods at full employment* _____ .

7. On the two axes of the production-possibility diagram, we put _____ *quantity of good A and quantity of good B* _____ .

8. On this graph, the rate at which the commodity on one axis is sacrificed to obtain more of the other is shown by _____ *the slope* _____ .

9. If an economy is considered to be operating at a position *inside* the boundary, it indicates one or both of two situations: a. _____ *unemployment* _____ ;
   b. _____ *bad distribution* _____ .

1

10. The only way an economy can attain a production point *outside* of the boundary is
_____ *unlimited resources* _____ *growth of economic capacity* ___.

11. That part of economics dealing with resource allocation and with the question of what, how much of, and how commodities are produced is called ___ *micro* ___.

12. A policy of noninterference by government in the economy is often called a policy of _____ *free market* _____. *laissez-faire*

13. When the government intervenes with an economic policy measure, the economist should ask what the specific _____ *goal* _____ of the measure is.

_____

    If you have not answered all questions correctly, review the text in order to be sure that you have all of the important concepts clearly in mind before going on to the next chapter.

1. scarce; unlimited 2. impossible; choice 3. opportunity cost 4. resource allocation 5. production-possibility diagram 6. attainable combinations of goods at full employment 7. amounts of two alternate or competing kinds of goods 8. the slope of the boundary line 9. unemployment; inefficiency in the use of resources 10. growth of economic capacity 11. microeconomics 12. laissez-faire 13. objective or goal

MULTIPLE-CHOICE QUESTIONS

1. The fundamental problem of economics is, in short,
   (a) too many poor people
   (b) finding jobs for all
   (c) the scarcity of resources relative to wants
   (d) constantly rising prices

2. Scarcity is a problem that
   (a) proper use of resources could eliminate
   (b) will probably exist as long as man finds new wants to be satisfied
   (c) the twentieth century has solved
   (d) is confined to poor countries

3. Drawing a production-possibility boundary for swords and plowshares will help us to
   (a) estimate how much it is necessary to spend on defense (swords)
   (b) estimate the amount of unemployment that is likely to result from a given federal expenditure on housing (plowshares)
   (c) illustrate the cost of defense (swords) in terms of the expenditure on nondefense commodities (plowshares) that will have to be forgone
   (d) show the relative desires of the public for plowshares and guns

4. Opportunity cost
   (a) is measured by how much of one commodity you have to forgo in order to get some stated amount of another commodity
   (b) measures how many different opportunities you have to spend your money
   (c) measures opportunities in terms of their relative prices
   (d) is the same as money cost

5. If tuition plus other costs of going to college come to $2,500 per year, and you could have earned $4,000 per year working instead, the *opportunity cost* of your college year is
   (a) $2,500
   (b) $4,000
   (c) $6,500
   (d) $1,500

6. If a commodity can be produced without sacrificing the production of anything else,
   (a) its opportunity cost is zero
   (b) the economy is on its production-possibility boundary
   (c) the opportunity-cost concept is irrelevant and meaningless
   (d) its opportunity cost is infinite
   (e) its opportunity cost equals its money cost

7. Points to the left of the current production-possibility boundary
   (a) are currently unobtainable and are expected to remain so
   (b) will be obtainable if there is economic growth
   (c) will result if some factors of production are unemployed or used inefficiently
   (d) have lower opportunity costs

8. A country's production-possibility boundary shows
   (a) what percentage of its resources is currently unemployed
   (b) what choices in production and consumption are currently open to it
   (c) what it is actually producing
   (d) the available methods of production

9. A shift outward in the production-possibility boundary
   (a) would result if more of one product and less of another were chosen
   (b) could reflect higher prices for goods
   (c) could reflect increased unemployment
   (d) could result from the increased productivity of resources

10. The question of what goods and services are produced, and how much of them, is covered by the general term
   (a) resource allocation
   (b) macroeconomics
   (c) consumption
   (d) scarcity

11. The causes of general unemployment and inflation are topics studied in
   (a) resource allocation
   (b) macroeconomics
   (c) opportunity costs
   (d) production possibilities

12. Even government policy measures have "opportunity costs," which means
   (a) higher taxes will be necessary
   (b) moving toward one goal may require moving away from another goal
   (c) government action is usually inefficient
   (d) government action provides new opportunities

EXERCISES

1. Chapter 1 gives a six-way classification of economic problems. List them here in the order presented, numbering them from 1 to 6. Then, after each of the topics listed below, place the appropriate number indicating in which classification it belongs.
   (1) _____
   (2) _____
   (3) _____
   (4) _____
   _____
   (5) _____
   _____
   (6) _____
   _____

4   Chapter 1

(a) A blight hits the corn crop; harvest is 15 percent below previous year. ( )
(b) Farmers are seeking a different kind of corn seed to plant in order to avoid blight, but it is more expensive. ( )
(c) Unemployment rose in most of the nation in 1972. ( )
(d) Statistics indicate that the distribution of income has become somewhat less unequal in recent years in Canada. ( )
(e) The standard of living in Canada, measured by real GNP per capita, has risen steadily over the last century. ( )
(f) The cost of living rose at about 4 percent per year during the latter part of the 1960s. ( )
(g) Neither the government nor private business was willing in the mid-1950s to go ahead with building the Avro Arrow jet fighter. ( )
(h) Whether our future power needs will be met by nuclear energy or by fossil-fuel plants depends not only on technology but also on the relative availability of uranium and petroleum. ( )

2. The following data show what combinations of corn and beef can be produced annually from a given piece of land.

Corn (bushels)	Beef (pounds)
10,000	0
8,000	500
6,000	1,000
4,000	1,300
2,000	1,400
0	1,500

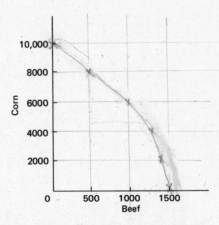

(a) On the graph above, draw the production-possibility boundary for this piece of land.
(b) Can this acreage produce 5,000 bushels of corn and 500 pounds of beef?

(c) Can this acreage produce 8,000 bushels of corn and 900 pounds of beef?

(d) What is the opportunity cost of expanding beef production from 500 to 1,200 pounds per annum?

(e) What would the production of 5,000 bushels of corn and 500 pounds of beef suggest about the use of this acreage?

(f) What would be required for this community to go beyond the production-possibility boundary?

PROBLEM

EXPENDITURE FOR THE ENVIRONMENT

In spite of the widespread feeling that pollution abatement is a priority goal for Canadian society, there are those who argue against spending vast sums of money on improving the quality of the environment. It has been estimated by the federal Department of the Environment that roughly one and one-half billion dollars per annum will have to be spent in Canada to achieve a significant reduction in pollution by 1980.

Those arguing against such expenditure claim that if the government spends the money, other "important" goals such as health and education programs will have to be reduced if taxes are not to rise too high.

Questions

1. What is the basic concept referred to by the above statement?

2. How is the cost of pollution abatement being measured?

3. Label the production-possibility curve below for the above argument and indicate the move that more pollution abatement would imply.

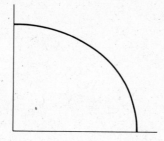

   4. If taxes were increased to pay for pollution abatement, there would be less personal income for expenditure on automobiles, vacations, and other private goods. Label the production-possibility curve below to show this, and indicate the move that more pollution abatement would imply.

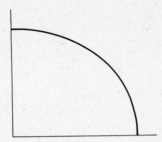

   5. Some people argue that by imposing pollution control on firms, the price of products produced by these firms will rise and less will be purchased, resulting in lower production and unemployment. What is the fallacy in this argument?

Chapter Two
Economics as
a Social Science

CHECKLIST	Make certain that you understand the following concepts: positive statements; normative statements; scientific method; a priori; economic theory; hypothesis.

REVIEW QUESTIONS

1. After each phrase below, write *P* or *N* to indicate whether a positive or normative statement is being described.
   (a) a statement of fact that is actually wrong   _P_
   (b) a value judgment   _N_
   (c) a prediction that an event will happen   _P_
   (d) a statement about what the author thinks *ought* to be   _N_
   (e) a statement that can be tested by evidence   _P_

2. The scientific method involves testing the factual accuracy of (positive/normative) statements.

3. Even though individuals singly may take odd and unlikely actions, human behavior in general can be predicted, thanks to the "law" of __large numbers__.

4. An attempt to explain the process of a sequence of economic events is called a hypothesis or a ___theory___.

5. A theory that turns out to explain cause and effect well and that is shown by events to fit the observed facts will indicate to us the consequences of a particular event or policy measure, and thus be useful for the purpose of ___prediction___.

6. In order to theorize in economics, it is usually necessary to simplify complex reality by setting certain conditions, or ___assumption___.

7. A problem in testing economic theories that is not the case with laboratory sciences is that the environment for the experiments cannot be ___controlled___.

If you have not answered all questions correctly, review the text in order to be sure that you have all of the important concepts clearly in mind before going on to the next chapter.

1. *P; N; P; N; P* 2. positive 3. large numbers 4. theory 5. prediction 6. assumptions 7. controlled

MULTIPLE-CHOICE QUESTIONS

1. Which of the following statements is most appropriate for economic theories?
   (a) The most reliable test of a theory is the realism of its assumptions.
   (b) The best kind of theory is worded so that it can pass any test to which it could be put.
   (c) The most important thing about the scientific approach is that it uses mathematics heavily.
   (d) We expect our theories to hold only with some margin of error.

2. Positive statements concern what is; normative statements concern
   (a) what was
   (b) what is the normal situation
   (c) what will be
   (d) what ought to be

3. A natural science that has much the same problem as economics in testing theories is
   (a) animal psychology
   (b) astronomy
   (c) microbiology
   (d) organic chemistry

4. We do not want value judgments incorporated in scientific theories because
   (a) they are too complex
   (b) they are too unrealistic because they are generally idealistic
   (c) they cannot be tested by an appeal to evidence
   (d) they cannot be expressed mathematically

5. The significance of the normal curve of error for social scientists is that
   (a) it shows that physical scientists make mistakes too
   (b) it shows that experimentation is not necessary
   (c) it shows how futile it is to bother measuring accurately
   (d) it aids in making predictions from a large number of observations

6. A theory may contain all but one of the following:
   (a) an unorganized collection of facts about the real world
   (b) a set of definitions of the terms used
   (c) a set of assumptions defining the conditions under which the theory will be operative
   (d) one or more hypotheses about how the world behaves
   (e) implications about empirical behavior that are deduced from the assumptions

7. The term "empirically testable" means that a theory
   (a) is a priori obvious and therefore needs no testing
   (b) is capable of being shown to be a probable explanation of a given event
   (c) is proven to be true
   (d) is not testable, really

EXERCISE

The following information is made available to you.

Annual Change in Housing Starts in Province X	Annual Change in the Average Mortgage Rate
-10,000	+1.2%
-10,000	+1.5%
+8,000	-1.0%
-5,000	+0.5%
+13,000	-2.0%
+10,000	-1.1%

(a) What can you say about the relationship, in general, between housing starts and the mortgage interest rate?

(b) Would these data enable you to test the hypothesis that, "For every 1 percent change in the mortgage interest rate there is always an opposite change of 10,000 in building starts"?

PROBLEM

THE NORMATIVE VERSUS THE POSITIVE

1. Classify each of the statements below as positive (P) or normative (N).

(a) "That environmental pollution is the major cause of elevated levels of mercury in fish is shown by the 100-fold increase in mercury in certain species of fish in Lake St. Clair between 1935 and 1970." (*Environment*, May 1971) _____

(b) "While government must assume a major role in economic management, the bulk of productive and distributive activity should be carried on by the private enterprise units. . . ." (*Growth, Employment and Price Stability*, Report of the Standing Senate Committee on National Finance, Information Canada, 1971) _____

(c) "In the long-term interests of the economy as a whole, it is essential for us to continue our efforts to maintain reasonable price stability in Canada." (HON. J. Turner, Minister of Finance, *House of Commons Debates*, Vol. 116, No. 47, May 8, 1972)

_____

(d) "During the high growth period of the 1960's capital imports amounted to a relatively low percentage of GNP." (Economic Council of Canada, *Performance and Potential: mid 1950's to mid 1970's*, Information Canada, 1970, p. 35) _____

(e) "One of the best-established facts about the American economy is the long-run tendency for prices on the average to rise at about the same rate as unit labor costs on the average." (Council of Economic Advisers, Inflation Alert, December 1, 1970)

_____ (f) "300,000,000 Americans Would Be Wrong" (Title of an article advocating voluntary population limitation, by David E. Lilienthal, *New York Times Sunday Magazine*, January 6, 1966) _____

2. (a) Indicate how the positive statements above might be tested.

(b) What value judgments and assumptions of fact might have led to each normative statement?

Chapter Three
The Methods
of Economics

REVIEW QUESTIONS

1. The expression $Q = f(P)$ may be read that quantity is a _____*function*_____ of price. Q and P in this expression are ___*variable*_____.

2. The amount of income earned per year is a (stock/flow) because it has a _____ ____*flow*_____ dimension. The size of one's bank account is a ___*time*_____.

3. Economic theories usually treat weather (measured by temperature, rainfall, etc.) as an (endogenous/exogenous) variable because the theory (does/does not) attempt to explain weather. Such a variable may be helpful in economic theory to explain the price of wheat, an _____ variable.

4. The hypothesis that the amount of skis sold (Y) depends upon their price (P) and the amount of snow (X) can be expressed _____. In such a theory, X is an _____ variable.

5. To say that the amount borrowed is a decreasing function of the interest rate paid means that borrowing varies (directly/inversely) with the interest rate.

6. All theories and measurements (are/are not) subject to error. In functional notation, this can be shown by adding an _____ term.

7. In deducing the implications of a theory, three methods—verbal, geometrical, and _____—can be used.

8. The purpose of statistical analysis is to _____ theories and to _____ quantitative relations between economic variables.

9. In laboratory sciences, experiments (can/cannot) be controlled; in economics, factors (can/cannot) actually be isolated one at a time.

10. If two related economic variables such as beef consumption and income are plotted on a scatter diagram, the points "scatter" rather than form a line for primarily two reasons: _____ and _____.

11. Usually, a hypothesis (can/cannot) be proved absolutely wrong or right. But the probability that it is wrong or right (can/cannot) be estimated, if available data meet certain sampling criteria.

    If you have not answered all questions correctly, review the text in order to be sure that you have all of the important concepts clearly in mind before going on to the next chapter.

1. function; variables 2. flow; time; stock 3. exogenous; does not; endogenous 4. $Y = f(P,X)$; exogenous 5. inversely 6. are; error 7. mathematical 8. test; measure 9. can; cannot 10. errors of observation; omitted causal variables 11. cannot; can

---

MULTIPLE-CHOICE QUESTIONS

1. If the demand for snowmobiles is higher, the lower the average temperature,
   (a) the demand for snowmobiles is an increasing function of the average temperature
   (b) the demand for snowmobiles is a decreasing function of the average temperature
   (c) the demand for snowmobiles varies directly with the average temperature
   (d) both (a) and (c) are correct

2. We must remember that for every real-world economic function there is
   (a) an exact equation
   (b) demand and supply
   (c) an error term, whether explicit or implicit
   (d) a direct relationship between the variables

3. Which of the following equations is consistent with the hypothesis that beef consumption (Q) is an increasing function of income (Y), a decreasing function of price (P), and an increasing function of the price of pork (K)?
   (a) $Q = 25YP/K$
   (b) $Q = 25 - 1.85P + .08Y + .6K$
   (c) $Q = 25 + .08Y + 1.85P + .6K$
   (d) $Q = 25 - .6K - 1.85P + .08Y$

4. Economists use mathematics because
   (a) mathematics is the only good economic tool
   (b) mathematics puts variables in relationships of cause and effect
   (c) mathematics can definitely prove hypotheses for the economist
   (d) mathematics is a relatively short and clear language for expressing complicated relationships

5. As part of a study of campus opinion concerning careers in industry, which sampling method will probably yield the best results?
   (a) interviewing students on the steps of the business administration building
   (b) randomly drawing a sample of students' names from the dormitory residence lists
   (c) throwing darts blindfolded at a complete list of student numbers or names
   (d) obtaining a comprehensive list of officers of student organizations

6. The relationship between two variables on a scatter diagram
   (a) may be obscured by the movement of another variable
   (b) cannot be significant because of errors of observation
   (c) will show a wavelike pattern if the variables are related to time
   (d) will usually be a straight line

7. A single observation will not refute a hypothesis because
   (a) our theory may be wrong
   (b) errors of observation are possible
   (c) economic theories are deterministic
   (d) the observation may not have come from a random sample

8. Many economic data are similar to those relating high death rates to prolonged
   cigarette smoking in the following respect(s):
   (a) they do not depend primarily on controlled experiments in which all causes ex-
       cept one are held constant during each individual experiment
   (b) more than two variables are likely to be involved
   (c) they represent observations taken over a period of time
   (d) all of the above

9. If the consumer price index rises from 104 to 106, the percentage increase is
   (a) exactly 2
   (b) sufficiently low to refute the hypothesis of galloping inflation
   (c) slightly less than 2
   (d) sufficient to confirm the hypothesis of creeping inflation

10. A substantial rise in the consumer price index means
    (a) that it is more expensive for everyone to live
    (b) that a weighted average of prices for a particular set of goods and services
        has risen
    (c) very little; not really significant errors are large
    (d) that all prices of consumer goods and services are necessarily higher

11. A rising straight line on a semilog scale between a variable and time indicates
    (a) growth by a constant percentage rate
    (b) growth by the same numerical amount each year
    (c) no change in the value of the variable
    (d) growth by a constant percentage rate but a decreasing absolute rate

EXERCISES

1. On the graph at the top of the next page, plot the following equation, assuming
   that X and Y are positive numbers.

$$X = 9 + 1.5Y$$

(a) What is the slope of this line?

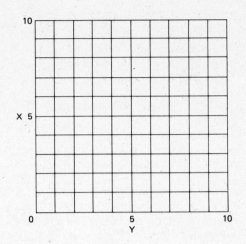

(b) Why is Y the exogenous variable?

2. Given the following relation between saving (S) and income (Y), $S = -\$100 + .10Y$, what is the amount of S for each of the indicated values of Y? Plot S on the graph.

Y	S
0	
500	
1,000	
1,500	
2,000	

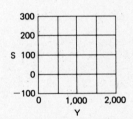

3. Put the following statements in the form of equations (use symbols as suggested).
   (a) The amount of saving (S) out of income (Y) averages 7 percent.
   (b) A certain household will spend $1,000 on consumption ($C$) at zero income ($Y$), plus 95 percent of any income it receives.
   (c) Cost per unit (c) equals total cost (C) divided by output (Q).
   (d) Total revenue (R) equals price (P) times quantity sold (Q).
   (e) Profit (Π) is the difference between total revenue (R) and total cost (C).

4. Indicate whether you would expect the pairs of variables below to vary directly or inversely with each other (other things being equal).
   (a) savings, income   _____
   (b) price, quantity demanded   _____
   (c) temperature, use of air conditioners   _____
   (d) sales of hot dogs, sales of hot dog rolls   _____
   (e) total income, income tax receipts of government _____

5. Regardless of the number of visitors to a recreation park, there are certain fixed expenses of $500 that must be met for gate attendants, light, and basic security. The cost of cleanup, however, does depend on the number of visitors and is equal to $0.10 per visitor.

   (a) If TC is the total cost of running the park and N is the number of visitors, write the equation for the total cost of the park operation.

(b) Graph the two different cost relationships (the one for the fixed costs and the one for the cleanup costs) on the graph below.

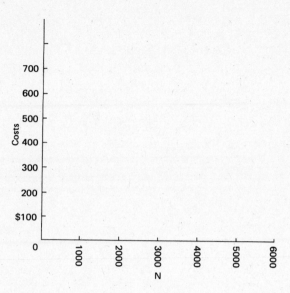

PROBLEMS

1. *SCATTERED INCOME AND TIME SERIES PLOTS*

    Time series data similar to those in the text on real personal disposable income and real consumer expenditure (in per capita terms) are shown below.

Year	*C* Consumption Expenditure (constant dollars)	Y_d Disposable Income (constant dollars)
1950	1142	1217
1951	1127	1252
1952	1167	1300
1953	1216	1253
1954	1224	1300
1955	1294	1366
1956	1358	1450
1957	1364	1450
1958	1374	1470
1959	1418	1485
1960	1435	1500
1961	1411	1475
1962	1458	1560
1963	1501	1598
1964	1561	1635
1965	1627	1719
1966	1679	1791
1967	1728	1834
1968	1786	1883
1969	1841	1932

Questions

1. Plot this information on a scatter diagram.

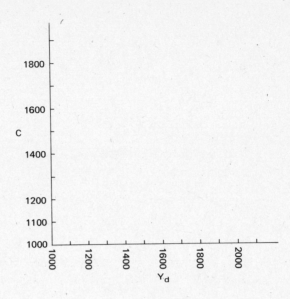

2. Draw a line through these observations to obtain some idea of the relationship between consumption spending and disposable income.

3. What (roughly) is the slope of the line you have drawn?

4. How good does the "fit" of this relationship seem to be?

5. If you had set out, as a hypothesis, that $C = f(Y_d)$, would you accept or reject your hypothesis? Why?

2.   THE SPENDING VERSUS THE INCOME PLOT

As a contrast to the time series data on consumption and disposable income in the previous question, the table below gives cross-sectional data on family disposable income in a given year—1969—in Canada. These data are obtained by Statistics Canada through a sample survey of Canadian families.

Family Disposable Income	Family Spending Goods and Services, and Taxes
$ 1,834	$ 2,370
3,283	3,615
4,133	4,475
4,940	5,047
5,794	5,852
6,586	6,450
7,389	7,196
8,182	7,613
8,966	8,352
9,813	8,976
11,147	9,571
16,237	12,801

Questions

1. Plot these data on a scatter diagram.

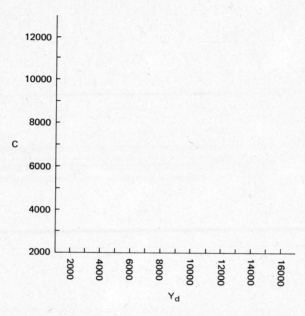

2. Can the relationship between the two variables be explained by a straight (linear) or curved (nonlinear) line drawn through the points on the scatter diagram?

3. If the latter, what is happening to the slope of the line as disposable income and consumption increase?

4. Does the evidence from the data above cause you to reject or to accept the hypothesis that family consumer spending is a function of disposable income?

Chapter Four
An Overview
of the Economy

CHECKLIST | Make certain that you understand the following concepts: market mechanisms; price system; free-market economy; command economy; mixed economy; circular flow of income; withdrawals from the circular flow; injections to the circular flow; household; firm; central authority; factor market; product market.

REVIEW QUESTIONS

1. Three basic types of economic decision makers are ___firm households___, ___household firms___ and ___central authorities public agency___. The initial assumption is that households seek to maximize ___satisfaction___, that firms seek to maximize ___profits___, and that central authorities have (one/more than one) objective.

2. Commodities for the use of households are sold in ___product___ markets. The services of households are sold in ___factor___ markets.

3. A change in the willingness of the consumer to purchase a particular product because of a change in something other than price is called a change in ___market mechanisms___.

4. When consumers' tastes were assumed to shift toward brussels sprouts and away from carrots, eventually a ___reallocation___ of resources took place through a sequence of events that included the following: a ___rise___ in the price of brussels sprouts; a ___fall___ in the price of carrots; the prospects of ___large___ profits in sprout production and ___low___ profits in carrot production; the movement of additional resources toward ___sprouts___ production and away from ___carrot___ production.

5. The events in question 4 (include/do not include) an increase in supply because an increase in supply of a product (is/is not) defined as resulting from an increase in price.

6. Prices are determined by both ___demand___ and ___supply___. A change in either the demand for or supply of a commodity will usually result in ___price___ changes, which act as ___signals___ for households and firms on how to alter their behavior.

7. The amount of money is a (flow/stock), and (is/is not) equal to flow of total income.

8. The fact that households do not spend all of their income and that firms may retain profits lead to _____ *withdraws* _____ from the circular flow.

9. When withdrawals from and injections into the circular flow are the same, we predict that income will be _____ *same* _____ .

    If you have not answered all questions correctly, review the text in order to be sure that you have all of the important concepts clearly in mind before going to to the next chapter.

1. households, firms, central authorities; satisfaction or utility, profits, more than one 2. product; factor 3. demand 4. reallocation (or shift); rise; fall; greater; smaller; sprouts, carrot 5. do not include; is not 6. demand; supply; price, signals or information 7. stock; is not 8. withdrawals 9. unchanged

---

MULTIPLE-CHOICE QUESTIONS

1. An increase in supply, as the term is used in this chapter, is
   (a) an increase in the efficiency of transporting commodities to market
   (b) an increased willingness of firms to produce a commodity for reasons other than its price
   (c) a glut, or surplus
   (d) an increase in the amount consumers want to buy

2. A change in consumers' preferences toward chicken and away from pork may be predicted to lead to
   (a) a rise in the price of chicken
   (b) a fall in the production of pork
   (c) a fall in the incomes of owners of land particularly well suited for raising pigs but not chickens
   (d) all of the above

3. A fall in the price of peas could result from
   (a) a shift in producers' preferences, with an increased willingness to grow string beans and a decreased willingness to grow peas
   (b) decreases in the amount of land available for growing vegetables through the expansion of suburbs
   (c) a shift in consumers' preferences, with an increased willingness to eat string beans and a decreased willingness to eat peas
   (d) an unusually small crop of peas because of adverse weather conditions

4. The circular flow of real goods and services
   (a) refers to actual dollars exchanged
   (b) refers only to the products sold by firms
   (c) moves in the same directions as monetary flows
   (d) refers to outputs of firms and to the factor services of households

5. An example of an injection into the circular flow of income is
   (a) the purchase of General Motors stock by a household
   (b) government expenditure on the Trans-Canada Highway
   (c) increased purchases of hypodermic needles
   (d) the decision of a liberated wife to seek a job

EXERCISES

1. Given the circular flow diagram below, indicate where the following should be placed.
   (a) family expenditure on clothing and food = $25 M
   (b) man-hours worked at textile plants and food processors = 10,000 hours
   (c) production of yards of clothing = 5,000 pounds
   (d) production of food = 2,000 pounds
   (e) wages and salaries paid to employees in food and clothing = $40 M

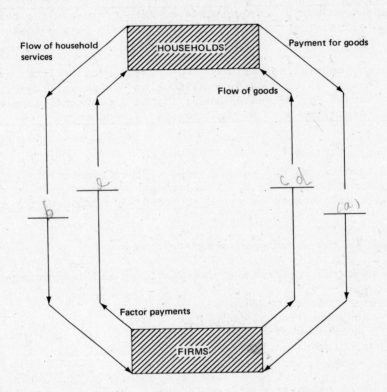

2. Indicate the initial effects on the price of beef, profits in the beef industry, and resources employed in the beef industry as a consequence of the following.

	Price	Profit	Employment of Resources
1. A steady decline in the price of pork and poultry	↓	↓	↓
2. Increased desire on the part of consumers for steak and roast beef	↑	↑	↑
3. A general decline in household income	↓	↓	↓
4. A substantial rise in the cost of feed for beef cattle	↑	↓	↓

Chapter Five
Demand, Supply,
and Price

<table>
<tr><td>CHECKLIST</td><td>Make certain that you understand the following concepts: demand; demand function; demand schedule; shift of demand curve; supply; supply function; supply schedule or curve; shift in supply schedule; movement along demand or supply schedule; inferior good; equilibrium price; shortage; surplus.</td></tr>
</table>

REVIEW QUESTIONS

1. The amount of a commodity that households wish to purchase at various prices is called the ____demand____ for the commodity.

2. The quantity demanded depends upon consumers' tastes and preferences, population size, ____household income____, the distribution of ____income____, the commodity's own price, and the ____price____ of many other commodities.

3. The demand curve is a representation of the functional relation between ____price____ and ____Q^D____. It differs from the demand function because values of the other determinants of demand are assumed to be ____constant____. This assumption is frequently described by the Latin term ____ceteris paribus____.

4. A shift in the demand curve may be caused by changes in any determinant of the demand function except the ____price____ of the commodity.

√5. When an increase in the price of another good causes an increase in the demand for a commodity, the other good is called a ____substitute____; if it causes a decrease, the other good is called a ____complement____.

6. A movement along a demand curve is the equivalent of a change in ____price____ and therefore in the quantity ____demanded____.

7. Neither the quantity demanded nor the quantity supplied is a stock but rather a ____flow____, and each is expressed as a quantity per ____year (time period)____.

8. The quantity supplied depends upon the goals of the ____profit firm____; the initial assumption is that the goal is to ____maximize____ profits.

9. The quantity supplied also depends on the state of _____technology_____, the price of the commodity, the prices of all other _____goods_____, and the prices of the factors of _____production_____.

10. The supply schedule shows the _____quantity_____ that will be supplied at every _____price_____.

_____

If you have not answered all questions correctly, review the text in order to be sure that you have all of the important concepts clearly in mind before going on to the next chapter.

1. demand 2. income; income; prices 3. price, quantity; constant; *ceteris paribus*
4. price 5. substitute; complement 6. price; demanded 7. flow; time period 8. firm; maximize 9. technology; commodities; production 10. quantity; price
_____

MULTIPLE-CHOICE QUESTIONS

1. An increase in supply, as the term is used in this chapter, is
   (a) an increased willingness of firms to produce a commodity for reasons other than its price
   (b) the creation of glut or surplus
   (c) an increase in the amount consumers want to buy
   (d) a description of the increased quantities supplied at higher prices

2. A decrease in income can be predicted to
   (a) invariably cause leftward shifts in demand curves
   (b) increase the quantity demanded of an "inferior good"
   (c) invariably cause rightward shifts in demand curves
   (d) decrease the quantity demanded of an "inferior good"

3. In Canada, an increasing proportion of economic activity is taking place
   (a) in agriculture and forestry
   (b) in mining and manufacturing
   (c) in wholesale and retail trade
   (d) in the production of other services

4. When we draw a market demand curve, we
   (a) ignore tastes and incomes and all other prices
   (b) assume that tastes, incomes, and all other prices do not matter
   (c) assume that tastes, incomes, and all other prices change in the same way prices change
   (d) assume that tastes, incomes, and all other prices stay constant

5. A leftward shift in the demand curve for Corn Flakes would be predicted from
   (a) an increase in the average number of breakfast eaters
   (b) a change in tastes away from hot cereals
   (c) a rise in the price of Corn Flakes
   (d) a fall in the price of Wheaties

6. Consumer tastes and preferences are
   (a) always treated as exogenous to the economic system
   (b) always treated as endogenous to the economic system
   (c) so unpredictable that demand analysis is virtually impossible
   (d) altered by such economic activities as advertising and demonstration effects

7. The supply curve of houses would probably shift to the left if
   (a) construction workers' wages increased
   (b) cheaper methods of prefabrication were developed
   (c) the demand for houses showed a marked increase
   (d) the population stopped growing

8. A rise in the price of washing-machine components would probably lead to
   (a) a fall in the demand for washing machines
   (b) a rise in the supply of washing machines
   (c) a leftward shift in the supply curve of washing machines
   (d) a rightward shift in the demand curve for washing machines

EXERCISES

1. The demand and supply schedules for good X are hypothesized to be as follows:

(1) Price per Unit	(2) Quantity Demanded (units per time period)	(3) Quantity Supplied (units per time period)	(4) Excess Demand (+) Excess Supply (−) (units per time period)
$1.00	1	25	—
.90	3	21	—
.80	5	19	—
.70	8	15	—
.60	12	12	0
.50	18	9	+
.40	26	6	+

(a) Using the grid below, label the axes and plot the demand and supply curves. Indicate the equilibrium level of price and quantity of X.

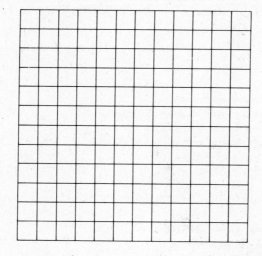

(b) Fill in column (4) for values of excess demand and excess supply. What is the value of excess demand (supply) at equilibrium?

(c) Indicate and explain the likely direction of change in the price of X if excess demand exists. Do the same for excess supply.

2. *The Hypotheses of Demand and Supply*
   Fill in the table below. Draw new curves on the graphs to aid you. Show the *initial* effects predicted by the hypotheses of the indicated events on the markets. For changes in demand and supply (meaning shifts in the curve), equilibrium price, and quantity, use + or - to show increase or decrease; for no change, use 0. If effect cannot be deduced from the information, use U.

Market	Event	D	S	P	Q
1. Canadian wine	Early frost destroys a large percentage of the grape crop in British Columbia.	0	-	+	-
2. Copper wire	The Bell Telephone Co. greatly increases orders for wire to satisfy transmission needs.	+	0	+	+
3. Pine antique furniture	"Antique hunting" becomes popular and Canadians attempt to furnish their homes with antique pine chairs and tables.	+	0	+	+
4. Auto tires	Incomes and population rise as synthetic rubber, cheaper than natural rubber, is invented.	+	+	-	U

Market	Event	D	S	P	Q

5. Cigarettes   A new law requires this notice on each park: "Warning: The Department of National Health and Welfare advises that danger to health increases with amount smoked."

6. Automobile fuel   Middle East oil producers restrict the total amount of crude oil going to North America.

PROBLEMS

1. *THE CHANGING APPETITES OF CANADIANS*

In this problem, you are asked to formulate hypotheses concerning the most important elements in the demand functions for various types of food that are consistent with the data given and that might be tested against further facts. The data here can be found in the *National Income and Expenditure Accounts* published by Statistics Canada.

Table 1 Food and Consumption Expenditures

	1950	1960	1970	1970 ÷ 1950
Total consumption expenditures (billions of dollars)	12.5	25.5	50.0	4.0
Total expenditures on food[a] (billions of dollars)	2.7	4.8	7.9	2.9
Food expenditures as a percentage of total consumption	21.6	18.8	15.8	

[a]Excluding alcoholic beverages

Table 2 Price Indexes, Population, and Income

	1950	1960	1970	1970 ÷ 1950
Consumer price index--food[a]	102.6	128.3	166.8	1.63
Consumer price index--all items except food[a]	101.0	128.6	166.2	1.65
Canadian population (millions)	13.7	17.9	21.4	1.56
Per capita disposable income (current dollars)	971.0	1486.0	2523.0	2.60
Per capita disposable income (1958 dollars)	946.0	1158.0	1518.0	1.60

[a]1949 = 100

Table 3   Per Capita Canadian Consumption and Average Retail Prices: Selected Foods[a]

	1950		1960		1970		1970 ÷ 1950	
	Q	P	Q	P	Q	P	Q	P
1. Beef (round steak)	50.5	78.6¢	69.2	89 ¢	84.0	$1.27	1.66	1.62
2. Pork (rib chops)	60.8	28.5¢	55.2	74 ¢	55.3	98.3¢	.91	3.45
3. Eggs (dozen)	19.7	56.5¢	23	52 ¢	21.8	54.5¢	1.11	.96
4. Butter	20.2	60.3¢	16.9	69.8¢	15.5	71.8¢	.77	1.19

[a]1, 2, and 4 are given in pounds.
Source: *Prices and Price Indices* and *Handbook of Agricultural Statistics*.

Questions

1. (a) From 1950 on, the percentage of disposable income spent on food has declined. This is reflected in the lower percentage of total consumption expenditures represented by food expenditures. What hypothesis might explain this?

(b) Suggest a modification of this hypothesis that would account for a larger percentage spent on food in 1950 than in the war years 1939-1945.

2. A simple hypothesis is that the consumption of a commodity will vary proportionally with the number of people. This would indicate that over time the per capita figures would be reasonably _____. This hypothesis would be confirmed, accepting 10 percent as a reasonable variation, only for two products: _____ and _____.

3. Dieticians among you will recognize that items 1 and 2 in Table 3 are major sources of protein, and 3 and 4, of fats. Formulate a general hypothesis incorporating the variables of income and price to explain relative consumption of protein and fats. Do the data above support the hypothesis? Explain.

2. *EFFECTS OF IMPORTED WINE*
    ON CANADIAN SALES

    The Liquor Control Board of Ontario stated in early 1975 that the prices of French wines in the United States would decline dramatically while less spectacular declines would occur in Canada.
    The reasons given for these expectations were:
    (i) the growing acceptance in the United States of California wines.
    (ii) the excellent grape crop in France in 1973 and 1974.

Question
    1. Using basic supply and demand analysis, explain how each of the above factors operates to reduce the expected price of French wines. (Use the simple supply and demand diagram.

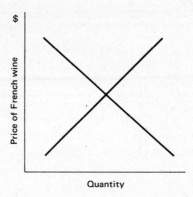

3. *ARABS RAISE PRICES*

    Suppose there were an open world market for crude oil and that the price of Middle East oil and Canadian oil in various parts of Canada were as follows, the differences reflecting transportation costs.

	Middle East	Canadian
Maritimes	$5.00/bbl	$6.50/bbl
Central	5.50/bbl	6.00/bbl
Western	6.00/bbl	5.00/bbl

The price of Middle East oil suddenly rises by 100 percent.

Questions
    1. Given that the supply for both sources in the short run is fixed, what will happen to the demand for Canadian oil? To the demand for Middle East oil?

    2. What will happen to the price of Canadian oil? To the price of Middle East oil?

Chapter Six
Elasticity of Demand and Supply

CHECKLIST	Make certain that you understand the following concepts: elasticity of demand; elastic demand schedule; inelastic demand schedule; income elasticity of demand; normal goods; inferior goods; cross-elasticity of demand. *Appendix:* arc elasticity; point elasticity.

REVIEW QUESTIONS

1. *Elasticity* of demand (or supply) measures the degree of response of quantity demanded (or supplied) to changes in ____price____ .

2. If for a fall in price, the quantity of a commodity demanded increases, elasticity of demand is greater than ____0____ .

3. If for a fall in price, the percentage increase in quantity demanded is greater than the percentage change in price, elasticity of demand is greater than ____1____ .

4. If, when the price of a good falls, the total revenues received by the industry rise, elasticity of demand is greater than ____1____ .

5. (a) The term "elastic demand" means one whose elasticity is ____0 > 1____ .
   (b) The term "inelastic demand" means one whose elasticity is ____1 < 0____ .
   (c) The term "unitary elasticity" of demand means one whose elasticity equals __1__ .

6. If elasticity is unitary, a fall in price will cause total revenue to ____remain____ ____unchanged____ .

7. If, when the price of a commodity is increased, total revenues also increase, *ceteris paribus*, elasticity of demand must be ____inelastic____ .

8. If there are few available substitutes for a good that is a necessity, elasticity of demand would probably be ____inelastic____ .

9. (a) If, as an individual seller in a market, you think you can sell all you can produce at the going market price, then for you the elasticity of demand seems ____infinity____ .
   (b) On the diagram this demand curve would appear ____horizontal____ .

10. (a) If buyers are totally impervious to price, and continue to buy the same quantity no matter what the price, elasticity of demand is ___*zero elasticity*___.
    (b) On the graph this demand curve would be ___*vertical*___.

11. *Income elasticity* measures the response of quantity demanded to ___*income*___.

12. If a rise of 10 percent in income is associated with a 5 percent increase in the sale of shoes, income elasticity is ___*positive 5%*___.

13. If a fall in the price of Y results in a decrease in the sale of X, the two goods appear to be (substitutes/complements) and the cross-elasticity would be (positive/negative).

14. If a small rise in price of a good results in a large increase in the amount supplied, we should say that the supply is ___*elastic*___.

Appendix

15. Of two parallel, downward-sloping demand curves, the more elastic one would be (further from/ closer to) the origin.

16. Given a straight-line downward-sloping demand curve, the elasticity of demand becomes greater as the price (rises/falls).

17. When price and quantity changes are small, we can use a simpler formula than that given for arc elasticity in Chapter 6, namely, ___$\frac{\Delta q}{\Delta p} \times \frac{p}{q}$___, where p and q are taken as the _____ rather than the average amounts.

18. The slope of a downward-sloping straight-line demand can be symbolized as:

    ___$\frac{\Delta p}{\Delta q}$___; that of a tangent to a point on a curve can be symbolized as: ___$\frac{dp}{dq}$___.

_____
    If you have not answered all questions correctly, review the text in order to be sure that you have all of the important concepts clearly in mind before going on to the next chapter.

1. price 2. zero 3. one 4. one 5. greater than one; between zero and one; one 6. remain unchanged 7. inelastic or less than one 8. inelastic or less than one 9. infinite; horizontal 10. zero; vertical 11. changes in income 12. 0.5 13. substitutes; positive 14. elastic 15. closer to 16. rises 17. $\frac{\Delta q}{\Delta p} \times \frac{p}{q}$; original 18. $\frac{\Delta p}{\Delta q}$, $\frac{dp}{dq}$
_____

MULTIPLE-CHOICE QUESTIONS

1. To say that the demand for a commodity is *elastic* means
   (a) that the demand curve slopes downward to the right
   (b) that more is sold at a lower price
   (c) that a rise in price will increase total revenue
   (d) that the change in quantity sold is proportionally greater than the change in price

2. When the demand is elastic,
   (a) a fall in price is more than offset by an increase in quantity sold, so that total revenue rises
   (b) the good is probably a necessity
   (c) a rise in price will increase total revenue, even though less is sold
   (d) buyers are not much influenced by prices of competing products

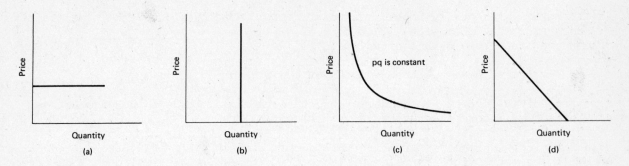

3. The demand curve with an elasticity of 0 is
   (a) a
   (b) b
   (c) c
   (d) d

4. The demand curve with an elasticity of 1 is
   (a) a
   (b) b
   (c) c
   (d) d

5. The demand curve with an elasticity varying from 0 to ∞ depending on price is
   (a) a
   (b) b
   (c) c
   (d) d

6. The demand curve with an elasticity of ∞ is
   (a) a
   (b) b
   (c) c
   (d) d

7. The demand for vegetables is probably more elastic than the demand for
   (a) food
   (b) carrots
   (c) spinach
   (d) Fords

8. A demand curve is completely inelastic if
   (a) a rise in price causes a fall in quantity demanded
   (b) a fall in price causes a rise in sellers' total receipts
   (c) the commodity in question is highly perishable, like fresh strawberries
   (d) a change in price does not change quantity demanded

9. If a small rise in the price of graduation dance tickets led to some decrease in total dollar sales,
   (a) demand was inelastic
   (b) demand was infinitely elastic
   (c) demand was elastic
   (d) the price rise caused a shift in demand for the tickets, so it is impossible to say

10. Which of the following would you expect to have the highest income elasticity:
    (a) spaghetti
    (b) bus rides
    (c) skis
    (d) baby carriages

11. Inferior commodities
    (a) have zero income elasticities of demand
    (b) have negative cross-elasticities of demand
    (c) have negative elasticities of supply
    (d) have negative income elasticities of demand

12. Margarine and butter probably have
    (a) the same income elasticities of demand
    (b) very low price elasticities of demand
    (c) negative cross-elasticities of demand with respect to each other
    (d) positive cross-elasticities of demand with respect to each other

13. If price elasticity of demand for a product is 0.5, this means that
    (a) a change in price changes demand by 50 percent
    (b) a 1 percent increase in quantity sold is associated with a 0.5 percent fall in price
    (c) a 1 percent increase in quantity sold is associated with a 2 percent fall in price
    (d) a 0.5 percent change in price will cause a 0.5 percent change in quantity sold

14. If, when incomes rise by 5 percent, the quantity sold of a commodity rises by 10 percent, income elasticity is
    (a) -2
    (b) 2
    (c) -½
    (d) ½

15. In a certain market, when the price of hotdogs rose from 76 cents per pound to 84 cents per pound, the quantity of hotdog buns sold went from 11,000 to 9,000. Indicated cross-elasticity of demand is
    (a) ½
    (b) -½
    (c) 2
    (d) -2

16. Price elasticity of demand for a commodity tends to be greater
    (a) the more of a necessity it is
    (b) the closer substitutes there are for it
    (c) the less important it is in our budget
    (d) the lower the price

EXERCISES

1. Fill out the following table:

	Price Elasticity	Change in Price	Change in Total Revenue (up, down, or none)
(a)	2	up	↑ down
(b)	1	down	none
(c)	1	up	none
(d)	0	down	down
(e)	.6	↓ up	up

2. *Demand Elasticities and Total Revenue*

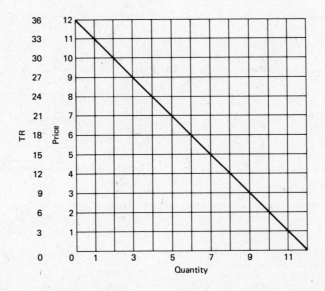

(a) You are given the demand curve in the diagram above, for which several points are contained in the table below. Its equation can be written $Q = 12 - P$. Note that $\Delta Q/\Delta P = -1$. Calculate the arc elasticities for the segments between the points, the point elasticities, and the total revenue. Draw in the total revenue curve on the diagram above, and enter the elasticities along the demand curve (note separate scale).

P	Q	Elasticities Arc	Elasticities Point	TR
$11	1		_____	_____
9	3	_____	_____	_____
7	5	_____	_____	_____
5	7	_____	_____	_____
3	9	_____	_____	_____
1	11	_____	_____	_____

(b) What is the relationship between total revenue and elasticity?

(c) Assume that the demand curve shifts to the right with two more units sold at every price. Calculate two or three elasticities to illustrate the general proposition that the new demand curve is less elastic than the old at each price.

3. *Riders for Nippon's Monorail*

In October 1968, the Tokyo Monorail Company denied that it was facing bankruptcy. It stated that its operating results were much improved since it had reduced its fare from 250 yen to 150 yen (70 cents to 42 cents) on its 12-mile run from Tokyo airport to the center of the city and by equivalent percentages on shorter commuter runs.

Assume that this price cut was completely responsible for its increase in revenues from 460,000,000 yen in 1966 to 640,000,000 yen in 1967. Calculate the indicated arc elasticity of demand. (*Hint:* As a unit for quantity, use the full-trip equivalent.)

	P	Q	Revenue	Elasticity
1966	250	_____	460,000,000	
1967	150	_____	640,000,000	_____

4. *Toronto Public Transit*

In 1973 the Transportation Commission in Toronto voted to abolish the "two-fare" system whereby some people, because of where they lived, had to pay the fare twice to reach downtown.

Those opposed to the change stated that the transit system would lose money because of the lower fare paid by some people. Those in favor argued that the quantity of transit service demanded would increase sharply, thereby offsetting any revenue loss due to lower fares.

(a) What might the advocates of the new proposal be thinking about the elasticity of demand for public transit?

(b) How will they know if their assumption about the elasticity was correct?

(c) If total revenue rises, what might one forecast for the price of automobile parking spaces downtown?

PROBLEMS

1. RAISING THE RATES ON WATER

To pay for the treatment of sewage and thus avoid pollution, it has been suggested that water rates be increased, and in some Canadian cities this has occurred. Suppose water rates in a community are doubled and revenue is expected to double also, but in actual fact revenues only increase one and one-half times.

Questions
1. What was the expected elasticity of demand for water in the community?

2. What actually was the elasticity of demand? (Give the numerical value.)

3. If rates were quadrupled, would you expect the elasticity of demand to be the same as it was in question 2 above?

2. RAISING UNIVERSITY TUITION RATES

The Board of Regents at the University of Wisconsin reduced the tuition fees for undergraduate students at two colleges in 1974. At one college, tuition fell from $515 to $180 per annum, and enrollment increased by 23 percent. At the other, tuition was reduced from $476 to $150, and enrollment increased by 47 percent.

Questions
1. What do these statistics say about the price elasticity of demand for university education in these two areas?

2. Who would bear the cost of such a reduction in tuition fees?

Chapter Seven
Price Controls and
the Agricultural Problem

CHECKLIST | Make certain that you understand the following concepts: black market; price ceiling; floor price; crop restriction.

REVIEW QUESTIONS

1. If a government sets an enforceable price ceiling on a good below the equilibrium price, a (shortage/surplus) of the good will result. At the ceiling price, the amount demanded (exceeds/is less than) the amount supplied.

2. If a government sets a price ceiling on a good below the equilibrium price but wishes everyone to be able to obtain some of it, it must be prepared to set up a system of _____ *rationing* _____.

3. If a government sets a legal minimum price on a good or service, a surplus will develop if the price is (below/above) the equilibrium price because the amount demanded will (exceed/be less than) the amount supplied.

4. If a minimum wage is set above the equilibrium wage, there will be a (surplus/shortage) of workers available at that time.

5. The gap between the desire to produce goods and a change in actual production is called the _____ *supply* _____ lag.

6. If the Canadian Wheat Board agrees to buy wheat from farmers at a fixed price, farmers face a perfectly _____ *elastic* _____ demand curve.

7. Farmers' short-run supply curves are very (elastic/inelastic).

8. Demand curves for many farm products seem to be quite (inelastic/elastic). This reflects the probable fact that if food prices fell by 10 percent, you probably (would/would not) increase the amount you eat by 10 percent.

9. Demand inelasticity coupled with fluctuating supply has tended to make farm prices historically (stable/unstable).

10. Government policy to aid farmers most often has been to put a floor under (prices/incomes), which has resulted in (shortages/surpluses). In order to prevent surpluses from increasing, the government may resort to _____quota_____ such as acreage restrictions.

11. Technological developments such as pesticides, agricultural machinery, and improved crop varieties have permitted individual farmers to raise more crops, thus shifting supply curves to the _____right_____. At the same time, demand has risen (less than/more than) proportionally to the rises in income.

12. These developments have led to the problem of reallocating resources (into/out of) agriculture and have tended to keep agricultural incomes (below/above) average incomes.

_____

    If you have not answered all questions correctly, review the text in order to be sure that you have all of the important concepts clearly in mind before going on to the next chapter.

1. shortage; exceeds 2. rationing 3. above; be less than 4. surplus 5. supply
6. elastic 7. inelastic 8. inelastic; would not 9. unstable 10. prices; surpluses; quotas 11. right; less than 12. out of; below

_____

MULTIPLE-CHOICE QUESTIONS

1. Both maximum and minimum price controls, when effective,
   (a) lead to production controls
   (b) lead to rationing
   (c) lead to a drop in quality
   (d) lead to a reduction in quantity bought and sold

2. In a free-market economy, the rationing of scarce goods is done by
   (a) the price mechanism
   (b) the government
   (c) business
   (d) consumers

3. One prediction made about minimum-wage legislation is that
   (a) it will reduce employment in those industries affected by it, given competition in the labor market
   (b) no one benefits in the long run
   (c) it will actually lower wages
   (d) it will raise productivity

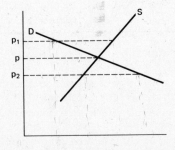

4. If p_1 is a minimum price,

   (a) it will have no effect
   (b) it will lead to shortages and probably to black-market activity
   (c) it will lead to surpluses and possibly to undercutting of the minimum price
   (d) it would represent a response to Nader's Raiders

5. If p_2 is a minimum price,

   (a) it will have no effect
   (b) it will lead to shortages and probably to black-market activity
   (c) it will lead to surpluses and possibly to undercutting of the minimum price
   (d) it would represent a response to Nader's Raiders

6. If p_1 is a maximum price,

   (a) it will have no effect
   (b) it will lead to shortages and probably to black-market activity
   (c) it will lead to surpluses and possibly to undercutting of the minimum price
   (d) it would represent a response to Nader's Raiders

7. If p_2 is a maximum price,

   (a) it will have no effect
   (b) it will lead to shortages and probably to black-market activity
   (c) it will lead to surpluses and possibly to undercutting of the minimum price
   (d) it would represent a response to Nader's Raiders

8. A cobweb cycle for an agricultural product means
   (a) there will be excess supply
   (b) there will be excess demand
   (c) price will be unstable for a period
   (d) demand never changes

9. The main reason for price supports is to
   (a) stabilize farm incomes
   (b) make certain there are always extra stocks of goods on hand
   (c) give the government control over agriculture
   (d) reduce competition

10. If the government support price for a commodity is above the long-run equilibrium price,
    (a) farm incomes will fall
    (b) price of the commodity will decline
    (c) unsold stocks will accumulate
    (d) price of the commodity will rise

11. Unplanned fluctuations in the supply of agricultural produce
    (a) cause larger price changes when demand is elastic than when it is inelastic
    (b) cause price variations that are in the same direction as the fluctuations
    (c) make the supply more elastic
    (d) cause price fluctuations that will be larger the more inelastic demand is

12. A price completely stabilized by government's buying surpluses and selling its stocks when there are shortages means that
    (a) poor farmers will benefit the most
    (b) there will be no storage costs
    (c) farmers' revenues will be proportional to output
    (d) all farms will have satisfactory incomes

13. Agricultural output in Canada has increased substantially since World War II mainly because
    (a) many people are going back to farming
    (b) productivity and yields have risen
    (c) rising demand has kept prices steadily increasing
    (d) it has had good growing weather

14. The long-run problem of overproduction in Canadian agriculture is intensified by
    (a) the population explosion
    (b) low income elasticity of demand for agricultural products
    (c) the continued use of cheap hand labor
    (d) increased foreign demand

EXERCISES

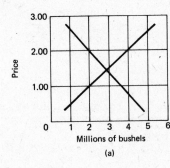

(a)

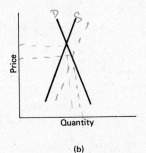

Quantity

(b)

1. On graph (a), illustrate the effects of the government's setting a minimum price of $2.00 per bushel. Label all significant points of interest. (Assume that the government maintains the price by purchasing any surpluses, and that there are no acreage controls.)
    (a) Farmers' total revenue: _____8_____
    (b) Consumers will get _____2_____ bushels at $2.00 per bushel.
    (c) The government will have to buy _____2_____ bushels at a total cost of _____4_____.
    (d) At the equilibrium price, consumers would have bought _____3_____ bushels at about what price? _____1.5_____

2. Show by drawing a new curve on graph (b)
    (a) a large shift in agricultural supply due to great technological improvements in agriculture. What has happened to farmers' total revenue, judging from the graph?

    (b) a shift in the demand for agricultural products due to rising population. In the long run, which shift, (a) or (b), has the more serious implications for the world?

3. *Farm Price Supports: Price vs. Income*

     D represents the demand curve for an agricultural commodity whose normal supply curve is S (the supply available for marketing would be S_ni); in poor crop years the supply actually available for marketing is S_1g; in bumper crop years it is S_2k. The dashed line labeled $\eta = 1$ has unitary elasticity.

     In answering the following questions, use letters to designate line segments, such as oc for price and oi for the corresponding quantity. Circle the most appropriate term within parentheses.

    I. First assume that no price or income maintenance controls are used.
       (a) In a normal year the predicted price is _____oc_____; the predicted quantity is _____oi_____.
       (b) In a year of bumper crops the predicted price is _____oe_____; the predicted quantity is _____ok_____; farmers' revenues will be (greater than/less than) normal because the demand curve is (elastic/inelastic).

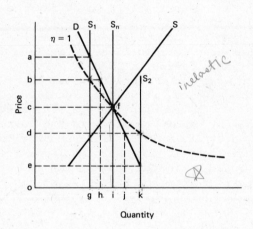

II. Now assume that the government seeks to maintain the price that in a normal year would just clear the market.
    (a) Why will it not be enough for the government simply to specify that no sales below that price are legal?

pressure to sell surplus

    (b) In the year of a bumper crop the government will have to (purchase/sell) quantity _____ik_____.
    (c) In the year of a poor crop it will have to (purchase/sell) quantity _____gi_____.

III. An alternative policy is to maintain farmers' total revenues, rather than to maintain one fixed price.
    (a) In this case, in a bumper crop year the price could be allowed to drop to _____od_____ and the government would have to (purchase/sell) quantity _____ik_____.
    (b) In a poor crop year the price could rise to _____ob_____ and the government would (purchase/sell) quantity _____gi_____.
    (c) Why might the government actually make money under this arrangement? Why in any case will the government's expenses be less under III than under II?

IV. Can either system above *successfully* meet the long-run problem of supply increasing much faster than demand because of technological advances in agriculture since World War II? Picture the S curve moving to the right on the diagram, and consider the consequences for government programs II and III. What
modifications and further requirements will the government have to make in its
support system?

PROBLEMS

1. *CANADIAN WHEAT SUPPLIES*

Warm winds will soon be blowing across Canada's Prairies, melting snow and
thawing some of the richest farmland in the world. Already farmers are tinkering
with tractors, readying them for the day when they will move out onto the land to
work the soil for this year's crop.

The crop this year, however, will be far different from any other in recent
memory. While wheat has historically been by far the biggest single crop in the
mix of agricultural products on Canada's Prairies, if the Federal Government's
recently announced plan to induce farmers to take up to 22 million acres out of
wheat production this year were to have its maximum impact, practically no wheat
would be grown in Western Canada in 1970.

This situation would be a complete reversal of that which existed only a few
years ago. In the mid-sixties, it will be recalled, contracts for the sale of huge
quantities of wheat negotiated with the U.S.S.R. and China caused concern over
Canada's ability to meet export commitments and farmers were urged to increase
production. Now, with export sales falling and world wheat markets glutted, Canadian wheat stocks have been rising sharply. In fact, the Minister responsible for
the Canadian Wheat Board estimates that at the end of the current crop year
(July 31, 1970) stocks of wheat on hand will still amount to 950 million bushels,
nearly double estimated annual domestic consumption and expected export sales.*

Questions

1. Given that the world demand curve for wheat is downward sloping, what would
happen to the price of wheat if the Wheat Board were to place the stocks of wheat on the
market?

* Source: *Business Review*, Bank of Montreal, March 25, 1970.

2. By inducing farmers to take acreage out of wheat production, what is the government attempting to achieve?

3. If farmers do not grow wheat but instead plant oats and barley, what will happen to the price of these crops if (a) their demand does not change; (b) their demand increases greatly?

2. *THE FEDERAL BEEF SUBSIDY*

In March 1974, the federal government introduced a subsidy of $7.00 per hundred-weight on premium beef, when marketed, as a means of supplying more beef to the market at a lower price to the consumer. Among other things, the need for this subsidy suggests that beef producers were not willing to market more cattle because of the effect such action would have on the price and total revenue they would receive.

Questions

1. What does this imply about the elasticity of the demand schedule for beef?

2. Illustrate the effect of the subsidy on beef prices to the consumer and the revenue to the producer if the demand schedule is: (a) inelastic; (b) elastic. (Consider this a short-run situation where the *actual* supply of beef put on the market and the *potential* supply are inelastic.)

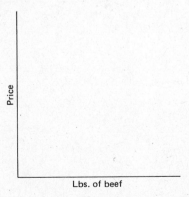

3. THE FLUID MILK SUBSIDY

In early 1975, the federal government removed the 6-cent-a-quart subsidy on fluid milk while maintaining its 34-cent-a-pound (or 8.5-cent-a-quart equivalent) subsidy on skim milk powder.

Questions

1. What would you predict about the demand for fuild milk and milk powder following the removal of the subsidy?

2. If fluid skim milk was retailing for 40 cents a quart before the subsidy was removed, and the elasticity of demand for fluid milk is estimated at 0.62, what would be the percentage decline in fluid milk consumption if the subsidy removal was reflected in a price rise of 6 cents a quart?

3. Does it make any difference at all to the dairy farmer whether the subsidy is given to fluid or skim milk production? Justify your answer.

Chapter Eight
Household
Consumption
Behavior

> **CHECKLIST** Make certain that you understand the following concepts: budget line or isocost; relative price; absolute price; money income; real income; price level; indifference curve; marginal rate of substitution; income consumption line; price consumption line; marginal utility; total utility; free good; paradox of value; substitution effect; income effect.

REVIEW QUESTIONS

1. The budget line shows combinations of two types of commodities obtainable, given household _____*income*_____ and the commodities' _____*price*_____. It shows a household's purchasing power, or _____*real*_____ income.

2. The budget line's slope reflects the ratio of the _*relative price*_ of the two types of commodities shown; because it also represents the rate at which one commodity must be given up to gain more of another, it shows the _____*opportunity*_____ cost of a particular combination.

3. To find out where the budget line intersects the vertical, or Y, axis, household money income is divided by _____*the price of y*_____.

4. How would the following events be pictured on the budget-line diagram, *ceteris paribus*:
   (a) household money income rises _____*parallel shift outward*_____
   (b) relative prices of commodities change _____*slope*_____
   (c) income rises, price level rises by equal percent _____*no change*_____
   (d) income rises, price level rises by greater percent _____*line shifts to left*_____

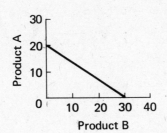

5. The budget line on the accompanying diagram is drawn for an income of $300 per week. Referring to it, determine the following:
   (a) price of product A-- _____15_____
   (b) price of product B-- _____10_____
   (c) To buy one more unit of A, if the household is spending all of its income, it must give up how much B? _____
   (d) opportunity cost of A, in terms of B-- _____

6. Show on the diagram the effect of the following changes, and tell whether real income has risen or fallen or whether we have insufficient information to know:
   (a) money income becomes $400; real income _____
   (b) money income = $300, P_A = $20, P_B = $12; real income _____
   (c) money income = $330, P_A = $12, P_B = $15; real income _____

7. An indifference curve shows various combinations of two commodities that give to the buyer _____equal satisfaction_____ .

8. An indifference curve farther from the origin than another shows points where total satisfaction is _____greater_____ than the other.

9. (a) The slope of an indifference curve shows what we call the marginal _____rate_____ _____of substitution_____ .
   (b) If a household is indifferent between 21 units of food, 30 of clothing and 20 of food, 32 of clothing, the rate of substitution of food for clothing is _____

10. (a) Satisfaction is maximized at the point where an indifference curve is tangent to a _____budget line_____ .
    (b) At this point, the marginal rate of substitution must be equal to the ratio of _____prices_____ .

11. A rise in the price of one commodity, *ceteris paribus*, will move the budget line to a point of tangency with a (lower/higher) indifference curve.

12. Successive increases in real income will shift the budget line _____outward_____ , and the several points of tangency with (higher/lower) indifference curves will enable us to derive a line called an _____income-consumption_____ line.

13. (a) To construct a demand curve for a certain commodity A from an indifference map, we put on the two axes of the map: _____quantity of A_____ and _____value of all other goods_____ .
    (b) As the price of A falls, the budget line's tangencies with (higher/lower) indifference curves produce a line called _____price-consumption-line_____ .

14. Consumers tend to value a commodity less the more of it they have; this is called diminishing ___marginal utility___. Thus, with constant incomes, consumers are usually unwilling to buy more of a product beyond their present rate unless ___the price falls___.

15. (a) If the marginal utility of a good is zero, a household will be willing to pay a price of ___zero___ for it.
    (b) A free good, one so plentiful as to have no price, will be used up to the point where its marginal utility is ___zero___.

16. A household maximizing the utility or satisfaction obtained with a given income will allocate its spending among commodities so that the last dollar spent on each brings equal ___marginal utility___.

17. The more rapidly the marginal utility of extra units of a particular good falls, the (greater/less) will be the elasticity of demand.

Appendix
18. A fall in the price of a commodity, *ceteris paribus,* will lead to more of it being sold as a result of two effects: ___income___ and ___substitution___.

19. The substitution effect of a price fall always leaves the amount demanded either the same or ___greater___ than before.

20. The income effect of a price fall, if positive, will result in a (greater/smaller) quantity demanded.

21. For a good to have an upward-sloping demand curve, the income effect must be both ___large___ and ___negative___ than the substitution effect.

_____

    If you have not answered all questions correctly, review the text in order to be sure that you have all of the important concepts clearly in mind before going on to the next chapter.

1. income, prices; real 2. prices; opportunity 3. the price of Y 4. parallel shift outward; slope of line changes; no change; line shifts to left 5. $15; $10; 1½B; 1½B 6. has risen; has fallen; cannot tell 7. the same total satisfaction 8. greater 9. rate of substitution; ½ 10. budget line; prices 11. lower 12. outward; higher; income consumption 13. quantity of A, value of all other goods; higher, price-consumption line 14. marginal utility; the price falls 15. zero; zero 16. marginal utility 17. less 18. substitution; income 19. greater 20. greater 21. negative; larger

MULTIPLE-CHOICE QUESTIONS

1. A change in household income will always shift the budget line parallel to itself if
   (a) money prices stay constant
   (b) relative prices stay constant with money prices changing by the same percentage as income
   (c) real income stays constant
   (d) prices change in the same direction

2. Halving all absolute prices, *ceteris paribus,* has the effect of
   (a) halving real income
   (b) halving money income
   (c) changing relative prices
   (d) doubling real income

3. A change in one absolute price, with all other things remaining constant, will
    (a) shift the budget line parallel to itself
    (b) change money income
    (c) cause the budget line to change its slope
    (d) have no effect on real income

4. An indifference curve includes
    (a) constant quantities of one good with varying quantities of another
    (b) the prices and quantities of two goods that can be purchased for a given sum of money
    (c) all combinations of two goods that will give the same level of satisfaction to the household
    (d) combinations of goods whose marginal utilities are equal

5. Households may attain consumption on a higher indifference curve by all but which of the following:
    (a) an increase in money income
    (b) a reduction in absolute prices
    (c) a proportionate increase in money income and in absolute prices
    (d) a change in relative prices caused by a reduction in one price

6. The slope of the budget line with product y on the vertical axis and product x on the horizontal axis is
    (a) $-(P_y/P_x)$
    (b) $-(x/y)$
    (c) $-(y/x)$
    (d) $-(P_x/P_y)$

7. Where the budget line is tangent to an indifference curve,
    (a) equal amounts of goods give equal satisfaction
    (b) the ratio of prices of the goods must equal the marginal rate of substitution
    (c) the prices of the goods are equal
    (d) the household has revealed a preference for that combination of goods

8. Indifference curve theory assumes that
    (a) buyers can measure satisfaction
    (b) buyers can identify preferred combinations of goods, without necessarily being able to measure their satisfaction
    (c) buyers always behave consistently
    (d) all buyers have the same preference patterns

9. The hypothesis of diminishing marginal utility states that
    (a) the less of a commodity one is consuming, the less the utility obtained by an increase in its consumption
    (b) the more of a commodity one is consuming, the more the utility obtained by an increase in its consumption
    (c) the more of a commodity one is consuming, the less the utility obtained by an increase in its consumption
    (d) marginal utility cannot be measured, but total utility can

10. According to utility theory, for a consumer who is maximizing total satisfaction, MU_a/MU_b
    (a) equals p_a/p_b
    (b) equals p_b/p_a
    (c) will not necessarily be related to relative prices
    (d) equals TU_a/TU_b

11. Elasticity of demand
   (a) varies inversely with total utility
   (b) varies inversely with marginal utility
   (c) is less, the greater the substitution effect
   (d) is greater when marginal utility declines slowly rather than rapidly

12. The "paradox of value" is that
   (a) people are irrational in consumption choices
   (b) the total utilities yielded by commodities do not necessarily have a relation-
       ship to their market values
   (c) value has no relationship to utility schedules
   (d) free goods are goods that are essential to life

EXERCISES

1. *Budgeting and Price Changes*
      From 1920 to 1940, consumer prices were generally declining or stable; from
   1940 to 1970, consumer prices were occasionally stable but usually rose. This is
   shown in the table below for food and for all items but food, where prices are expressed in 1957—1959 dollars (i.e., 1957—1959 index = 100). Representative budgets
   based on the disposable income for an employed family are also shown.

   (a) Draw budget lines for 1920, 1940, and 1970 on the graph and complete the table
       below. Each unit of food and of items other than food is the amount that could
       be purchased in 1957—1959 for $1. For example, for each $100 of income,
       100/.70 or 143 units of food could be bought in 1920.

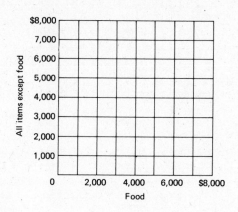

| | Price Indexes | | Family | Food | "Other" |
	Food	"Other"	Income	Intercepts	Intercepts
1920	70	70	$ 2,200	_____	_____
1940	40	52	2,000	_____	_____
1970	135	135	10,000	_____	_____

(b) Does the graph indicate that absolute price declines can be the equivalent of rises in income? Explain briefly.

(c) The budget line for which year is the least steep? _____ Explain.

2. Deriving Household Demand Curves from Indifference Maps

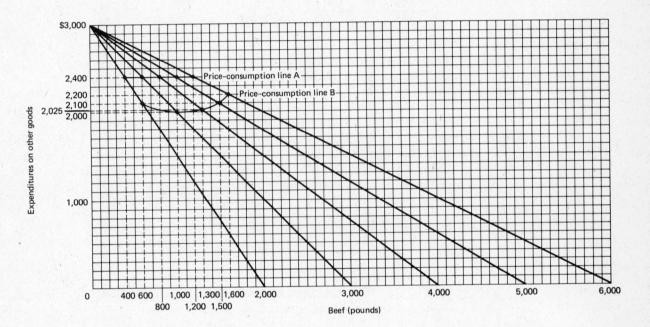

(a) On the graph above, sketch in (using two different colors) indifference maps that could lead to price-consumption lines A and B.

(b) From the price-consumption lines, derive demand curves A and B and enter on the chart below.

P	Q_A	Q_B	Total Expenditure on Beef A	B
$1.50	400	600	600	900
1.00	600	1000	600	1000
.75	___	___	___	___
.60	___	___	___	___
.50	___	___	___	___

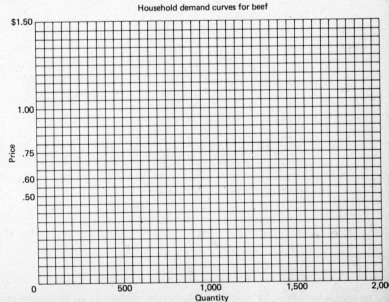

Household demand curves for beef

(c) 1. What is price elasticity of demand for household A? _____
    2. At what price does elasticity of demand for household B approach 1?

TR maximum

PROBLEMS

1. CHANGES IN FAMILY CONSUMPTION PATTERNS

The following table shows how a "typical" family in the income range $7000-$8000 spent their income on certain items, for the years 1959 and 1969. (Assume that the family nominal income is $7500.)

	1959	1969
Food	$1575	$1500
Clothing	750	580
Transportation	460	1005
Alcohol and Tobacco	315	290

Source: Family Expenditure Survey,
1959 and 1969, Statistics Canada.

Over the same period, the percentage increases in the price index for these commodities and services were as follows:

Food	26%
Clothing	28%
Transportation	22%
Alcohol and Tobacco	27%

Questions

1. Over this period the general increase in the price level was 28 percent; hence a family with income of $7500 in 1969 was less wealthy than in 1959. How has the real consumption pattern for these goods changed over this period?

2. Can you estimate the price elasticity of demand for these goods with the data that you have? If so, indicate how you would make the estimate. If not, indicate why it cannot be done.

2. THE SWITCH TO BREAD

An April 3, 1975, report in *The Globe and Mail* stated that:

In the past 15 years, with rising disposable income per capita consumption of bread was decreasing and consumption of meat increasing but the tren has levelled off. . . . With meat prices too high . . . we've all arranged our food budget a little.

The report went on to say that per capita bread consumption had declined over the past 15 years from 90 to 75 pounds but was now on the increase.

Questions

1. Using indifference-curve analysis, illustrate what has been happening as money income rises and meat becomes relatively more expensive in recent years. (Assume that, for the first two periods, the relative prices of meat and bread do not change and that, in the third period, the change occurs.)

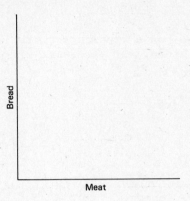

2. With reference to bread, what is the direction of the income effect between the first and second periods?

3. If, because of the recent recession (1974-1975), nominal incomes were to fall, what do you think would happen to the amount of bread consumed per capita, assuming no change in relative prices?

Chapter Nine
Measuring
Demand

REVIEW QUESTIONS

1. The most common use of the theory of demand is to predict the market behavior of (individual households/the aggregate of all households).

2. The downward slope of the demand curve requires that (all/most/some) households behave according to the theory.

3. (a) An unward-sloping demand curve would mean that, if the price of a good rose, people would buy (more/less) of it.
   (b) This may be true of a few goods called _____ goods, which are (normal/inferior) goods that take a (large/small) part of the household budget.

4. (a) Evidence indicates that income elasticities are (fairly stable/very unstable) over time.
   (b) Income elasticities seem to follow (the same/different) patterns in different countries of the West.

5. Low income elasticity for food seems to be (the rule/the exception) in most advanced industrial countries.

6. In production, machines and their operators are used together, so they are _____ _____ goods; a fall in the price of one leads to a _____ in the demand for the other.

7. Changes in taste are (measurable/unmeasurable); we (should avoid using/feel free to use) them to explain every departure from what the theory of demand would predict.

8. In the attempt to measure and plot actual demand curves, use of pairs of actual price and quantity sold will result in an "identification problem" if there has been a shift in (the demand curve/the supply curve/both curves).

9. A new theory of demand suggests that consumers get satisfaction from (the quantity of goods consumed/the characteristics or effects of the goods).

If you have not answered all questions correctly, review the text in order to be sure that you have all of the important concepts clearly in mind before going on to the next chapter.

1. the aggregate of all households 2. most 3. more; "Giffen," inferior, large
4. fairly stable; the same 5. the rule 6. complementary; rise 7. unmeasurable; should avoid using 8. both curves 9. the characteristics or effects of the goods

MULTIPLE-CHOICE QUESTIONS

1. Which one of the following variables, which cannot be measured directly, could be easily misused as an alibi whenever it appeared that the theory of demand had been refuted?
   (a) income
   (b) supply
   (c) tastes
   (d) price

2. A series of observations in which the lower the price, the lower the quantity sold, could represent all but one of the following:
   (a) an unchanged supply with a changing demand
   (b) a conventional demand with a changing supply
   (c) the demand for a "Giffen" good with a changing supply
   (d) a changing supply and a changing demand

3. To demonstrate that elasticities are not stable, it is necessary to
   (a) give at least three or four good reasons why they should not be stable
   (b) show that two elasticities of demand for the same commodity are not exactly the same
   (c) demonstrate their instability by logical, deductive reasoning
   (d) investigate the matter by measuring elasticities over time

4. Demand studies have indicated that the price elasticities of demand for most food-stuffs
   (a) are less than 1
   (b) are greater than 1
   (c) are of unitary elasticity
   (d) have no general tendency that has been noted

5. The category of expenditures classed as meals purchased at restaurants
   (a) has been observed to have low income elasticities
   (b) has been observed to have high income elasticities
   (c) has been observed to have negative income elasticities
   (d) shows no consistent relationship with income

6. Some recent thinking in demand theory stresses
   (a) characteristics of the products as the objects of demand
   (b) indifference curves that are concave to the origin
   (c) upward-rising demand curves
   (d) commodities rather than services

EXERCISES

1. *What Has Happened to the Razor Strop?*

The leading producer of razor strops (whose major use is in sharpening straight razors) compiled these price and sales figures for the industry. Of 11 U.S. producers in 1915, only 4 were left by 1949.

Year	Unit Sales	Est. Price
1900	800,000	$1.00
1915	1,750,000	1.50
1930	400,000	1.85
1945	100,000	2.10
1948	80,000	2.10

(a) What, if anything, could you conclude about the price elasticity of demand?

(b) Show on the accompanying graph what probably has happened to the demand curve for strops. How compatible are these events with your diagram: a trend toward more shaving at home after 1900, and widespread acceptance of the safety razor after 1915?

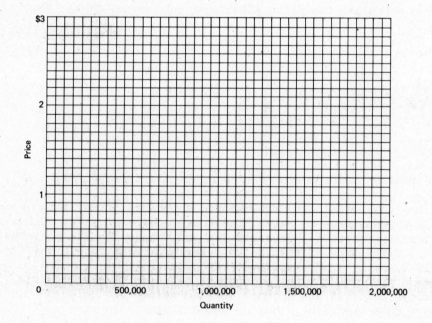

2. Suppose you had the following information concerning the purchase of a product over some time period of years.

Year	Price per Unit	Quantity Bought
1	$1.50	2700
2	1.25	2500
3	1.00	2200
4	0.75	2500
5	1.00	2000
6	1.50	1555

(a) Plot the above relationship between quantity purchased and average price.

(b) Can you calculate the price elasticity of demand? If so, how? If not, explain.

PROBLEM

IDENTIFYING A DEMAND RELATIONSHIP BETWEEN SALES AND ADVERTISING

One of the most difficult problems for a business firm is to ascertain the effect of advertising expenditures on sales. There are qualitative variations in the effectiveness of particular promotional expenditures and changes in the policies of competitors that add to the difficulty of setting up *ceteris paribus* conditions. These are accentuated in many cases by an "identification" problem.

The demand function for the product to be identified in $Q = f(A)$, when all other variables such as price of the product (P) and income are held constant. A is defined as expenditures on advertising. Then we would expect Q to rise as A rises. But if the firm determines how much its advertising should be on the basis of current sales, we have what amounts to a supply curve for expenditures on advertising that is a function of the quantity sold: $A = kQP$, where k is some constant.

Questions

Suppose that a firm has the following observations with price fixed at $10.

Period	A	Sales
1	$1,000,000	$10,000,000
2	1,200,000	12,000,000
3	1,400,000	14,000,000
4	1,500,000	15,000,000

1. What apparently is the relationship between the quantity demanded and advertising?

2. Suppose the firm wishes to predict the effect of advertising expenditures on their sales. Does it have an "identification" problem? Explain.

Chapter Ten
The Firm, Production, and Cost

> **CHECKLIST** Make certain that you understand the following concepts: firm; single proprietorship; partnership; corporation; limited liability; profit; opportunity cost; dividends; factors of production (inputs); capital and capital goods; roundabout production; technical efficiency; economic efficiency; cost; imputed cost; depreciation; normal profit. *Appendix:* balance sheet; income statement.

REVIEW QUESTIONS

1. In predicting the behavior of firms in the market, it is assumed that large firms have (the same/different) motivation than small ones do.

2. If a person owns his own business, it is called a _____ single proprietorship _____.

3. In a general partnership firm of two partners, one of them would be liable for (all/half) of the firm's debts.

4. To collect an unpaid debt from a corporation, one would sue (the owners/the company).

5. (a) The most important aspect of a corporation from the point of view of its owners is that their liability is _____ limited _____.
   (b) This means that the risk of putting your money into shares of a corporation would tend to be (greater/less) than investing in a partnership.

6. It is assumed that firms make decisions so as to make their profits (satisfactory/a maximum).

7. Basically, all production is made with the services of three kinds of inputs or factors: _____ land _____, _____ labor _____, _____ capital _____.

8. The process of producing machines with which to produce other machines with which to produce consumer goods is called _____ roundabout method _____.

9. If an electric typewriter permits a student to type 10 percent faster than with a mechanical typewriter, it is _____ technological _____ efficient but not necessarily _____ economically _____ efficient.

10. Because economic efficiency is affected by the costs of inputs, the firm must consider not only the technical efficiency of various methods but also the _prices_ _____ of the inputs.

11. Profits from production consist of the difference between the value of the outputs and the _____ _value of the inputs_ _____.

12. If you own a summer cottage which you could rent for July and August to some family for a net gain of $600 after expenses and taxes, the opportunity cost of living in it yourself for the summer is _____ _600_ _____.

13. The cost of using owned rather than purchased or hired factors in production is called an _____ _imputed_ _____ cost; it is estimated by the earnings they could have received in _____ _their best alternative use_ _____.

14. If a firm's machinery has no possible alternative use, its opportunity cost is _____ _zero_ _____.

15. The loss in value of a capital asset over time is called _____ _depreciation_ __.

16. In making profit-maximizing decisions, a firm should compare present and expected returns or benefits with (past/present and future) costs.

17. The extra return on money put into a venture to compensate for the possibility of not getting it back is considered a return for taking _____ _risk_ _____.

18. (a) If in its present production a firm is earning a lower rate of return than it could earn if its factors were used in their best alternative use, an economist would say that its profits are _____ _negative_ _____.
    (b) If that same firm shows an excess of revenues over money costs, its owners will probably consider that profits are _____ _positive_ _____ but inadequate.

19. To most economists, dividend payments sufficient to keep shareholders from taking their invested money capital out of the business would be included in (cost/profit). Some economists would refer to such dividend payments as _____ _normal profit_ __.

20. (a) In a free market with profit-maximizing firms, it is predicted that resources will be reallocated into an industry where economic profits are (zero/positive).
    (b) A firm that shows profits to an accountant or to the Internal Revenue Service is not necessarily making _____ _economic_ _____ profits.

Appendix
21. (a) Balance sheets report the assets and liabilities of a firm (over a period/at a moment) of time; they thus measure a (stock/flow).
    (b) Income statements show the stream of revenues and expenditures (over a period/ at a moment) of time; they thus measure a (stock/flow).

22. Mr. Maykby's company showed a profit on its income statement because he had neglected these imputed costs: (a) _____ ; (b) _____ _____ ; (c) _____ .

If you have not answered all questions correctly, review the text in order to be sure that you have all of the important concepts clearly in mind before going on to the next chapter.

1. the same 2. single proprietorship 3. all 4. the company 5. limited; less 6. a maximum 7. land; labor; capital 8. roundabout 9. technically; economically 10. prices 11. value of the inputs 12. $600 13. imputed; their best alternative employment 14. zero 15. depreciation 16. present and future 17. risks 18. negative; positive 19. cost; normal profits 20. positive; economic 21. at a moment; stock; over a period; flow 22. his own services; interest on his own money; part of depreciation

---

MULTIPLE-CHOICE QUESTIONS

1. Economically efficient methods of production have which of the following relationships to technologically efficient methods?
   (a) All technologically efficient methods are economically efficient.
   (b) All economically efficient methods are technologically efficient.
   (c) Some economically efficient methods are not technologically efficient.
   (d) Both (a) and (b) are true because economically efficient and technologically efficient methods must coincide.

2. Which of the following groups of claimants would be the last to have their claims honored in a bankruptcy?
   (a) bondholders
   (b) commercial creditors
   (c) common stockholders
   (d) employees owed back wages

3. Limited liability for the claims against a firm is an advantage for
   (a) single proprietors
   (b) corporate shareholders
   (c) paid employees
   (d) general partners in a partnership

4. Which of the following is *not* an advantage of the corporate form of business organization?
   (a) limited liability
   (b) separate legal existence
   (c) close identification of owners with management
   (d) relative ease of obtaining capital funds

5. The difference between economic profits and normal profits is that
   (a) normal profits are smaller
   (b) normal profits are necessarily larger for all firms
   (c) normal profits are part of opportunity cost, whereas economic profits are returns in excess of opportunity costs
   (d) normal profits take into account monopoly power; economic profits do not

6. The major cost for most students in attending college is
   (a) tuition and fees
   (b) room and board
   (c) the income they could have received from employment
   (d) social and miscellaneous expenses

7. We can be *certain* of the usefulness of opportunity-cost concepts when our purpose is
   (a) to help a firm make the best decision it can to achieve maximum profits
   (b) to predict the responses of the firm to a change in conditions
   (c) to describe the firm's actual behavior
   (d) to predict the money costs of a firm's activities

8. The major role of economic profits, as seen in this chapter, is
   (a) to provide income for shareholders
   (b) to provide income for entrepreneurs
   (c) to act as a signal to firms concerning the desirability of devoting resources
       to a particular activity
   (d) to encourage labor to reform the system

9. "Profits are necessary for the survival of Canadian business." This chapter
   (a) disagrees with this viewpoint entirely
   (b) accepts this viewpoint but defines the necessary profits as costs
   (c) accepts this viewpoint without qualification or clarification
   (d) does not consider the subject

10. Inputs to productive processes
    (a) can be the outputs of other firms
    (b) are solely land and labor
    (c) can be clearly distinguished from factors of production
    (d) consist primarily of capital equipment in a capitalistic society

11. Economic theory frequently assumes that firms try to maximize profits
    (a) because firms always maximize profits
    (b) because firms ought to maximize profits to be fair to their stockholders
    (c) because use of this simple assumption has frequently led to accurate predictions
    (d) because economists wish thus to criticize the greed of firms

12. Depreciation is defined as the loss of value of an asset associated with its use in
    production, and thus it
    (a) is clearly a cash cost
    (b) is a function only of wear and tear in use
    (c) is not an economic cost if the asset has no market value or alternative use
    (d) does not apply to used equipment

EXERCISE

Assume that there are two basic methods of producing vegetables for sale from a
garden plot, and that the grower can sell all output at a given price. One method
involves hand tools and labour, the other, power tools and labour. The following
information gives an idea of the production processes involved. (Output from the
garden is proportional to the size of the lot.)

Garden Size	Man-Hours to Produce Output	
(square feet)	Hand Tools	Power Tools
200	50	20
500	125	50
1000	250	100
2000	500	200

Note: (1) The hand tools are depreciated at $10 per year; (2) the power tools are
         depreciated at $300 per year; (3) labour cost is $4 per hour.

(a) At what garden size is it economically efficient to use power tools?

(b) If the price of labour declined to $3 per hour, would this affect the answer in (a)? How?

PROBLEMS

1. *DIAMOND'S FOR RENT*

In the early 1960s, B. G. Diamond changed the location of his jewelry store to a newly developed suburban shopping area, where he built a new store in a corner location for $50,000. His operations were successful there, and his stated profits increased substantially. Diamond's 1968 statement follows:

Gross margin (sales—cost of goods sold)		$45,000
Wages and salaries (including $10,000 salary for himself)	$22,000	
Taxes, depreciation, and insurance on store	4,000	
Interest paid on bank loans of $50,000 @ 6%	3,000	
Other expenses	4,000	33,000
		$12,000

In late 1968, one of the rapidly growing national jewelry chains offered Diamond $1,500 a month rent on his store under a long-term lease* and an opportunity to sell out his inventory and fixtures for $80,000. He could retire his bank loan and invest the other $30,000 at 6 percent and take a standing offer of $12,000 to join a downtown department store as manager of its jewelry department.

B. G. Diamond estimated that his store's future results would be similar to those in 1968, because, although business had been increasing, the national chain was likely to locate somewhere in the area and its competition would reduce gains.

Question

Revise his income statement to estimate economic profits and predict his decision.

---

*Diamond would have to meet the expense items: taxes, insurance, and depreciation.

2. STOCKS AND BONDS

Listed below are selected stock and bond prices, and other information relating to certain securities listed on the Toronto Stock Exchange.

STOCKS

1975				Recent	Last Price	Latest
High	Low	Company		Dividend	6/17/75	Price
48 3/8	43 3/4	Bell Telephone		$3.44	45	
44 3/4	34 5/8	Bank of Nova Scotia		1.60	44 3/4	
29 3/4	26	Steel Co. of Canada		1.30	27 5/8	
4.10	2.75	Koffler		0.10	3.45	

BONDS

Corporation or Government	Recent Bid Price	Contractual Interest	Latest Bid Price
Government of Alberta (1991)	$ 86.00	7 7/8%	
Seagrams Distillers (1995)	102.50	10 7/8%	
Government of Canada (1983)	80.38	4 1/2%	
Ontario Hydro (2000)	102.25	10 1/4%	

Questions

1. For the stocks above, what was the dividend as a percent of price on June 17, 1975? Find out the latest stock price and estimate the dividend as a percent of this latest price.

2. What might you infer about Bell Telephone from its dividend and its price fluctuations? What about Koffler?

3. Compute the present rate of return on the bonds listed above (contractual interest divided by the latest bond price). Why do you think that Government of Canada bonds yield the lowest rate? Compare these returns using the latest bid price on the above bonds.

4. Why do you think it is usually the case that the actual rate of return on stocks, measured by dividend divided by price, is less than the rate of return on bonds?

Chapter Eleven
Cost and Supply
in the Short Run

<table>
<tr><td>CHECKLIST</td><td>Make certain that you understand the following concepts: short run; fixed factors; variable factors; long run; very long run; production function; total product; average product; point of diminishing average productivity; marginal product; point of diminishing marginal productivity; total cost; fixed costs; variable costs; average total cost; average fixed costs; marginal cost; capacity; excess capacity; marginal revenue; industry; short-run supply curve; diminishing returns; law of variable proportions.</td></tr>
</table>

REVIEW QUESTIONS

1. A production function relates the amount of output to _the quantity of input used_ .

2. The period of time over which one or more inputs cannot be varied is called the _short run_ .

3. The period of time over which all inputs may be varied, but technological methods of production are fixed, is called the _long run_ .

4. The period of time long enough for basic production methods to be varied is called the _very long run_ .

5. Factors and costs that do not vary in the short run, regardless of the amount of output produced, are called _fixed_ factors and _fixed_ costs. Factors and costs that change in amount as quantity of output changes are called _variable_ costs.

6. In the short run, total output or product can be increased by adding variable factors to fixed factors. The amount added to total product by adding one more variable factor is called the _marginal product_ of that factor. Total produce divided by the quantities of variable factors used to produce it is called the _average product_ of those factors.

7. The hypothesis of eventually diminishing returns states that, as variable factors are added to fixed factors, there will be at some point a decline in first the _____ *Marginal* _____ and then the _____ *Average* _____ product. When diminishing returns have set in, the proportions of factors being used are (more/less) efficient and the factors are (more/less) productive than at lower outputs.

8. The average product rises when the marginal product is (higher/lower) than the average, and falls when it is (higher/lower) than the average.

9. By applying factor prices paid or imputed to factor quantities used in production, we get _____ *product cost* _____.

10. (a) To get *average cost* we divide _____ *Total Cost* _____ by _____ *total* _____ *output in units* _____.
    (b) "Spreading overhead costs" is demonstrated by dividing increasing amounts of output *into* _____ *fixed costs* _____.
    (c) Average fixed costs plus average variable costs equal _____ *ATC* _____.
    (d) Marginal costs are not affected by changes in (variable/fixed) costs.

11. At low levels of output, average costs usually fall because _____ *average fixed* _____ costs are falling rapidly; as output increases, this is often offset by rising _____ *average variable* _____ costs, so that average costs eventually (rise/fall) in the short run.

12. When average product per variable factor is a maximum, average variable cost will be _____ *at a minimum* _____.

13. The level of output at which short-run average cost is at a minimum is called _____ *plant capacity* _____.

14. By the "rules" of profit maximization, a firm in the short run would not produce at all unless the price is equal at least to _____ *AVC* _____ cost. At this point, he is incurring (profit/losses) equal to the amount of _____ *fixed* _____ costs.

15. A firm which is trying to maximize profits will expand output as long as the additional revenues per additional unit exceed the _____ *marginal cost* _____ of that unit.

16. Average and marginal costs usually rise beyond a certain level of output because of _____ *diminishing returns* _____. As a result, supply curves slope _____ *upward* _____ in the short run.

If you have not answered all questions correctly, review the text in order to be sure that you have all of the important concepts clearly in mind before going on to the next chapter.

1. the quantity of inputs used 2. short run 3. long run 4. very long run 5. fixed, fixed; variable or direct 6. marginal product; average product 7. marginal, average; less, less 8. higher; lower 9. production costs 10. (a) total cost, total output in units; (b) fixed costs; (c) average total costs, or average cost; (d) fixed 11. average fixed, average variable, rise 12. at a minimum 13. plant capacity 14. average variable; losses, fixed 15. marginal cost 16. diminishing returns; upward

MULTIPLE-CHOICE QUESTIONS

1. The production function relates
   (a) cost to input
   (b) cost to output
   (c) wages to profits
   (d) inputs to outputs

2. Which of the following is an example of a production decision in the short run?
   (a) a contractor buys two additional cement mixers and hires two new drivers for them
   (b) a contractor decides to work his crew overtime to finish a job
   (c) a railroad decides to eliminate all passenger service
   (d) a paper company takes only three weeks to install antipollution equipment

3. Short-run average costs eventually rise because of
   (a) rising overhead costs
   (b) rising factor prices
   (c) falling marginal and average productivity
   (d) decreasing returns to scale

4. The hypothesis of eventually diminishing returns applies to production function
   (a) having at least one fixed factor
   (b) in the long run only
   (c) in the very long run preferably
   (d) in which inputs are applied in fixed proportions

5. Long-run decisions
   (a) do not affect short-run decisions
   (b) can consider all factors variable
   (c) are not very important because the long run is a succession of short runs
   (d) are taken with fewer alternatives open than in the case of short-run decisions

6. Plant capacity is
   (a) the output at which unit costs are a minimum
   (b) the maximum output possible for a firm
   (c) where unit costs are a maximum
   (d) where marginal cost begins to rise

7. In the short run a firm wishing to maximize profits or minimize losses will
   (a) shut down unless fixed costs are met by revenue
   (b) produce as much as possible
   (c) operate at the plant's capacity whenever possible
   (d) produce as long as revenue exceeds all variable costs

8. Which of the following necessarily declines continuously?
   (a) marginal cost
   (b) average fixed cost
   (c) average variable cost
   (d) total fixed cost

9. When average cost is declining,
   (a) marginal cost must be declining
   (b) marginal cost must be above average cost
   (c) marginal cost must be below average cost
   (d) marginal cost must be rising

10. The "law of diminishing returns" describes
    (a) the fact of inevitable eventual unprofitability
    (b) the reduction in revenue resulting from falling prices
    (c) the declining marginal productivity of productive factors
    (d) the decline in total output from a given production function

EXERCISES

1. Using the vegetable garden example of Chapter 10, we can show the relationship between productivity and cost. The data below illustrate what happens if additional
   man-hours (the variable input or factor) are applied to a fixed input (land). The
   cost of the variable factor is $1 per unit, and fixed costs are $20.

Variable Input	Total Output	Average Product	Marginal Product	Average Cost	Marginal Cost
0	0		0	0	0
10	30	3	3	13	1
20	60	3	3	.67	
30	80	2.7	2		
40	90	2.25	1		
50	90	1.8	0		
60	90	1.5	0		

(a) Calculate the marginal and average product and the marginal and average cost.

(b) Graph the average- and marginal-
    product curves.

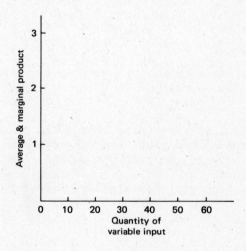

(c) Graph the average- and marginal-
      cost schedules.

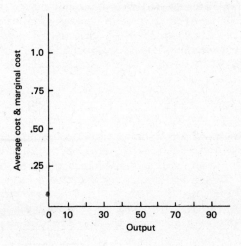

2. With fixed costs of $2, the marginal-cost
   schedule of a firm producing good X is
   shown in the graph at bottom right.

   (a) Calculate the total cost and average
       cost and plot them (approximately)
       on the graph at top right.

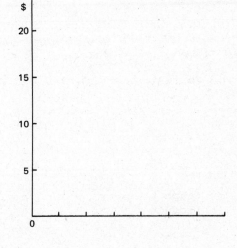

AC=TC-FC

AVC
vc

   (b) Calculate the average variable cost
       schedule and plot this (approxi-
       mately) on the graph at bottom right.

   (c) At what output levels will this firm
       be willing to produce? Why?

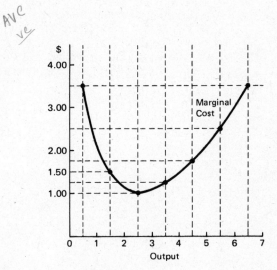

   (d) If the market price for good X is $2.50,
       will this firm produce good X? If so,
       what level of output?

3. Suppose the following costs apply to a single flight from Toronto to Vancouver on a Boeing 707 with 180 seats.

Maintenance and depreciation	$1200
Fuel	2600
Salary for Crew	3600
Administration salaries	2100
Sales and publicity	1100
Office rent	2800
Interest on debt	3500

(a) What are the average fixed costs (AFC) and the average variable costs (AVC) for this flight.

(b) In establishing fares, the government regulation agency sets the price per seat at the level which allows the airline to cover AFC when operating at 50 percent of capacity. What will be the regular fare per person on this run?

(c) Given this price, what is the marginal cost to the airline of carrying the ninety-first passenger on the flight?

(d) Should the airline agree to supply a charter flight for a group that offers to guarantee the sale of 140 tickets at $60 per seat? Explain.

4. A producer of a particular commodity finds that he has a total cost curve that can be described by the equation:

$$TC = \$50 + \$3Q + \$Q^2$$

(a) Complete the columns below. [*Hint*: $(3Q + Q^2)$ is obviously variable costs, and $50 is the fixed cost.]

Q	FC	VC	TC	MC	AFC	AVC	ATC
0	50	0	50	4	0	0	80
1	80	4	54	6	50	4	54
2	80	10	60		25	5	30
3	80						
4	80						
5							
6							
7							
8							
9							
10							
...	80						
20							

(b) At what output are total costs per unit (ATC) at a minimum?

(c) What is the marginal cost at this output?

(d) If, as shown above, there were only variable costs and no fixed costs, would MC be affected? *no effect* *VC*

(e) By examining the table above, explain why ATC decreases to a minimum value and then starts to rise.

PROBLEM

THE RISING COST OF DRIVING AN AUTOMOBILE

A. On June 13, 1971, the *New York Times* reported that the American Automobile Association's "cost-of-driving index" had risen to $1,550, an increase of $102 over the 1969 level. The $1,550 assumed 10,000 miles driven (the national average), made the calculations for full-sized Chevrolets (Impalas) with automatic transmission and power steering, and based the depreciation on a trade-in after four years.
The average costs were as follows:

Variable Costs	Average per Mile (cents)	
	1971	1969
Gas and oil	2.96	2.76
Maintenance	.73	.68
Tires	.56	.51
Total per mile	4.25	3.95
Fixed Costs	Annually (dollars)	
Fire and theft insurance	$ 62	$ 44
Collision insurance	125	102
Liability insurance	175	154
Licence and registration	25	24
Depreciation	738	729
Total per year	$1,125	$1,053

Questions

1. Assuming that the total variable costs vary proportionally with output (this means that AVC = MC; why?), complete this cost output table for 1971.

Output in Miles	TFC (dollars)	TVC	TTC	AFC	AVC = MC (cents)	ATC
5,000	$1,125				4.25	
10,000	$1,125				4.25	
15,000	$1,125				4.25	

2. Is it fair that firms should pay their employees 11 cents per mile for travel expenditures in view of the average cost of driving?

Chapter Twelve
Cost and Supply
in the Long Run

> **CHECKLIST** Make certain that you understand the following concepts: cost minimization; principle of substitution; long-run average cost curve; short-run average cost; increasing returns; decreasing returns; constant returns; envelope cost curve; long-run supply curve; rising supply price; replication. *Appendix:* isoquant; isoquant map; isocost line; returns to scale; returns to substitution; pecuniary returns to cost; returns to cost; minimal efficient scale.

REVIEW QUESTIONS

1. The "long run" is defined as a situation in which ___*all factors can be varied*___.

2. A profit-maximizing firm will always try to choose the method of production of a given output that costs ___*least*___. This means that it will equate the ratios of the marginal products of the factors of production to the ratio of ___*their prices*___.

3. If the marginal product of capital rises, *ceteris paribus,* the firm will tend to use relatively (more/less) of it. If the price of labor rises, *ceteris paribus,* the firm will tend to substitute ___*capital*___ for it.

4. The principle of substitution results in the greater use of factors that are (abundant/scarce) and therefore relatively (cheap/expensive). Thus the price system in a market economy acts to allocate factors so as to (waste/economize scarce resources.

5. The long-run cost curve is determined by factor ___*price*___ and by the state of ___*technology*___ in the industry.

6. Increasing returns mean that as output increases long-run average costs are ___*decreasing*___. This must be caused by either ___*fall in factor price*___ or ___*more efficient method*___, or both.

7. Decreasing returns mean that as output is increased long-run average costs ___*increasing*___. This must be caused by ___*rise in factor price*___,

because no one would deliberately choose to expand with a less efficient plant than is already attainable.

8. If in the long run, with constant factor prices, output increases at exactly the same rate as inputs, average costs and returns will be _____*constant*_____.

9. Except for the point of tangency between them, the short-run average cost curve will be (above/below) the long-run average cost curve.

10. A rise in the price of any factor will shift all cost curves (upward/downward). Technological changes will shift cost curves (upward/downward).

11. The long-run supply curve's shape depends on what happens to _____*AC*____ as output of the firm and industry expands. The expansion takes place in two ways: _____*entry of new firms*_____ and _____*existing firms*_____.

_____

If you have not answered all questions correctly, review the text in order to be sure that you have all of the important concepts clearly in mind before going on to the next chapter.

1. all factors can be varied 2. least; their prices 3. more; capital 4. abundant, cheap; economize 5. prices, technology 6. decreasing; more efficient methods of production, lower factor prices 7. increase; rising factor prices 8. constant 9. above 10. upward; downward 11. average cost; entry of new firms, existing firms building new plants
_____

MULTIPLE-CHOICE QUESTIONS

1. The long-run average cost curve
   (a) shows total output related to total input
   (b) assumes constant factor proportions throughout
   (c) reflects the least-cost production method for each output level
   (d) rises because of the "law" of diminishing returns

2. Constant long-run average costs for a firm mean that
   (a) there are greater advantages to small- rather than large-scale plants
   (b) an unlimited amount will be produced
   (c) any scale of production is as cheap per unit as any other
   (d) no addition of factors is taking place

3. Decreasing average costs for a firm as it expands plant size and output
   (a) result from decreasing returns to scale
   (b) results usually from the effects of increased mechanization and specialization
   (c) result from the increased complexity and confusion of rapid expansion
   (d) are a very rare case caused by exogenous events

4. If the marginal product of capital is six times that of labor and the price of capital is three times that of labor,
   (a) capital will be substituted for labor
   (b) labor will be substituted for capital
   (c) the price of capital will fall, of labor will rise
   (d) twice as much capital as labor will be employed

5. The long-run average cost curve is determined by
   (a) long-run demand
   (b) long-run supply
   (c) population growth and inflation
   (d) technology and input prices

6. Long-run decreasing returns are evidently the result of
   (a) rising factor prices
   (b) replication
   (c) "spreading the overhead"
   (d) incompetent management

7. A rise in labor cost relative to capital costs in an industry, *ceteris paribus*, will
   (a) lead to replacement of some workers by machines where possible
   (b) cause the industry to be unprofitable
   (c) necessarily increase long-run costs
   (d) tend to be offset by rising labor productivity

8. A firm facing long-run increasing returns should expand by
   (a) substituting labor for capital
   (b) replication
   (c) building smaller plants
   (d) building larger plants

Appendix

9. An isocost line for two factors C and L (their respective prices are P_C and P_L) could have which of the following equations?
   (a) $LC = \$100$
   (b) $\$100 = P_C + P_L$
   (c) $\$100 = P_L L + P_C C$
   (d) $\$100 = P_L P_C$

10. With factors C and L graphed in the same unit scale with C on the vertical axis, an isocost line has the slope = -2; therefore,
    (a) $P_L = 2P_C$
    (b) $P_C/P_L = 2$
    (c) $C = 2L$
    (d) $L = 2C$

least-cost method

11. At the point of tangency of this isocost line with an isoquant,
    (a) the desired factor combination has $2C$ for each L
    (b) the marginal product of labor is twice that of capital
    (c) the desired factor combination has $2L$ for each C
    (d) the marginal product of capital is twice that of labor

$$\frac{MPL}{MPk} = \frac{Pk}{PL}$$

12. If firms are profit maximizers, we should not expect to find a competitive firm expanding its scale if it faces
    (a) increasing returns to scale
    (b) decreasing returns to scale
    (c) constant returns to scale
    (d) pecuniary returns to cost

EXERCISES

1. At the beginning of some time period, it is observed that a firm producing 10,000 bottles of wine per month uses the following inputs of capital (K) and labour (L) per month:

$$K = 50 \text{ units}$$
$$L = 1000 \text{ units}$$

The price of capital per unit is $20, and for labour the price is $4.

As the firm increases its output over time, the following changes in the use of capital and labour are observed:

Outper per Month	K	L	
20,000	100	1800	0.46
40,000	180	3000	0.3
60,000	250	4000	0.3
80,000	400	7200	0.46
100,000	600	10000	0.52

(a) Calculate and graph the long-run average-cost curve.

(b) At what output level do increasing returns come to an end?

(c) What happens to the ratio of capital to labour inputs as output expands?

$$\frac{P_K}{P_L}$$

(d) If the price of labour were increasing steadily over time, what might happen to the mix of labour and capital inputs as the firm expands? Justify your answer.

2. Below is a table showing hypothetical costs for a firm as it expands output and plant size.

Output (units)	100,000	200,000	300,000	400,000	500,000
Materials	$ 50,000	$100,000	$150,000	$200,000	$250,000
Labour	$100,000	$180,000	$260,000	$340,000	$440,000
Capital (interest and depreciation)	$ 50,000	$ 90,000	$130,000	$170,000	$220,000
Average cost	2	1.85	1.8	1.78	1.82

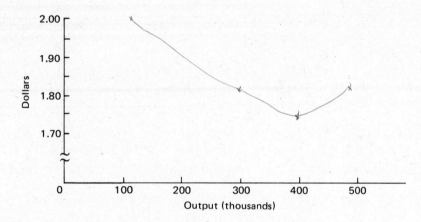

(a) Calculate the average cost for each level of output above and plot it on the graph.

(b) Returns to scale continue until what output is reached? _____400_____

(c) Would you says that there seems to be substitution occurring, or not? _constant_

(d) Judging from these figures, what would you recommend that this firm do if it wants to produce output of 800,000 units?

bruet two plant

(e) Under what circumstances might long-run supply of 1,600,000 require a cost greater than $1.78 per unit?

3. *(Appendix)* The diagram to the right illustrates how various levels of output can be
   produced by different combinations of
   capital and labour.

   (a) If the ratio of the price of capital
       to that of labour were

       $$\frac{L}{K} = \frac{1}{1}$$

       how many units of capital and labour
       will the firm use to produce 100 units
       of output?

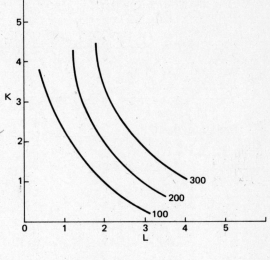

   alternative way to produce
   6 unit
   6 · 8 = √LK

   (b) If the price of capital per unit were to fall by 100 percent and the firm wished
       to produce 200 units of output, approximately how much capital and labour would
       it employ?

4. Suppose the input-output data for a firm are as shown in the table below.

		Labour Inputs			
		1	2	3	4	5
	1					
Capital Inputs	2		100*	100	100	100
	3		100	150	150	150
	4		100	150	200	200
	5		100	150	200	

*Units of output.

(a) Draw the isoquant map for the three levels of output.

(b) What impact would a change in the relative factor prices have on the mix of capital and labour used in the firm? Justify your answer.

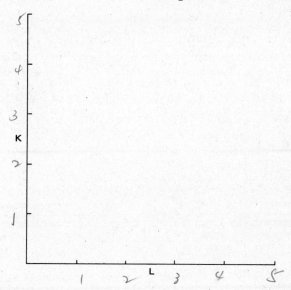

Chapter Thirteen
The Very Long Run: Progress and Pollution

CHECKLIST Make certain that you understand the following concepts: productivity; invention; innovation; private cost; social cost; externalities (third-party effects); common property resource.

REVIEW QUESTIONS

1. Three kinds of changes affect the production function in the very long run. They are changes in: _available techniques of production_, ~~types of good & services produced~~ and _quality of inputs_ .

2. The use of tractors instead of horses on farms is an example of a change in ___available technique of production___

3. A rise in the average number of years of education of the work force is an example of a change in _____ _quality of input_ .

4. At the time they were invented and introduced, phonograph records would have been an example of a change in _types of goods & services produced_

5. By *productivity* we mean a measure of output per unit of ___input___ . *Labour* productivity is measured by output per ___man-hour___ .

6. Since World War II, labour productivity in the United States has been rising at an average annual rate of almost ___2___ percent.

7. For the machines, production processes, and transportation requirements of a modern industrial society, the basic need is sources of ___energy or power___ .

8. When an invention is put to use in production, ___innovation___ has occurred.

9. Because innovation occurs when it seems profitable, it is an (endogenous/exogenous) ✓ process.

10. If the act of invention is responsive to financial incentives, it would be considered (endogenous/exogenous).

11. Dismal predictions of population growth outrunning the supply of food and other resources were implied by the "law" of _____ *plentiful* _____. Instead, until now, living standards improved as a result of _____.

12. The value of the best alternative uses of resources that are available to the whole society is called _____ *social cost* _____.

13. *Externalities* discussed in this chapter result when social costs (exceed/are less than) _____.

14. One way for society to induce a polluting firm to adopt antipollution devices is by providing incentives such as _____ *penalties* _____.

15. If anti-air-pollution regulations cause a firm to close down because of the cost, there may be a conflict between the goals of cleaner air and *local employment*.

16. The examples of social costs and externalities given in the book indicate that they are incurred (always/only sometimes) because of the profit motive.

17. Governmental intervention is more likely when the difference between private and social costs is (large/small).

18. In deciding how many resources to put into the fight against pollution, the economic answer would be to compare the benefits to be gained with the _____ *cost* of the action.

If you have not answered all questions correctly, review the text in order to be sure that you have all of the important concepts clearly in mind before going on to the next chapter.

1. available techniques of production; types of goods and services produced; quality of inputs 2. available techniques of production 3. quality of inputs 4. types of goods and services produced 5. input; man-hour 6. 3 7. energy or power 8. innovation 9. endogenous 10. endogenous 11. plentiful, cheap; less than 12. cleaning up afterward; changing the techniques; prohibiting the activity 13. cost 14. penalties or fines for polluting 15. local employment 16. only sometimes 17. large 18. cost

---

MULTIPLE-CHOICE QUESTIONS

1. A major source of the large increase in the standard of living in this century is
   (a) population growth
   (b) advertising
   (c) an increase in output per unit of input
   (d) increases in production keeping pace with population growth

2. Aspects of production functions that have been altered by technological change are
   (a) types of inputs
   (b) production processes
   (c) kinds of output
   (d) all of the above

3. We need not consider the explanation of the introduction of new techniques into the productive process as part of the theory of supply if
   (a) they are endogenous to the firm's decisions
   (b) we know that invention is a random process
   (c) we are considering an underdeveloped economy
   (d) we decide that innovation is completely exogenous

4. Population growth may lead directly to increased productivity through
   (a) substitution of capital for labor
   (b) increases in the quality of inputs
   (c) scale effects
   (d) substitution of labor for capital

5. Innovation is defined as
   (a) any particularly important invention
   (b) an invention whose source is endogenous to the firm
   (c) a change in output per unit of input
   (d) the initial introduction of a significant change in a production function.

6. Private efficiency
   (a) economizes the use of all resources
   (b) economizes the use of resources the firm pays for
   (c) does not involve any economizing process
   (d) in a market economy will always correspond with social efficiency

7. Air pollution has as its most important cause in the United States
   (a) industrial activity including electrical power generation
   (b) the widespread and increasing use of automobiles
   (c) the home-heating requirements of larger populations
   (d) such natural processes as volcanic activity and forest pollen

8. Considerations of social efficiency
   (a) call for the elimination of all water and air pollution
   (b) require the abandonment of market incentives
   (c) indicate the need for a variety of interventions into markets
   (d) mitigate against attempts to increase productivity

EXERCISES

1. Productivity in Agriculture

	Index of Farm Production (1967 = 100)	Crop Production per Acre (1967 = 100)	Man-hours of Farm Labor Number (billions)	Man-hours of Farm Labor Index (1967 = 100)	Index of Total Inputs (1967 = 100)	Index of Fertilizer Input (1967 = 100)	Index of Mechanical Power and Machinery (1967 = 10
1930	53	52	22.9	315	89	10	36
1940	59	62	20.5	282	89	14	38
1950	73	69	15.1	208	93	33	77
1960	90	89	9.8	135	93	55	93
1970	103	103	6.7	92	104	114	104

Sources: U.S. Department of Agriculture. Reported in *Economic Report of the President.*

(a) Which of the columns is a productivity index?

(b) What might you conclude from the figures in columns 1 and 2 about the amount of land in the United States used for agriculture in 1970 compared with 1930?

(c) The increase in what input seems particularly associated with the increase in crop production per acre of land? What evidence is there to suggest the possible applicability of the hypothesis of diminishing returns?

(d) Between 1930 and 1970, agricultural production almost doubled and labor input decreased to substantially less than one-third of that of 1930. Therefore, labor productivity in agriculture in 1970 was more than _____ times as great as in 1930.

(e) What evidence is there above of the technological changes responsible for this?

(f) Why would it be misleading to say that overall productivity in agriculture increased over six times between 1930 and 1970?

(g) Construct a labor productivity index for agriculture (1967 = 100); 1930 _____ _____; 1940 _____; 1950 _____; 1960 _____; 1970 _____.

(h) Over what part of this period was the change so rapid as to suggest the term "revolution"?

2. The following schedule shows (1) how the cost of resources increases as a pulp and paper firm expands output and (2) the effect of pollution from the firm on commercial fishing in the area.

Output (tons/wk)	Total Private Cost	Dollar Value of Fishing Loss Due to Pollution
0	0	0
1	500	100
2	550	225
3	620	365
4	710	515
5	820	675
6	1050	845
7	1350	1025

(a) Complete the table below and graph your results.

Average Private Cost (APC)	Marginal Private Cost (MC)	Average Social Cost (ASC)	Marginal Social Cost (MSC)

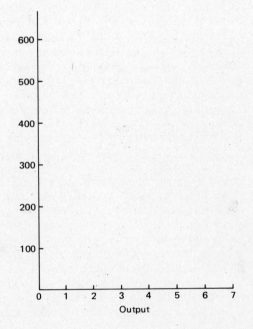

(b) If the firm were producing four tons of output per week, what price would they require to cover their private cost? What price would they require to cover the social cost?

(c) If pricing were based on the average costs and *all* costs of producing pulp and paper were considered, then the price of pulp and paper would always be _____ than the case where only private costs are considered.

PROBLEMS

1. THE ECONOMICS OF POLLUTION

A. The Canada Water Act

In 1970, the Federal Government of Canada passed legislation that established the Canada Water Act. The following remarks are by the Honorable J. J. Greene, Minister of Energy, Mines and Resources, delivered during the second reading of the Bill in 1969.*

Waste disposal is not necessarily an illegitimate use for water and it does not necessarily interfere with other uses for water because our waterways, if not overloaded, can purify themselves. It is only when the natural ability of water to cleanse itself is surpassed that we find this use of water interfering with other uses of that precious resource.

All of this makes one point very clear. Our water must be so used as to ensure the maximum stream of benefits to all of the users for all of the purposes for which water is requried. This optimization can only occur if we have comprehensive planning to achieve our goal of multi-purpose use. We must look at each basin as an integrated whole. We must examine all the uses which can be made of each basin. We must plan for the future so as to achieve the greatest long-term net social benefit of our water resources. The Canada water bill will allow us to do this—to plan together with the provinces firstly the optimum utilization of our water resources, taking into account all the uses which can be made of our water; and secondly, the re-establishment of water quality to preserve the best balance among these uses.

. . . we are facing a costly problem and we shall not avoid it. It will cost Canadian society some billions of dollars over a period of time to deal with its water resources in a rational way, and to undo the damage we have done in the last hundred years. But let us think of the alternate cost, that of doing nothing. To begin with, doing nothing is a threat to our entire way of life, and, yes, perhaps to life itself. Eventually, if we do not act to clean up air and water pollution, if we allow our environment to run down further we may upset the ecological and climatological balances of nature upon which life itself depends.

But even if the problem we face has not yet reached this peak, there are huge social costs involved. It is not hard to imagine the day—not far off if we do not act—when there will be no place within easy range of our cities where a person can go to swim in a natural river or lake, or any accessible place where fish can still live, or any place to just walk beside a pleasant stream. Our society will have its two cars in every garage but there will be no fit outdoor

* Canada, *House of Commons Debates*, Nov. 20, 1969.

place in which to drive them. Yes, we will have our superclean, automatically washed clothes, but will there be any place fit to walk in these snow white garments? These are staggering social costs, costs that neither we nor our children will have to pay, if we act now.

Then, too, there are the purely monetary costs. Water despoiled by man must be cleaned again for his own use. The cost of purifying the water we have first made dirty is high. How much better to clean up our effluents before we put them into our rivers. For we then have the double benefit of clean water while it is in the stream, and drastically lowered purification costs when we want to use it again.

There are other monetary costs as well. The salmon run in certain maritime rivers may be dying because of our pollution. With it would die a source of revenue as well as of pleasure. Our other fisheries are also threatened by pollution, and with them would go the livelihood and the way of life of thousands of Canadians. Our tourist industry depends in no small part on the cleanliness of our streams, rivers and lakes . . . Without the use of our most important single resource, water, the future of the industry would be a bleak one indeed!

The problem has arisen from the unwise use of resources that come to us free of charge. The lesson which we can learn from the past is a vital one. It is simply this, that the unplanned and uncontrolled use of our resources, even though they come free, as does water, can lead us to disaster. The first principle of the Canada water bill, and of the thinking of experts of all persuasions across Canada, is that no longer can we afford the unplanned and uncontrolled use of our water resources. No longer can each individual, each industry, each municipality, use our water resources as each sees fit. In that absolute and laissez-faire freedom lies the mistake of the past, and the disaster of the future. Those who use our waters must pay for that use, either by cleaning up what they discharge into our river basins, or by paying others to clean it up for them. This is the very gist of the Canada Water Act and the essence of its structure, that the user must pay for cleaning the water, for putting it back into the condition in which he found it and for improving it if indeed it requires improvement. The result, it is true, may be higher direct costs for certain goods and services. But as we look at these costs, we must remember that there will be savings to other users of the water who also have a right to expect that the water they receive will be clean and in good condition when it reaches them. We must remember, too, that there is no way we can avoid these costs and still maintain the quality of life. Everyone in society must eventually pay; this is the thing we must remember, and all society will thereby gain.

Questions

1. Why is it that the "social costs" referred to by Mr. Greene cannot normally be considered part of the total production costs of any polluting activity?

2. Why do you think man uses "free" resources unwisely?

B. Effluent Charges

Section 13(1) subsection (c)(iv) of the Canada Water Act reads that water quality management agencies will recommend ". . . as to the appropriate effluent discharge fees to be paid by persons for the deposit of waste in those waters. . . ."

Questions

1. What factors do you feel should be considered in setting the amount of the fee?

2. What problems do you envisage in making these fees workable?

2. THE NOISY FACTORY

Consider a factory which is causing such excessive noise that it seriously affects the enjoyment of living for residents in three houses nearby. The residents file a complaint, and, in the hearing which follows, the following information is revealed:

1. The cost to the factory to reduce the noise would be $150,000.
2. The expense of relocating the three homes would be $100,000.

Questions

1. If you had to decide on efficiency grounds *alone,* what should be done? What would you recommend? Why?

2. If the law were such that it was a person's "right" to have a quiet place of residence, why would the factory probably pay for the relocation of the homes?

Chapter Fourteen
Pricing in
Competitive
Markets

CHECKLIST	Make certain that you understand the following concepts: market structure; equilibrium; price taker; freedom of entry and exit; perfect competition; short-run supply curve of competitive firm and industry; short-run equilibrium; long-run equilibrium.

REVIEW QUESTIONS

1. The number of firms in a market and the similarity of their products are two aspects of ___*market structures*___.

2. A behavioral rule for a profit-maximizing firm is that it should not produce at all unless total revenue exceeds or equals total ___*variable cost*___.

3. A firm in perfect competition (has/has no) influence over the price it receives for its product; hence, it is called a ___*price taker*___.

4. Such a firm can sell any amount of output, limited only by its capacity to produce, without lowering its price below the market price, but it will make no sales at all if it raises its price above the market, so its demand curve is ___*horizontal*___ and its elasticity is, for all practical purposes, ___*infinite*___. Its marginal revenue curve is the same as its ___*demand curve*___.

5. In most cases, beyond a certain output each additional unit adds more to costs than did the previous unit; in other words, ___*marginal*___ cost is ___*rising*___.

6. Therefore, if a firm wishes to maximize profits, it will expand or contract its output to the amount at which the marginal cost of that extra output ___*equals*___ the price at which it can sell the extra output.

7. Whether or not the firm produces any output, it still has incurred ___*fixed*___ costs. In deciding whether to produce at all in the short run, the profit-maximizing firm will (ignore/insist on covering) these costs. It will insist that its selling price at least covers average ___*VC*___ cost.

8. If, for instance, production costs are $1 per unit in addition to the $1,000 of fixed costs already incurred, a selling price of ___*$1*___ would be the minimum for which the firm should produce. If the firm did not produce, the total losses would be ___*1000*___. If the market price were 80 cents and this firm produced 1,000 units, its total losses would be ___*1200*___. The firm would lose (more/less) by not producing at all.

9. The firm's short-run supply curve has the same shape as the firm's ___*M*___ cost curve to the right of its intersection with the minimum of the average ___*VC*___ cost curve.

10. If one store has much more business than another because it has a much better location, it incurs (more/less) rent than the other. If one firm has a manager more effective in keeping production costs down than has another firm, that manager will have a (higher/lower) salary. Thus, these factor advantages are costs to the advantaged firm, and we can therefore say that, according to this opportunity-cost principle, firms in a perfectly competitive industry will have (the same/differing) average costs.

11. In short-run equilibrium, with price = marginal cost, the firm will be making profits if market price exceeds average ___*T*___ costs.

12. With such profits the ___*entry*___ of new firms can be predicted until the price is driven down to the level of ___*average total*___ costs. Short-run losses, on the other hand, should lead to the ___*exit*___ of firms.

   If you have not answered all questions correctly, review the text in order to be sure that you have all of the important concepts clearly in mind before going on to the next chapter.

1. market structure 2. variable cost 3. has no; price taker 4. horizontal, infinite; demand curve 5. marginal; rising 6. equals 7. fixed; ignore; variable 8. $1; $1,000; $1,200; less 9. marginal; variable 10. more; higher; the same 11. total 12. entry, average total; exit

---

MULTIPLE-CHOICE QUESTIONS

1. A perfectly competitive firm does not try to sell more of its product by lowering its price below the market price because
   (a) this would be considered unethical price chiseling
   (b) its competitors will not permit it
   (c) its demand curve is inelastic, so total revenue will decline
   (d) it can sell all it wants to at the market price

2. If the market demand for wheat has an elasticity of 0.25,
   (a) an individual wheat farmer can increase his revenue by reducing output
   (b) nothing can be said about the elasticity of demand for a wheat farmer
   (c) revenue from wheat sales will rise with an increase of industry production
   (d) each wheat farmer, nevertheless, faces a highly elastic demand

3. Which is *not* a required characteristic of a perfectly competitive industry?
   (a) Consumers have no reason to prefer one firm's product to another.
   (b) There are enough firms so none can influence market price.
   (c) Any firm can enter or leave the industry.
   (d) Industry demand is highly elastic.

4. Long-run profits are incompatible with a perfectly competitive industry because
    (a) new firms will enter the industry and eliminate them
    (b) corporate income taxes eliminate such excess profits
    (c) competitive industries are too inefficient to be profitable
    (d) long-run increasing costs eliminate profits

5. In long-run equilibrium in an industry of perfectly competitive, profit-maximizing firms,
    (a) price will equal average variable cost
    (b) price will exceed marginal cost
    (c) price will equal average total cost
    (d) average fixed cost will be at a minimum

6. The conditions for long-run competitive equilibrium include all but one of the following for all firms:
    (a) $P = AVC$
    (b) $P = MC$
    (c) $P = AVC + AFC$
    (d) $P = LRATC$

7. If several firms in a competitive industry could achieve economies of large scale by doubling their outputs,
    (a) we predict that equilibrium will occur at double the present output
    (b) we predict there can be no equilibrium
    (c) we can say that the industry is not now in equilibrium and perhaps there will be no competitive equilibrium
    (d) we predict that the firms will prefer their present output rather than glut the market

8. In the short run, a profit-maximizing firm will produce additional units of a product as long as
    (a) price covers at least average fixed cost
    (b) additional revenue per unit exceeds additional cost per unit
    (c) total revenue is increasing
    (d) elasticity of demand is infinite

9. Equilibrium price and output in a market
    (a) are established where the amount people wish to buy equals the amount people wish to sell
    (b) depend entirely on cost
    (c) depend entirely on demand
    (d) are best described as the price existing at a particular time

EXERCISES

1. At present output levels, a competitive firm finds itself with the following:

    Output: 5,000 units   Fixed costs: $2,000   Marginal cost: $1.25 and
    Market price: $1.00   Variable costs: $2,500   rising

    (a) Is it maximizing profits? Why? no p ≠ MC
    (b) Should it produce more, produce less, or stay the same? _____ produce less _____

2. The graph shows the short-run cost situation of a hypothetical perfectly competitive, profit-maximizing firm. Fill in the blanks below.

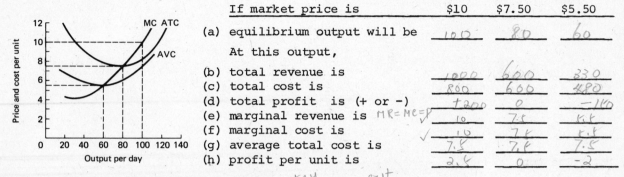

If market price is	$10	$7.50	$5.50
(a) equilibrium output will be	100	80	60
At this output,			
(b) total revenue is	1000	600	330
(c) total cost is	800	600	480
(d) total profit is (+ or -)	+200	0	-150
(e) marginal revenue is MR=Mc=P ✓	10	7.5	5.5
(f) marginal cost is ✓	10	7.5	5.5
(g) average total cost is	7.5	7.5	7.5
(h) profit per unit is	2.5	0	-2

(i) Why would we expect that neither $10 nor $5.50 will be the long-run market price?   *entry   exit*

3. Another competitive firm has the following:

Output: 80 units   Average total costs are at minimum and
Market Price: $10   are equal to $7.50.

(a) What is marginal cost at this output? _____ 7.5 _____
(b) Is the firm making profits? ___ yes ___
(c) Is it making maximum profits? ___ no ___
(d) Should it change its output? ___ yes ___
    (Refer to the diagram accompanying exercise 2.) 100

4. The diagram at right illustrates the cost position of a firm operating in a perfectly competitive market, immediately following the introduction of a cost-saving innovation.

(a) What initial advantage is this firm enjoying?

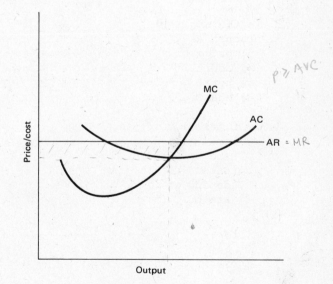

(b) Can this advantage remain? Justify your answer by noting what will be taking place in the market as a whole.   NO entry of firm

5. The supply (S) and demand (D) schedules for an industry are shown below in the figure on the left. The cost schedule for one firm in this industry is shown in the figure on the right.

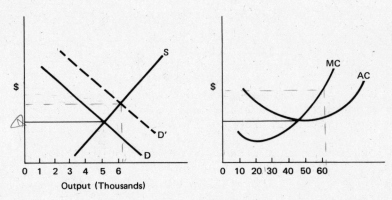

Output (Thousands)

(a) Does the above information suggest that the industry is a perfectly competitive one? Give your reasons. *yes*

price-taker

no abnormal profit

(b) If the market demand schedule were to shift to D', what is the initial impact on the price of output in this industry and on the profits of the firm?

increase in price

" " quantity

(c) What change in the above diagram would be necessary to bring the firm back into a position of "normal" profits?

supply shift → meet demand

entry of new firm

PROBLEM

COMPETITION IN WORLD MARKETS

The "representative" Canadian firm in a perfectly competitive world market has the following cost and output schedule:

Output	Total Cost	Average Cost	Marginal Cost	Average Cost (with tax)
10,000	$ 40,000	$ 4	$ 0	$ 4.5
20,000	60,000	3	2	3.5
30,000	70,000	2.33	1	2.33
40,000	80,000	2	1	2.5
50,000	120,000	2.4	4	2.9
60,000	180,000	3	6	3.5

Questions

1. Calculate the average- and marginal-cost schedules.

2. If the world price is roughly $2.25, what output would this firm produce?

3. Why would Canadian firms in this market strongly oppose a federal sales tax of 0.50 per unit of output?

Calculate the average-cost schedule that would occur if it were imposed.

Chapter Fifteen
Pricing in
Monopoly Markets

> **CHECKLIST** Make certain that you understand the following concepts: monopoly; monopoly power; collusion; equilibrium of a monopoly firm; concentration ratio; price discrimination.

REVIEW QUESTIONS

1. The demand curve of a monopoly firm is the same as that of its ___*industry*___ . Therefore, it must slope ___*downward*___ .

2. If a monopoly firm aims to maximize its profits, its output will be set where its marginal ___*revenue*___ equals ___*marginal*___ cost.

3. The demand curve of a monopoly firm is the same as its ___*Average*___ revenue curve. Its marginal revenue curve will lie ___*below*___ the demand or average revenue curve.

4. Thus, at the price and output set by such a monopolist, the price will (exceed/ equal/be less than) the marginal cost.

5. There (is only/is more than) one price and output at which a firm may be making some profit. If price exceeds ___*average Total*___ cost, the firm will be earning profits.

6. Because marginal cost cannot be negative, the most profitable output for a monopolist will be where marginal revenue is (positive/negative) and thus where demand is (elastic/inelastic).

7. Monopoly and monopoly profits can persist in the long run because of ___*monetary*___ ___*barries entry*___ of new firms.

8. *Monopoly power* (varies in degree/means complete monopoly).

9. A firm's monopoly power will be greater, the (larger/smaller) the shifts in its demand caused by the actions of other sellers.

10. The share of total industry sales held by the four largest companies in an industry is called the ___*concentration ratio*___ .

11. Two different prices charged for the same product do not constitute price discrimination if they are based on differences in ____cost____.

12. (a) The downward-sloping demand curve indicates that there are (*some*/no) buyers willing to pay more than the going market price for a commodity.
    (b) The fact that these buyers pay a lower price than they would be willing to gives them the benefit that is called the ___consumer's surplus___.
    (c) If a monopoly firm can sell some of its output at prices corresponding to what these buyers are willing to pay, total revenue can be ___increased___.

13. Two conditions are necessary for a firm to be able to practice price discrimination:
    (a) ___control the supply___
    (b) ___unable to resale___

14. *Ceteris paribus,* a monopoly firm charging a single price will, compared to a firm charging discriminatory prices, receive (*more*/less) revenue and produce a (larger/*smaller*) output.

15. If the monopolist were able to achieve perfect price discrimination, his marginal revenue curve would become the same as his ___demand___ curve. His profit-maximizing output would as usual be where MR = ___MC___, which in this case would be (less than/*the same as*/more than) the output of a perfect competitor.

   If you have not answered all questions correctly, review the text in order to be sure that you have all of the important concepts clearly in mind before going on to the next chapter.

1. industry; downward 2. revenue; marginal 3. average; below 4. exceed 5. are more than; average total 6. positive; elastic 7. barriers to entry 8. varies in degree 9. smaller 10. concentration ratio 11. cost 12. some; consumer's surplus; increased 13. can control supply to particular buyer; can prevent resale 14. less; smaller 15. demand; MC, the same as

---

MULTIPLE-CHOICE QUESTIONS

1. If profits are to be maximized by a firm, whether a monopolist or a competitor,
   (a) output should be increased whenever marginal cost is below average cost
   (b) output should be increased whenever marginal revenue is less than marginal cost
   (c) output should be set where unit costs are at a minimum
   (d) output should be increased whenever marginal revenue exceeds marginal cost

2. A monopolist has a downward-sloping demand curve
   (a) because it has an inelastic demand
   (b) because, typically, it sells only to a few large buyers
   (c) because it is the same as the industry
   (d) because consumers prefer that product

3. At the profit-maximizing output for a nondiscriminating monopolist,
   (a) price equals marginal cost
   (b) price exceeds marginal cost
   (c) price exceeds average total cost
   (d) price equals marginal revenue

4. In a monopolized industry,
   (a) other firms have no incentive to enter
   (b) profits are inevitable
   (c) there must be barriers to entry if the monopoly is to persist
   (d) there will be less incentive to lower costs than under competition

5. Monopoly power
   (a) can be measured quite precisely
   (b) varies inversely with the concentration ratio
   (c) implies a degree of control over price
   (d) is a term used only for complete monopolies

6. Concentration ratios have been found
   (a) to have considerable correlation with profit rates
   (b) to have little usefulness where there are more than two firms
   (c) to have little relevance in measuring the degree of monopoly power in an industry
   (d) to be very low in the great majority of manufacturing industries

7. Price discrimination is possible only
   (a) in the case of perfect monopoly
   (b) if it is possible to keep it a secret
   (c) if it is possible to conspire with competitors
   (d) if it is possible to separate the buyers or units that can be sold at different prices

8. A monopoly firm will not have more than normal profits unless
   (a) it practices price discrimination
   (b) its price exceeds average total cost
   (c) its marginal revenue exceeds marginal cost
   (d) it faces an inelastic demand curve

9. Which sentence below best describes the behavior of a profit-maximizing monopolist?
   (a) He picks a price he knows will give him a profit and sells as much as he can.
   (b) He produces as much as he can and sets whatever price is necessary to sell it all.
   (c) He seeks to select a price at which the additional revenue associated with one more unit just equals the addition to cost.
   (d) He sets price equal to marginal cost at his most profitable output.

10. Output under price discrimination will
    (a) generally be larger than under single-price monopoly
    (b) be produced at higher average cost than under single-price monopoly
    (c) usually be the same as under perfect competition
    (d) be indeterminate because we cannot know what prices can be charged

EXERCISES

1. The diagram at the top of the next page shows the demand and average cost situation of a hypothetical monopoly firm.
   (a) What is the output where the firm's profits will be at a maximum? ___60___
   (b) What will be the price at this output? _____11_____
   (c) What will be the total revenue (at this output)? ___660___
   (d) What will be the total costs? ___480___
   (e) What will be the total profit? ___180___
   (f) Within what *range* of output and price will the firm also make at least *some* profit, though not maximum? 28-10   14.8-7.8
   (g) What price would limit the monopolist to competitive profits? ___7.8___

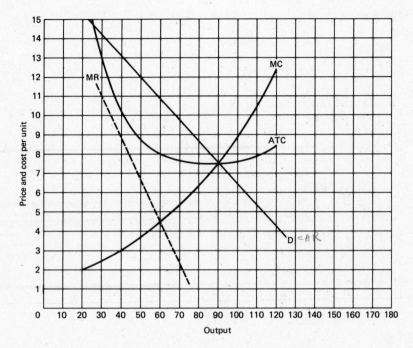

2. The data below relate to a pure monopolist and the product that he produces.

Output	Total Cost	Price	Quantity Demanded
0	$20	$14	0
1	24	12	2
2	27	10	4
3	32	8	6
4	39	6	8
5	48	4	10
6	59	2	12

(a) What additional cost and demand information do you need before you can calculate the profit-maximizing output and price for the monopolist?

(b) Calculate these additional schedules and plot them (roughly) below.

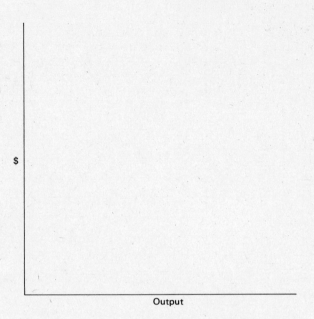

(c) What is the approximate profit-maximizing output?

(d) At what price will the monopolist sell his product?

(e) To calculate the monopolist's profits, what further cost schedule is necessary?

(f) Calculating this, what is the total monopoly profit in this case?

PROBLEM

THE NORTHERN DOCTOR

Dr. Lawrence practiced in a remote northern region over 50 miles from other medical services. To cover his family living expenditures and the fixed overhead expenses connected to his modest clinic required $20,000 gross income. (This amount was below the income he might command elsewhere but would be adequate.) In addition, he had expenses associated with visits estimated at $1.00 a visit. (This common unit, a visit, represents, of course, a considerable simplification of the variety of medical services he provided.)

The population of the area could be roughly divided into two groups. The first consisted of relatively prosperous oilmen, civil servants, merchants, and mining executives. The second, a lower income group, included those whose employment was based on fishing, hunting and trapping, as well as a few prospectors.

Assume that the demand for Dr. Lawrence's services is described by smoothly drawn curves through the points given in the table and that Dr. Lawrence can provide a maximum of 5,000 visits per year.

Hypothetical Demand Schedule for Dr. Lawrence's Services

Fee	Group I Visits	Group II Visits	Total Visits
$25	300	0	300
20	500	0	500
15	700	200	900
10	900	800	1,700
5	1,100	2,000	3,100
0	1,300	3,700	5,000

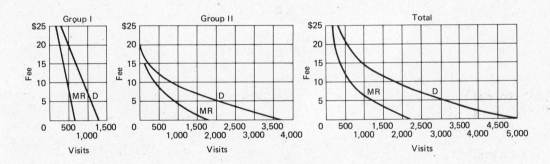

Note: The MR curves were plotted at interval midpoints as follows:
  Group I: $12.50 at an output of 400, $2.50 at 600, -$7.50 at 800.
  Group II: $15.00 at 100, $8.33 at 500, $1.67 at 1,400.
  Total: $8.75 at 700, $4.38 at 1,300, -$1.07 at 2,400.

Interested students may wish to work out reasons for this.

Questions

1. Evaluate the following pricing alternatives by the criteria below. To size up Dr. Lawrence's problem, draw the long-run average cost curve on the "total" graph, and to help in the evaluations draw the MC curve on all three diagrams.

	Price(s)	Output	TR	TVC	TC	TR - TC
(a) One-price system	____	____	____	____	____	____
(b) Two-price system						
I	____	____	____	____	xxx	xxx
II	____	____	____	____	xxx	xxx
Total	xxx	____	____	____	____	____
(c) Perfect price discrimination from	____	____	____	____	____	____
to	____	____	____	____	____	____

(approximate total revenue from areas on graph)

2. Recognizing that none of the alternatives above is fully possible [Dr. Lawrence would not have the perfect knowledge required for (c) and would find it professionally difficult to practice (a) and (b) without providing some free services and lower fees as well], what approach would you recommend?

3. Price discrimination in medical services probably has declined partly as influenced by government programs.
   (a) Some communities have subsidized the building of a clinic. How would this affect Dr. Lawrence's problem?
   (b) Would the provision of government payments of minimum fees under Medicare reduce discrimination?

Chapter Sixteen
Industrial
Organization
and Theories of
Imperfect Competition

REVIEW QUESTIONS

1. Two crucial features of perfect competition affecting market behavior are
   _____price-takers_____ and _____freedom of entry_____.

2. Except for the effect of extensive government intervention, agriculture most
   resembles the market structure of _____perfect Com_____.

3. A market structure where there are many sellers, free entry, but some control over
   price by each seller due to product differentiation is called _monopolist Com_.

4. A market structure dominated by a few big firms, all aware of their possible effects
   on each other's sales, and to which entry is difficult, is called ___oligopoly___.

5. The firm in a perfectly competitive market sees its demand curve as ____horizontal____
   _____, whereas the firm in imperfectly competitive markets has a demand
   curve that is _____sloping_____.

6. The more a firm can differentiate its product from others and create a brand
   preference for its product, the (more/less) elastic its demand curve will be.

7. The most profitable output and price for a firm in monopolistic competition is where
   _____M_____ cost equals marginal _____R_____. Price at equilibrium
   will be (higher than/lower than/the same as) under perfect competition.

8. (a) In the long run, any profits over opportunity costs in a monopolistically com-
    petitive industry will be eliminated by what process? _____ *entry* _____

    (b) Firm demand curves will be shifted to the (left/right) until price just covers
    _____ cost.

    (c) This point will occur at an output (below/beyond/at) the output where average
    costs are at a minimum.

    (d) Thus, the firms and the industry are producing below their most efficient level
    and a condition of _____ *excess* _____ capacity exists.

    (e) This inefficient situation has one possible advantage for the consumer compared
    to perfect competition: _____ *wide choice* _____ .

9. To increase its profits, a firm in imperfect competition must either lower its unit
    costs or increase its revenues by increasing its _____ *share of market* _____ .
    It attempts to do the latter not by changing its prices, but by _____ *nonprice*
    _____ *competition* _____ .

10. Profitable oligopolies do not turn into industries of monopolistic competition be-
    cause of _____ *natural barriers to entry* _____ .

11. In addition to considering its marginal cost and revenues in setting price and out-
    put, an oligopoly firm must consider _____ *the reactions of its rival* _____ .

12. There are several hypotheses about the conditions that will increase the tendency
    of oligopoly firms to attempt to maximize their combined or joint profits; for in-
    stance, the tendency is increased
    (a) the (smaller/larger) the number of sellers
    (b) the (more/less) similar are the rival products
    (c) the (greater/less) the barriers to new firms
    (d) when the industry or economy is (contracting/expanding)

13. In oligopolized industries, prices tend to be more inflexible
    (a) the (more/less) uncertainty exists as to rival reactions
    (b) the (more/less) effective is tacit agreement not to change them

14. Nonprice competition will tend to be more vigorous,
    (a) the (greater/less) the limitation on price competition
    (b) the (higher/lower) the other barriers to entry of new firms

15. Barriers to entry of new firms are greater,
    (a) the (smaller/larger) the minimum efficient scale of production
    (b) the (greater/less) the absolute cost advantage of existing firms over potential
    entrants

16. An oligopoly firm with a cost advantage could try to inhibit the entry of new firms
    by setting a price below the *limit price,* namely, below the entering firms'
    _____ *minimum AC* _____ cost.

17. Firms with low minimum efficient scale can still create barriers to entry by in-
    creasing the number of their _____ *brand* _____ and the amount of _____ *advertising* _____ .

18. The possibility of a "kink" in an oligopoly firm's demand curve arises if the curve
    is elastic (upward/downward) and inelastic (upward/downward).
    (a) This would be the case if its rivals (do/do not) follow a price rise and (do/
    do not) follow a price reduction.
    (b) Such a firm has a strong incentive to (raise/lower/leave unchanged) its price.

19. Referring to the table of Concentration Ratios in Selected Manufacturing Industries in this chapter of the text, decide in what market structure you would classify the following industries.
(a) cigarettes _____ *oligopoly*
(b) clothing _____ *mono*
(c) primary aluminum _____ *oli*
(d) automobiles _____ *olig mono*
(e) dairy products _____ *mono*
(f) sawmills _____ *mono*

_____

If you have not answered all questions correctly, review the text in order to be sure that you have all of the important concepts clearly in mind before going on to the next chapter.

1. price taking; free entry 2. perfect competition 3. monopolistic competition 4. oligopoly 5. horizontal; sloping 6. less 7. marginal, revenue; higher 8. entry of new firms; left, average; below; excess; wider choice of products 9. share of the market; nonprice competition (especially advertising) 10. natural or artificial barriers to entry 11. the reactions of its rivals 12. smaller; more; greater; expanding 13. more; more 14. greater; lower 15. larger; greater 16. minimum average 17. brands; advertising 18. upward, downward; do not, do; leave unchanged 19. oligopoly; monopolistic competition; oligopoly; oligopoly; monopolistic competition; monopolistic competition

MULTIPLE-CHOICE QUESTIONS

1. Many small firms are typical of all but which one of the following industries:
   (a) agriculture
   (b) restaurant
   (c) primary aluminum
   (d) retail trade

2. The important difference between our assumptions for monopolistic competition and those for perfect competition is that monopolistic competitors
   (a) do not try to maximize profits
   (b) worry about their influence on the market
   (c) have an inelastic demand curve facing them
   (d) sell similar but not identical products

3. An important prediction of monopolistic competition is that the equilibrium output of the firm occurs at an output
   (a) where price exceeds average cost
   (b) less than the one at which average cost is at a minimum
   (c) less than the one at which average cost equals average revenue
   (d) less than the one at which marginal cost equals marginal revenue

4. Which one of the following is *not* implied by the excess-capacity theorem for monopolistically competitive industries?
   (a) Prices and unit costs will be higher than they would have been under perfect competition.
   (b) Many firms will be operating at a loss.
   (c) The consumer pays for the privilege of having a wider choice.
   (d) The same total output could have been produced by fewer firms at a lower cost.

5. Which of the following is a seller *not* trying to do by giving out trading stamps?
   (a) shift his product's demand curve to the right
   (b) keep customers returning
   √(c) reduce his total costs
   (d) increase his share of the market

6. According to the theory, temporary profits of a monopolistic competitor are eliminated primarily by
   (a) production where average costs are above the minimum
   (b) nonprice competition
   (c) entry of new firms
   (d) price reductions to meet new competition

7. Long-run profits are possible in an oligopolistic industry primarily because
   (a) firms can always set the profit-maximizing price and output
   (b) oligopolistic firms use the most efficient production methods
   (c) the demand is typically quite elastic
   √(d) entry of new firms is difficult

8. In an oligopolistic industry, joint profit maximizing by setting prices through tacit agreement is
   (a) more likely the fewer the number of firms
   (b) more likely the less similar the products
   (c) more likely when prices are falling than when they are rising
   (d) invariably illegal under the anti-combines laws

9. According to our hypotheses, which of the following situations should give firms in an oligopolistic industry the best chance of reaching their profit-maximizing price and output?
   (a) a few firms, each with low minimum efficient scale
   (b) a few firms with similar products and very large fixed costs
   (c) a few firms, differing considerably in size and each with very unpredictable management
   (d) a few firms, one of which is managed by an aggressive price cutter

10. The "limit price" just below which an oligopolist might set his price to prevent new firms from entering is determined by
    (a) the oligopolist's lowest unit cost
    (b) the lowest price at which the oligopolist can still make a profit
    √(c) the lowest price at which a new entrant could cover costs
    (d) the price that can be set where marginal revenue equals marginal cost

11. About what percent of total Canadian manufacturing output is produced by industries with four-firm concentration ratios of over 50 percent?
    √(a) 50
    (b) 75
    (c) 10
    (d) 90

12. The price-quantity relationship cannot, in principle, be determined for an oligopolist
    (a) under the competitive *ceteris paribus* conditions
    (b) under any circumstances
    (c) because price is an unimportant factor in the oligopolist's sales
    (d) unless reactions by other firms in the industry are taken accurately into account

13. An industry frequently cited as an example of excess capacity because of monopolistic competition is
    (a) agriculture
    (b) gasoline retailing
    (c) steel
    (d) automobile manufacturing

EXERCISES

1. Below are hypothetical demand and cost curves for a monopolistic competitor.
   (a) What would be the profit-maximizing output? _____ q_1 _____ Price?
       _____ p_4 _____
   (b) How much profit does the firm make at this position? ___ $p_4 - p_3$ ___
   (c) How can you tell that this is not a long-run equilibrium position for the industry?

       firms enter

   (d) Which curves will be affected, and in which direction, if the firm now increases its advertising budget by a given amount, with the desired results?

       MC no affect
       Advertising cost is fixed

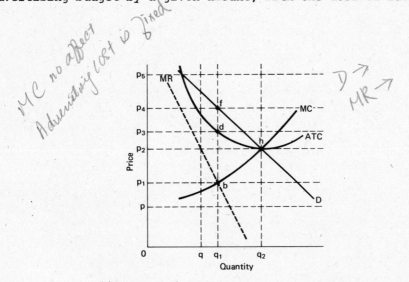

   (e) Suppose that new firms enter the industry. Show how the demand curve of this firm might appear in a long-run equilibrium position.

2. In the figure below, suppose that D is the demand curve for an oligopoly firm if all the firms in the industry act together, and that d is the demand curve for the firm when it alone in the industry varies its price. Assume that price is now at $2.

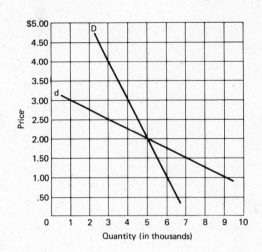

(a) If the firm lowers its price from $2 to $1.50 and no other firm does, its sales will go from _____5_____ to _____7_____, and total revenue will go from _____10_____ to _____10.5_____.

(b) If the firm lowers its price from $2 to $1.50 and every other firm does too, its sales will go from _____5_____ to _____5.5_____ and its total revenue from _____10_____ to _____8.25_____.

(c) If the firm raises its price from $2 to $2.50 and no other firm does, its sales will go from _____5_____ to _____3_____ and its total revenue from _____10_____ to _____7.5_____.

(d) If the firm raises its price from $2 to $2.50 and every other firm does too, its revenue will go from _____10_____ to _____.

(e) Assuming that this firm has fairly constant variable costs of about 75 cents in the relevant range of output, under what circumstances, if any, would the manager consider raising his price? Lowering it?

(f) Does this situation encourage collusive action by the firms in the industry to raise prices together? _____ To lower prices together? _____

PROBLEMS

1. SETTING THE PRICE OF FUEL OIL

In early 1974, the Nova Scotia Board of Commissioners of Public Utilities conducted hearings on fuel oil prices. An Imperial Oil executive told the hearings that, "Pricing is not a cost-plus formula. We don't determine in our pricing the cost of our products. We get what we can from the tone of the market at the time."

Questions
1. Is such a pricing policy consistent with perfect competition? Justify your answer.

2. Why is such a pricing policy inconsistent with a profit-maximizing producer in a setting of monopolistic competition?

3. Under what conditions would such a pricing policy call for government control of the "industry"?

4. If Imperial Oil really does operate in this manner, what are they trying to maximize? What form of industrial organization might best be depicted by such behavior?

2.   COOPERATION IN THE PULP AND PAPER INDUSTRY?

It was reported in early 1975 that Abitibi and Domtar pulp and paper producers closed their mills temporarily because of an inventory buildup. To continue producing would have necessitated lowering prices to eliminate excess inventories. The move to close the mills was hailed by the industry as a demonstration of price discipline in the industry.

Questions
1. What type of market structure for the pulp and paper industry does this action (and the comments on it) tend to suggest? Why?

2. If the industry were marked by perfect competition, would such action occur? Explain. What do you think would occur under perfect competition?

3. Because the "industry" is unwilling to reduce prices to unload excess inventory, what might this suggest about the price elasticity of demand for pulp and paper?

Chapter Seventeen
Price Theory
in Action

Make certain that you understand the following concepts: boycott; producers' cooperative; cartel.

REVIEW QUESTIONS

1. In theory, competitors can improve their profit position by jointly reducing (price/output) and increasing (price/output).

2. This will be particularly beneficial if market demand at competitive equilibrium is (elastic/inelastic).

3. By so doing, each firm will find its marginal revenue curve (higher/lower). Although its marginal cost curve is unchanged, the marginal cost of the last unit at the smaller output will be (less/greater) than before.

4. In a producers' organization like the Ontario Egg Marketing Board, voluntary quotas on output (to keep prices up) will not work because each producer can increase in revenue by _____.

5. Higher prices for haircuts in a town will not increase
   (a) barbers' revenues in the short run unless demand is _____.
   (b) barbers' profits in the long run unless _____ is limited.

6. The end result of higher prices is likely to be (more/fewer) barbers working (more/fewer) hours.

7. The recent trend toward much longer male hair would be diagrammed as a (shifting/elastic) demand curve for haircuts.

8. Heavy cigarette advertising seems to have two functions:
   (a) _____.
   (b) _____

9. The electrical equipment companies set prices by (tacit/explicit) agreement. The agreement fell apart apparently partly because of excess (demand/capacity) in the industry.

10. In the ball-point pen case, the initial but ineffective barrier to entry of other firms was a _____.

     If you have not answered all questions correctly, review the text in order to be sure that you have all of the important concepts clearly in mind before going on to the next chapter.

1. output; price 2. inelastic 3. higher; less 4. increasing his output 5. inelastic; entry of more barbers 6. more; fewer 7. shifting 8. nonprice competition; barriers to entry of new brands 9. explicit; capacity 10. patent

---

MULTIPLE-CHOICE QUESTIONS

1. If entry to an industry cannot be limited, we would predict in the long run
   (a) that excess capacity will necessarily result
   (b) that economic profits will approach zero
   (c) that the price will necessarily be the perfectly competitive price
   (d) that a cartel will be formed

2. The Reynolds International Pen Company
   (a) was able to rely on a patent monopoly to prevent entry and maintain profits
   (b) found its patent protection ineffective but succeeded in making substantial innovation profits
   (c) clearly made a mistake in judgment by offering the ball-point pen at too high a price
   (d) definitely overestimated its elasticity of demand in cutting prices

3. Of greatest use for barbers interested in increasing all incomes in the profession would be legislation
   (a) fixing the minimum price of haircuts at $3
   (b) making strict licensing requirements that would prevent any new entrants to the business
   (c) fixing the maximum price of haircuts at $3
   (d) eliminating licensing and price requirements for the industry

4. Which of these elements may have been significant in the great loss of market share suffered by the big three tobacco companies in the 1930s?
   (a) greater price consciousness by the consumer in a depression period
   (b) the large spread created between tobacco costs and cigarette prices in 1931
   (c) limited economies of scale, which had permitted the continued existence of small firms
   (d) all of the above

5. Oligopoly theory in the electrical equipment case is
   (a) most pertinent in explaining the formal price conspiracy in 1957
   (b) not useful at all because monopoly theory could predict the behavior of the 1950s
   (c) useful in understanding why joint profit maximization that worked in one period broke down in another
   (d) not at all necessary because the competitive model could predict the behavior of the 1950s

6. This chapter's examples of actual price and output behavior suggest that
   (a) there is a general preference among firms for strong price competition and expansion of output
   (b) agreements, whether tacit or explicit, to fix prices and divide markets are more apt to break down in good times than in bad
   (c) all firms in an industry can maximize profits by raising prices
   (d) raising prices in an industry, *ceteris paribus,* brings increased long-run profits only if entry can be restricted and output curtailed

EXERCISE

Two firms within an oligopoly have revenue schedules D_A and D_B as shown below (at least they *believe* that the demand schedules are as shown). The agreement in this industry is such that firm A produces an output of OQ_1 and firm B produces an output of OQ_2.

This produces a "stable" price in the industry. After some calculations, the two firms become more aware of their cost schedules (which are also shown in the diagrams below).

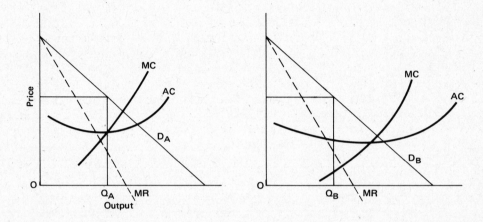

(a) Is there any incentive for the two firms to move away from the agreed-upon price and output? Why?

(b) Is there anything which might inhibit one or both of the firms from deviating from the agreed-upon price and output?

PROBLEM

WHY PRICES FALL

Four cases are presented in the chapter that involve price cuts or in one case an abortive attempt to raise prices:
1. the unsuccessful attempt in 1967 by the NFO to raise milk prices in the state of Wisconsin
2. the cutting of ball-point pen prices from mid-1946 to mid-1948
3. the price cuts by major cigarette companies following a raise in June 1931, that led to the entry of the "10¢ brands"
4. the drastic price cuts in turbine generators starting in mid-1958

As a step in analyzing similarities and contrasts in these situations, fill in, from information available, the structural and performance characteristics listed below.

	Milk	Pen	Cigarette	Turbine
Number of sellers				
Independence of sellers				
Homogeneity of product				
Entry possibilities				
Ratio of sales to capacity				
Ratio of price to costs				

Questions

1. Are there common characteristics in each of the situations according to the information given?

2. What combination of characteristics in each case seemed to lead to effective downward pressure on prices?

Chapter Eighteen
Monopoly Versus Competition: Implications About Performance and Policy

REVIEW QUESTIONS

1. Other things being equal, prices and quantities will change (less/more) in monopoly than in competition in response to a change in marginal costs.

2. According to classical analysis, if cost curves are the same under monopoly as under perfect competition, prices will be (higher/lower) and output will be (more/less).

3. This means an allocation of resources under monopoly that is considered (efficient/inefficient).

4. It is considered so because the monopoly price is (greater/less) than marginal cost, which means that the consumer is paying (more/less) for the last item purchased than the value of the additional resources being used.

5. If price exceeds marginal cost in all industries, it is theoretically (possible/impossible) to make some people better off without making others worse off, by changing some prices, outputs, and resource uses.

6. However, it is possible that, if a competitive industry is monopolized, economies of large scale will bring (lower/higher) unit costs, and price in the long run will be (lower/higher) and output (greater/less) than would have been possible under competition.

7. Unlike a competitive firm, a monopolist has a (long-run/short-run) incentive to innovate.

8. Providing temporary legal protection to the possible profits of a firm resulting from an innovating invention is one purpose of ____patent____ laws.

110

9. Monopolistic competition provides (greater/less) product variety than does perfect competition at (the same/increased) costs.

10. The examples of British radio and television suggest that (more/less) variety of product might be produced by a monopoly than by an oligopoly.

11. Monopoly power is predicted to lead to the employment of (fewer/more) resources in the industry compared with those used under competitive conditions, and usually to a (greater/smaller) relative share of national income for the monopolistic firms.

12. Two contrasting policies toward monopolistic firms are those of the _antitrust_ _____ laws and public-utility _regulation_ _____.

13. However, attempts by labor and farmers to organize and acquire monopoly power (are/are not) generally illegal under the antitrust laws.

14. The first antitrust law in the United States was the _____ Act in the year _____. This law prohibited _____ and _____.

15. Tying contracts and mergers were forbidden under the _____ Act if the effect might be to _____.

16. The prohibition of discriminatory pricing was brought into the Canadian _____ Act in the year _____.

17. In the Canadian Breweries case, the charge was dropped because changes in (market shares/pricing) had not established that an offense had been committed.

18. In the Carnation case, the charge of price discrimination was dropped because the company claimed its different regional prices were defensible on grounds of (meeting competition/different costs).

19. A "natural" monopoly reaches lowest unit cost at a very (large/small) output relative to the market.

20. If average costs are declining with output, regulation that sets price equal to marginal cost will result in _losses_ for the firm.

21. Problems in regulating utility rates have included determination of the proper value of investment, or _rate base_, and a fair rate of _return_ on investment.

_____

   If you have not answered all questions correctly, review the text in order to be sure that you have all of the important concepts clearly in mind before going on to the next chapter.

1. less 2. higher; less 3. inefficient 4. greater; more 5. possible 6. lower; lower; greater 7. long-run 8. patent 9. greater; increased 10. more 11. fewer; greater 12. antitrust; regulation 13. are not 14. Sherman, 1890; combination or conspiracy in restraint of trade, monopolizing or attempting to monopolize 15. Clayton; substantially lessen competition 16. Combines Investigation, 1935 17. market shares 18. meeting competition 19. large 20. losses 21. rate base; return

MULTIPLE-CHOICE QUESTIONS

1. Classical economists preferred perfect competition to monopoly because it fulfilled all but which one of the following basic goals?
   (a) consumer sovereignty
   (b) dispersion of economic power
   (c) virtual equality in income distribution
   (d) efficiency of resource allocation

2. So far as it affects consumer welfare, monopoly is potentially objectionable because
   (a) price = marginal revenue
   (b) price > marginal cost
   (c) marginal cost = marginal revenue
   (d) marginal revenue > marginal cost

3. Assuming that cost curves would be the same in an industry under either monopoly or competition, a monopoly will produce at equilibrium at a point where, compared to the competitive equilibrium,
   (a) output is larger but price is higher
   (b) output is less but price is higher
   (c) output is less but price is the same
   (d) output is the same but price is higher

4. In order to have the consumer pay for the last unit just what it cost to produce the last unit,
   (a) price should equal average cost
   (b) average cost must be at a minimum
   (c) marginal cost should equal price
   (d) marginal revenue should equal price

5. One reason that we cannot say for sure that, given the technology and resources at hand, welfare is maximized when price equals marginal cost in all industries is that
   (a) there are still poor people
   (b) marginal cost does not include possible social costs that may be substantial
   (c) it is never impossible to make someone better off without making someone worse off
   (d) we cannot measure either welfare or marginal cost, so they are not useful concepts

6. A monopoly may produce more efficiently than the same industry in competitive form because
   (a) there may be economies of scale that would not be achieved by a number of small firms
   (b) monopolies typically have better management
   (c) a monopoly does not have to worry about what its rival may do
   (d) a monopoly can concentrate on production rather than profits

7. Anti-combines cases in Canada have been highlighted by all except one of the following:
   (a) low fines for the guilty
   (b) few merger cases
   (c) few convictions
   (d) consistent appeal to economic questions

8. Conglomerate mergers are mergers of
   (a) firms with interlocking directorates
   (b) direct competitors in a market
   (c) firms whose products are not directly competitive
   (d) suppliers and their customers

9. The usual argument in favor of accepting a "natural" monopoly, if it is regulated, is that
   (a) regulation guarantees fair, low prices
   (b) more than one company would be obviously wasteful
   (c) it gives the same results as public ownership
   (d) regulation keeps it out of politics

10. Resale price maintenance was included in the Combines Investigation Act in
    (a) 1888
    (b) 1910
    (c) 1935
    (d) 1951

11. From the public's standpoint, a "fair rate of return" on a utility investment
    (a) should mean approximately the current rate on alternatives of similar risk
    (b) should be determined by historical costs
    (c) can always be earned, provided prices are set high enough
    (d) means what the stockholders think is fair

PROBLEMS

1. THE COST OF A FREE PRESS

     In 1974, the companies of K. C. Irving Ltd. and subsidiaries were convicted of operating a monopoly through their ownership of all English-language newspapers in the Province of New Brunswick. The companies were fined $160,000 and ordered to sell two of the five newspapers. K. C. Irving appealed the decision.
     On June 4, 1975, the Court of Appeal overturned the Supreme Court decision. The Court of Appeal judge stated in his report:

     I differ from the trial judge, however, in his statement that when a monopoly
     as defined in the dictionary occurs, detriment in law results.

     The Court of Appeal ruled that the conviction for monopoly must be based on evidence that the monopoly (in the dictionary sense) had harmed the public. As the Court decision stated:

     No evidence was adduced that any detriment to the public resulted. . . . This
     contention [that the five newspapers owned by one group was bad] was advanced
     . . . on a theoretical basis without supporting evidence of any actual lessening
     of competition.

What the Court of Appeal pointed out was that day-to-day control was in the hands of the publishers and editors and that they were as independent now as in the days before the takeover.

Questions
     1. Look up the definition of "monopoly" in a dictionary.

2. What "evidence" would you look for to determine if the ownership of these five newspapers by one group was detrimental to the public?

3. If this decision is appealed again to the Supreme Court of Canada, regardless of the outcome, what recommendation could the Court make concerning the interpretation of monopoly?

2.   EVIDENCE BEFORE THE RESTRICTIVE TRADE PRACTICES COMMISSION

In the early 1960s, the Director of Investigation and Research, Combines Investigation Branch, Government of Canada, alleged that the purchase of Wilson Boxes, a shipping container firm, by Bathurst Paper Ltd. was contrary to Canadian law in that it created a monopoly that was detrimental to public interest. Under the law at the time, such an allegation was brought before the Restrictive Trade Practices Commission for a hearing. Although an old case, it does give some idea of the problems involved in deciding upon the economic and public welfare implications of mergers.

Presented below are exerpts from the Report of the Commission to the Minister of Justice.

Allegations by the Director

4. It is alleged that the acquisition of WILSON by Bathurst Containers (Maritime) Limited, as hereinafter described, is a "merger, trust or monopoly" within the meaning of the Combines Investigation Act; that the said merger, trust or monopoly has operated and is likely to operate to the detriment or against the interest of the public, thereby constituting a "combine" within the meaning of the said Act; and that BATHURST is a party to such combine.

(Statement of Evidence, p. 1)

9. The general public detriment to which the merger gives rise is as described in paragraph 362 of Volume IV of the Shipping Containers Statement. In addition, the merger gives rise to particular detriment as a result of the excess of price over the company's net worh paid by BATHURST, which will have to be borne in the end by its customers and the general public. The merger also gives rise to the additional detriment that WILSON is now controlled by the company which exercises, over the only other shipping container manufacturer in the Maritimes, the influence and control described in paragraph 362(c)(5) of the Shipping Containers Statement, on page 903.

(Statement of Evidence, p. 4)

Paragraph 362 of Volume IV* of the Shipping Containers Statement of Evidence reads, in part, as follows:

362. Between 1945 and 1959, inclusive, various companies acquired control over or an interest in the whole of part of the business of another company, as listed in paragraph 7. These mergers must be regarded, not merely individually or in isolation, but in the light of the industry arrangements and practices described in this Statement as existing from the 1930's to 1959 inclusive. It is, in considerable measure, because of such continiuing arrangements and practices that the effects of the mergers have been, and will continue, detrimental. (Conversely, the arrangements and practices must be regarded, not only standing alone, but also in the light of the integrations, by way of mergers, which have taken place in the industry.) The detriment to the public common to all these mergers, except the acquisition of Canadian Western Box (Alberta) Limited by MARTIN PAPER, derives from the fact that in each case a shipping container manufacturer, formerly independent of the board mills in ownership and management, has been acquired by a board mill and has become part of its integrated operations. The competition arising from the divergent interests of the two branches of the industry, which in the absence of an agreement such as alleged in paragraphs 5 and 6 would safeguard the interests of users of shipping containers and of the general consuming public, has been *pro tanto* foreclosed. The process of integration has already proceeded to the extent that only a very small segment of the shipping container industry remains independent of the board mills. In consequence, even after the elimination of the agreement alleged in paragraphs 5 and 6, the possibility of future competition is impaired because:

(a) New entries into the industry of containerboard manufacturing will be discouraged by the fact that existing outlets for the sale of board have nearly all been absorbed by the present board manufacturers.

(b) The most likely importers of containerboard have been brought under the ownership and control of the containerboard manufacturers. The restraining influence of actual or potential competition from abroad is thereby curtailed.

(c) The most significant purchasers of containerboard have been brought under the ownership and control of the containerboard manufacturers and will not shop around among such manufacturers for their requirements.

(d) New entries into the industry of converting containerboard into boxes will be discouraged by the fact that all or most of the significant existing converters are integrated with containerboard manufacturers thus putting new entrants in danger of a "squeeze" between containerboard costs and box prices.

(e) The bulk of the business is now largely concentrated in a few integrated producers, all having a record of anti-competitive behaviour in this industry, and most of them in another sector of the pulp and paper industry. Two companies, BATHURST and ST. LAWRENCE, on the basis of 1958 figures, now account for approximately 60 per cent by volume of the total shipments of containers in Eastern Canada and are also important producers in the Prairies. Recent figures for containerboard are not in evidence, but the same two companies remain the leaders in the production of containerboard. Their combined market shipments, however, are a smaller proportion than would be indicated by the 1954 figures when they, together with HINDE & DAUCH, now wholly-owned by ST. LAWRENCE supplied 77 per cent of the total domestic shipments made in Canada as a whole. Under the market structure brought about by the mergers, anti-competitive behavior does not require forms of organization and methods of consultation which are readily capable of detection and correction.

---

*This is from an earlier study of the Investigation and Research Branch.

The detriment in respect of the expected merger lies in the elimination of competition, without any compensating advantages to the public, which it entailed. In addition to the general detriment referred to above, the various mergers gave rise to particular detriment as follows:

5. The acquisition of a minority stockholding and a voice in the management of MARITIME, together with a contractual right to purchase the shares of the majority stockholder in the event of its deciding to sell them, impaired potential future competition in the Maritimes, which heretofore secured its supplies solely from BATHURST, was placed in a position of potential squeeze between containerboard costs and box prices. Prior to the acquisition, MARITIME was one of the most likely companies to undertake independent competitive action, since it was less dependent upon the organized industry for board supplies, which it obtained principally from its major shareholder, MINAS BASIN.

Reply by Bathurst Paper Ltd. to the Allegations

1. Comparisons of the price paid for Wilson by Bathurst with the book value of Wilson are not valid because the book value is arrived at by taking as much depreciation as is permitted for income tax purposes.

2. Even the cost of reproduction less depreciation is not a valid measure of value. Because time is required for a new plant to reach peak efficiency, a newly built plant is worth less than one which has been operating for a while. Therefore "going value" must be added to any appraisal of a plant based on reproduction costs less depreciation.

3. The Director has not given sufficient weight to the value of goodwill, that is, the clientele and know-how, in relation to his allegation that an excessive price was paid for Wilson. Bathurst acquired control of Wilson precisely to obtain the latter's goodwill.

4. The Director has not taken sufficiently into account that the future prospects of a company may warrant an increase in the purchase price. Although the initial investment is large, an adequate return is secured later on.

5. Although Bathurst has, through taking over a number of companies, secured for itself 27.24 per cent of the total box market in Eastern Canada (Ontario, Quebec and Maritimes), it is in no position to exercise economic power virutally unaffected by competition.

6. There is no evidence to support the Director's allegation that Bathurst's policy was to eliminate independents so as to be able to dominate, together with other large companies, the market free from competition without the necessity of having any overt agreements between the various companies.

7. Bathurst's acquisitions and others represent a structural change brought about by economic forces. The acquisitions have rendered the industry more efficient and will eventually serve the Canadian public better by having products manufactured more cheaply and made available at the cheapest possible prices.

8. There is no link between the system as to costs among container manufacturers, as alleged by the Director, and Bathurst's acquisition of Wilson.

9. There is no evidence that Bathurst agreed with its competitors to integrate the industry.

Questions

1. What "particular detriment" is deemed to result from the allegation that Bathurst paid more than the net worth of Wilson?

2. By stating that new entrants into containerboard production will be discouraged by the control over sales outlets, what kind of barriers to competition is the Director suggesting?

3. Do you think that customers of shipping containers will not "shop around" for their requirement? What would prevent them from doing so?

4. Bathurst has challenged the allegation by stating that there is little evidence concerning certain points. What evidence *does* seem to be lacking?

5. How would it be possible for Bathurst to "serve the Canadian public better . . ." through its merger with Wilson?

Chapter Nineteen
Who Runs the Firm and for What Ends?

CHECKLIST	Make certain that you understand the following concepts: proxy; holding company; proxy fight; interlocking directorships; full-cost pricing; markup; organization theory; profit constraint; satisficing; tender offer; takeover bid consumerism; direct investment; extraterritoriality.

REVIEW QUESTIONS

1. Critics of the theory of behavior of firms question whether the goal of firms really is to _____.

2. U.S. ownership of Canadian industry is highest in the _____ industry and lowest in _____.

3. When one corporation controls another corporation by owning a controlling amount of its stock, it is called a _____.

4. The issue of ownership and control of firms affects the theory of the firm only if the firm's goals are thereby (different from/the same as) what the theory assumes.

5. If business managers do not know what marginal costs are, it is (impossible/still possible) for them to try to maximize their profits.

6. A producer is said to use full-cost pricing when he adds a _____ to his expected _____ costs.

7. (a) Under the theory of full-cost pricing, a decline in demand results in a price that (rises/falls/remains the same), sales will (fall/rise), inventories will (fall/rise), and production will probably be (increased/reduced).
   (b) However, if firms adjust their markup percentages downward or upward according to changes in (demand/supply), they must also adjust their (price/cost).

8. Some theorists believe that firms aim, not for maximum profits, but for _____ profits. This is (very/not) difficult to prove.

9. Another theory is that firms seek to maximize, not profits, but _____, assuming a minimum level of profits. This is more plausible if the firm is controlled by its (shareholders/managers).

10. Sales-maximizing behavior by a monopolistically competitive firm will result in (larger/smaller) output and (lower/higher) price than would its profit-maximizing behavior. It also implies setting price where demand elasticity is equal to _____.

11. Safarian and others feel that the major problem of Canadian industry is the _____ size of firms.

12. The application of U.S. laws to subsidiaries of U.S. companies in Canada is known as a problem of _____.

13. Two recent government reports dealing with foreign investment in Canada are the _____ and _____ reports.

    If you have not answered all questions correctly, review the text in order to be sure that you have all of the important concepts clearly in mind before going on to the next chapter.

1. maximize profits 2. automobile; transportation and utilities 3. holding company
4. different from 5. still possible 6. markup; average 7. remains the same, fall, rise, reduced; demand, price 8. satisfactory; very 9. sales; managers 10. larger, lower; one 11. inefficient 12. extraterritoriality 13. Watkins; Grey

MULTIPLE-CHOICE QUESTIONS

1. A characteristic of most modern large corporations is that
   (a) the stockholders really run the business
   (b) the board of directors really runs the business
   (c) hired managers run the business
   (d) the workers run the business

2. The full-cost pricing hypothesis
   (a) predicts market behavior and results better than the profit-maximizing hypothesis
   (b) means that the firm can never maximize profits
   (c) holds that the firm's pricing adjustments respond only to changes in costs
   (d) implies that firms will always be able to cover all their costs

3. If we find that one firm is content merely to make some level of satisfactory profits,
   (a) there is no specific prediction we can make about its equilibrium price and output
   (b) it is obviously a monopoly
   (c) it completely refutes our theory based on profit-maximizing assumptions
   (d) it will not long survive competition and change

4. If it would take ownership of 25 percent of the stock of Associated Gadgets to control it, and ownership of 20 percent of the holding company formed to hold the stock of Associated Gadgets to control that company, it would be necessary to have an amount of money equal to what percentage of the value of Associated Gadgets stock in order to control it? (Pick the minimum possible.)
   (a) 20
   (b) 25
   (c) 51
   (d) 5

5. The sales-maximizing hypothesis implies that
   (a) a firm will sell as many units as it can at a fixed price
   (b) firms are not interested in profits but only in growth
   (c) a firm will sell additional units by reducing price to the point where elasticity of demand is zero
   (d) a firm would reduce price to the point where marginal revenue is zero so long as a minimum satisfactory level of profits were achieved

6. Which of the following predictions is *not* implied by any of the theories discussed in this chapter? If an industry's labor costs rise, *ceteris paribus,*
   (a) a profit-maximizing firm will raise its price and reduce output
   (b) a satisficing firm may or may not change its price and output
   (c) a sales-maximizing firm will raise price and reduce output
   (d) a full-cost-pricing firm will raise its price

7. The firm's goals, according to Simon's satisficing hypothesis, would not include
   (a) maintenance of market share
   (b) achievement of a specified gain in sales
   (c) attaining a target level of profits
   (d) maximization of profits

8. Which statement best describes Galbraith's "new industrial state":
   (a) The U.S. federal government now has a great deal of control over American corporations.
   (b) American corporations are very responsive to the desires, needs, and best interests of the buying public.
   (c) Because of the power of unions and shareholders, U.S. industrial management has little real control.
   (d) The size and influence of large U.S. corporations give them too much power over government, consumers, markets, and other institutions.

9. The recommended approach in testing theories about firm behavior is to
   (a) ask business management whether they maximize profits, satisfice, or maximize sales
   (b) abstract from reality as much as possible
   (c) try to find evidence, facts, and figures to show what firms actually did in what circumstances
   (d) watch a business manager make a decision to see how he does it

EXERCISE

The diagram below represents demand and cost conditions for a firm.

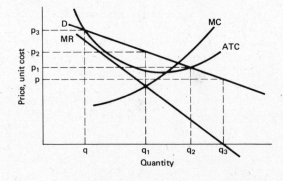

(a) What would be the choice of price and output for a profit maximizer?
_____

(b) What would be the range of price and output for a profit satisficer who is content to cover opportunity costs at a minimum? _____

(c) What would be the price and output of a sales maximizer who is willing to accept losses for short periods? _____

PROBLEM

THE NONREFILLABLE CONTAINER

This problem is linked with the issues discussed in Chapter 13. Before answering the questions, it would be useful to refresh your mind on the issues discussed in that chapter.

The *Solid Waste Task Force* (Ontario, 1974), from which the exerpt below is drawn, was established to examine all aspects of solid-waste disposal in Ontario and thus spent considerable time on the question of refillable versus nonrefillable containers. It summarized the debate as follows:

As non-refillable containers have become an important part of an increasingly convenience-oriented lifestyle, so have they also become one of the targets of a growing attack upon modern packaging methods by numerous environmental, conservation and consumer groups.

The basic argument against non-refillable containers centers about the fact that they replace refillable containers that can be re-used, up to 25 or more times depending upon the exact nature of their use, whether for soft drinks, beer, or, for that matter, milk. From this, it is argued that non-refillable beverage containers create additional solid waste, use up more energy and raw materials, and, as they have no return value, increase the amount of litter stemming from beverage containers.

Accordingly, say their critics, they should be banned in Ontario, or their use drastically reduced in favour of a major swing back to refillable bottles.

These demands are supported by a number of soft drink bottlers who say they will be forced out of business if non-refillables, particularly cans, continue to increase their share of the market.

A consumer argument against non-refillables arises from the fact that a given soft drink often costs more in a non-refillable container than in a refillable container.

The Counter Argument

Proposals to reduce the use of non-refillable soft drink containers by legislative means have been opposed primarily on economic grounds in terms of both lost capital investment, profits and job dislocation. In Ontario, as elsewhere, this opposition has primarily come from:

1. manufacturers of non-refillable containers, particularly those producing the can. (While the glass companies concerned would at least face some loss of employment, they would not be as severely affected as the can manufacturers because of the continued and increased use of refillable bottles.)

2. some soft drink companies with investments in canning systems.

3. vending companies that would have to convert existing machines or buy new equipment.

4. unions representing workers whose jobs might be affected.

5. many retailers for whom a greater use of refillable containers would mean additional handling and storage costs.

In addition to the economic aspect, proponents of the non-refillable container point out that it was readily accepted by the public when introduced and that its continued use has solely been the result of consumer demand. They maintain that increasing numbers of people have chosen the non-refillable for its convenience and are willing to pay the extra cost that may at times go with it.

Questions

1. In producing the nonrefillable container, the firm must price such a container in line with the costs of production. Does such a price reflect all the costs associated with nonrefillable container production?

2. Given the experience of most people, do you feel that consumers have had an adequate chance to illustrate their preference for one type of container over the other?

3. What would be the "true" test to see whether or not consumers are willing to pay for the "convenience" of nonrefillable containers as compared with refillable or recycled containers?

4. Proponents of the nonrefillable container have suggested, according to the report, that its continued use has ". . . solely been the result of consumer demand." Can you think of additional reasons why it is in continued use?

Chapter Twenty
The Distribution
of National
Income

CHECKLIST	Make certain that you understand the following concepts: functional distribution of income; Lorenz curve; derived demand; marginal-revenue product (MRP); marginal physical product (MPP); hypothesis of equal net advantage; marginal-productivity theory of distribution; factor mobility; labour force; supply of labour; dynamic (or disequilibrium) differential; equilibrium differential; transfer earnings; economic rent.

REVIEW QUESTIONS

1. The division of income among the three basic factors of production is called the _____functional_____ distribution of income.

2. A person who has a job, owns a house that he rents to another person, and owns a corporate bond receives three types of income: _____rent_____, ____interest____, and _____wage_____.

3. The distribution of income according to the amount of income of households is called the ____size____ distribution of income.

4. One indication of the inequality of income distribution in Canada is the fact that the lowest 20 percent of the population receive only about what percent of total income? _____

5. The functional distribution of income in Canada shows almost three-quarters of the total going to _____.

6. Price theory states that the competitive market price of a factor of production is determined by _____.

7. The demand for a factor of production will be more elastic
   (a) the (greater/lower) the elasticity of demand for the product it is used to make
   (b) the (larger/smaller) the proportion of total costs represented by payments to this factor
   (c) the (more/less) the substitutability of the factor for others in production

8. (a) The extra revenue a firm gains by using an additional unit of a factor is
       called its _____ marginal revenue product _____ .
   (b) It consists of the extra output, or _____ MPP _____ , added
       by using the extra factor multiplied by the value of the extra product, or
       _____ MR _____ .

9. A profit-maximizing firm will hire an additional unit of a factor only up to the
   point at which the extra cost of the factor does not exceed its ____ MRP ____
   _____ .

10. The MRP curve of a factor slopes _____ upwards _____ due to the effect of
    _____ diminish marginal return _____ . Thus, a producer is willing to hire
    additional units of a factor only at a progressively (lower/higher) price, so that
    the demand curve for a factor slopes _____ upward _____ and can be repre-
    sented by the _____ MRP _____ curve.

11. The prediction that owners of factors will wish to move them to uses the relative
    pay for which has (increased/decreased) results in factor supply curves that slope
    _____ upward _____ .

12. The elasticity of supply of a factor will be greater the (shorter/longer) the length
    of time allowed and the (greater/less) the mobility of the factor from one use to
    another.

13. The supply of land in a particular geographic location is totally (elastic/inelas-
    tic). But agricultural land is quite (mobile/immobile) from one crop year to the
    next, and therefore relatively (elastic/inelastic) in supply for different crop
    uses.

14. Capital in money form is much (more/less) mobile than in the form of plant or
    machinery.

15. If workers prefer more leisure time, a rise in wage rates may result in their
    supplying (more/fewer) hours of effort. As higher income taxes reduce people's
    net income, they may very likely want to work (more/less).

16. The productive factor most concerned about nonmonetary aspects of its uses is
    _____ labor _____ .

17. If labour were fully mobile, workers would shift positions until the net advantage
    of one job over another is _____ zero _____ .

18. List several natural barriers to the mobility of labour between occupations and jobs:
    _____ time _____

19. Man-made barriers to mobility of labour are such things as ____ training ____
    _____

20. To the extent that the relative pay differences between scientists and English
    teachers persuaded college students to switch to scientific careers, the differen-
    tial would be considered a _____ dynamic _____ one.

21. Skilled workers usually get paid more than unskilled because they are more
    (skilled/scarce), relatively.

22. The preference of professors for lower pay in academia than higher pay in
    industry is explained by what the text calls _____ nonmonetary _____ advan-
    tages of the former. The pay differential would be considered a(n) _____ disequilibrium _____
    _____ one.

23. *Ceteris paribus,* a person who enjoys his job will have (lower/~~higher~~) transfer earnings than one who does not. The former is also (more/~~less~~) likely to be receiving some economic rent than is the latter.

24. Ricardo said that high land rents (caused/were caused by) the high price of grain.

25. The steeper or more inelastic the supply curve of a factor, the (greater/less) the proportion of that factor income that will be economic rent rather than transfer earnings.

26. Assume that Rod Laver is willing to continue on the pro tennis circuit as long as he earns at least $40,000 per year. If in a particular year he earns $100,000, his economic rent is ____60,000____ and his transfer earnings are ____40,000____.

27. The marginal-productivity theory predicts that each of identical factors in a competitive market would be paid according to the value of (its services/the services of the last unit of the factor hired).

If you have not answered all questions correctly, review the text in order to be sure that you have all of the important concepts clearly in mind before going on to the next chapter.

1. functional 2. wages; rent; interest 3. size 4. 6 percent 5. wages and salaries
6. demand and supply 7. greater; larger; more 8. marginal-revenue product; marginal physical product, marginal revenue 9. marginal-revenue product 10. downward, diminishing marginal returns; lower, downward, MRP 11. increased; upward 12. longer; greater 13. inelastic; mobile, elastic 14. more 15. fewer; more 16. labor
17. zero 18. lack of ability, training, inclination, distance 19. pension plans, licensing, union limitations, racial and sex discrimination 20. dynamic 21. scarce
22. nonmonetary; equilibrium 23. lower; more 24. were caused by 25. greater
26. $60,000; $40,000 27. the services of the last unit of the factor hired

---

MULTIPLE-CHOICE QUESTIONS

1. The theory of factor prices in competitive markets says that
   (a) factors are paid what they are worth
   (b) factor prices are determined by supply and demand
   (c) factor prices depend on their cost of production
   (d) factors are not paid what they are worth

2. Which of the following statements is *not* true about the demand for a factor of production?
   (a) It is more elastic the more elastic is the demand for the final product.
   (b) It is more elastic in cases where technology dictates its use in fixed proportions with other factors.
   (c) It is less elastic the smaller a part it is of the total cost of the product.
   (d) The quantity demanded varies inversely with its price.

3. The marginal-revenue product of a factor is
   (a) marginal revenue minus marginal cost
   (b) marginal physical product times the units of factors used
   (c) marginal revenue minus factor price
   (d) marginal physical product times marginal revenue

4. The marginal-revenue product of a factor is
   (a) the amount added to revenue by the last hired unit of a factor
   (b) total output divided by units of factors, multiplied by price
   (c) less under competition than under monopoly, *ceteris paribus*
   (d) always equal to its price

5. The quantity demanded of a factor, *ceteris paribus,* will vary inversely
   (a) with income
   (b) with the price of the factor
   (c) with the prices of other factors
   (d) with changes in demand for the product

6. Empirical evidence indicates that historically, as real wage rates have risen in North America,
   (a) workers have shown a willingness to work longer hours
   (b) business has shown no actual tendency to substitute capital for labor
   (c) the average work week has declined (particularly before World War II)
   (d) the supply of effort has sloped upward to the right

7. If a firm is a price taker in factor markets, it means that
   (a) it is also a price taker in product markets
   (b) it can set the price it pays for factors
   (c) it pays the market rate for whatever quantities of factors it wishes
   (d) it is maximizing profits

8. The addition to the stock of capital each year is
   (a) equal to depreciation allowances
   (b) indicated by the amount of gross investment
   (c) indicated by the amount of net investment
   (d) equal to net investment minus replacement of capital used up

9. Economic rent is
   (a) the income of a landlord
   (b) earned only be factors in completely inelastic supply
   (c) the excess of income over transfer earnings
   (d) usually taxable under the income tax, whereas transfer earnings are not

10. A dynamic differential in factor earnings
    (a) can exist in equilibrium
    (b) will be more quickly eliminated if factor supply is inelastic rather than elastic
    (c) will tend to cause movements of factors
    (d) is greater the greater is the mobility of the factor

11. The need for the physical presence of the owner of the labour factor (the worker)
    (a) is comparable to that of owners of capital and land
    (b) is not economically significant
    (c) makes nonmonetary factors much more important for it than for other factors
    (d) has not been fully demonstrated

12. Which of the following will *not* shift the supply curve of labour?
    (a) an increase in the population
    (b) an increase in the proportion of people going to college
    (c) an increase in the wage level
    (d) increased preferences for leisure activities

13. The marginal-revenue product of labour declines more rapidly for a monopoly firm than for a competitive firm because
    (a) workers are apt to be less productive when they work for a monopoly
    (b) the industry demand for the product is less elastic
    (c) the monopoly deliberately curtails output
    (d) with the monopoly firm, marginal revenue declines; with the competitive firm, it does not

EXERCISES

1. Fill in the table below, and then answer the questions.

Suppose a firm can vary its number of employees and output as shown. What will be the marginal physical product and the marginal-revenue product of each additional worker? Note the difference between case (a) and case (b).

Number of Workers	Units of Output per Day	MPP	Case (a)			Case (b)	
			MR	MRP		MR	MRP
0	0	0	$2	0		$2.00	0
1	20	20	2	40		1.90	38
2	40	20	2	47		1.80	36
3	58	18	2	36		1.75	31.5
4	74	16	2	32		1.70	27.2
5	88	14	2	28		1.65	23.1
6	100	12	2	24		1.60	
7	110	10	2	20		1.55	
8	118	8	2	16		1.50	
9	124	6	2	12		1.45	
10	128	4	2	8		1.40	

(a) If the market wage that this firm must pay is $20 per day, how many workers will the firm hire to maximize profits? Case (a) ___7___ Case (b) __about 5__

(b) If the wage rises to $28 per day, how many will the firm hire?
Case (a) ___5___   Case (b) _____

(c) If in case (a) the market price of the product rises to $3 and the wage is $28 per day, how many workers will be hired? _____

(d) Why does the MPP decline?

diminishing return

(e) In case (b), why does the MR decline?

monopoly

2. The marginal-revenue productivity of a factor may depend on the costs saved by its substitution for another factor. In this exercise assume that a firm can accomplish a particular function by any of the following combinations of labour and capital. The costs involved are negligible enough so that the firm's product output decision is not significantly affected:

Units of Labour (man-years)	Units of Capital	MRS[a]	MRP[b] of Labour (dollars)
0	100	—	—
1	60	40	$40,000
2	45	15	15,000
3	35	10	10000
4	27	8	8000
5	20	7	7000
6	14	6	6000
7	9	5	5000
8	5	4	4000
9	2	3	3000
10	1	2	2000

[a]Units of capital substituted for by additional units of labour.
[b]Assume the price of capital expressed as an annual cost (which, as discussed in Chapter 21, is a function of the price of the capital good, its economic life, and the interest rate), is $1,000 per unit of capital.

(a) If the market wage that the firm must pay is $7,500 a year, how many workers will be hired? _____ (Assume man-years are indivisible.) In conjunction with how many units of capital? _____27_____

(b) If wages had increased to $8,500 a year, how many workers would have been hired? _____3_____

(c) The firm's demand for labour would shift to the _____ if the price of capital rose to $1,250 a unit, and at a wage of $8,500 it should result in the hiring of how many workers? _____

3. Suppose there are three adult persons in a hypothetical economy. Each individual has his own preferences for working and consuming leisure time. We have portrayed the labour supply curve of each person. The labour-supply curve depicts the number of hours per time period which the individual is willing to offer to the labour market at various wage rates.

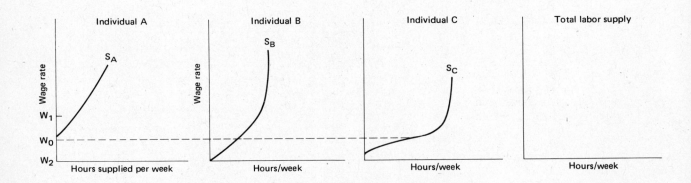

At wage rate w_0, A is not prepared to offer any hours per week, B is prepared to offer Oh_1, and C is willing to offer Oh_2 hours per week. Therefore, we can say that the total number of hours offered to the labour market is $Oh_1 + Oh_2$. Furthermore, two of the three members of population are willing to participate in the labour market. We say that the *participation rate* is two-thirds.

(a) Plot the total number of hours supplied per week at a wage rate of w_0.

(b) Taking a higher wate rate of w_1, determine the effect of the higher wage on hours supplied to the labour market. Has the number of hours increased? Why?

(c) What are your predictions regarding the magnitude of the participation rate at a wage of w_2?

PROBLEM

LORENZ CURVES AND INCOME DISTRIBUTIONS

The Lorenz curve is a graphical presentation permitting the comparison of income distributions (see text Figure 20-1). The vertical axis represents the cumulative percentage of total national income; the horizontal axis, the percentage of the population (here expressed as families) cumulated from the lowest to the highest income. Exact equality of income would be represented by the straight diagonal line running from the lower left (20 percent of the families would receive 20 percent of the income; 50 percent of the families, 50 percent of the income, etc.). The departure of the Lorenz curve from the diagonal is a measure of the inequality of income.

Table 20-3 of the text is the source of the figures in the table below.

	Income Share Canada, 1967 (percent)	Cumulative Percent of Income
Lowest fifth	6.4	_____
Second fifth	13.1	_____
Middle fifth	18.0	_____
Fourth fifth	23.6	_____
Highest fifth	38.9	_____

Questions

1. Graph this distribution as a Lorenz curve.

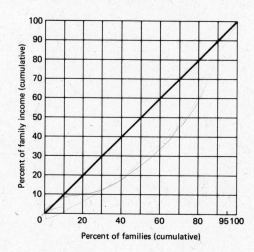

2. The following statistics were compiled by the World Bank for the year 1968.

Cumulative percentage of world's

GNP	Population
7	51
9	59
12	67
19	74
48	89
65	94
100	100

Sketch a Lorenz curve for the world. Comparing the world's Lorenz curve with that of Canada, which one more closely approaches absolute equality of income? Explain.

Chapter Twenty-one
Labor Unions,
Collective
Bargaining, and
the Determination of Wages

REVIEW QUESTIONS

1. When a union can set a wage level for its members, this can be shown diagrammatically, by a supply curve of labour whose elasticity is ___*perfectly elastic*___ up to the maximum number willing to work at that wage.

2. If a union pushes wages above the competitive equilibrium wage, the quantity of labour hired will be (more/less) than the quantity of labour supplied. The result will be a (surplus/shortage) of workers available.

3. (a) For a monopsony firm, which can set the wages of unorganized workers, an upward-sloping labour supply means that, if it hires additional workers, it will have to (raise/lower) wages.
   (b) This wage increase will be paid to (all workers/the last worker hired only). The marginal labour cost will be (higher/lower) than the average labour cost or wages paid since increases in hirings push wages up.
   (c) This monopsony firm, if a profit maximizer, will hire workers up to the point at which marginal labour cost equals ___*MRP*___.
   Compared with the case of competitive demand for labour, this firm would therefore employ (more/fewer) workers at a (lower/higher) wage.

4. The situation in which a monopsonistic buyer faces a monopolistic seller is called a case of ___*bilateral*___ monopoly. The resulting negotiated price (or wage) is influenced by the relative ___*power*___ of the two parties.

5. By forcing a profit-maximizing monopsonist to pay a higher wage than it otherwise would, a union can cause a (higher/lower) level of employment than would otherwise have occurred.

6. Unions of workers with similar skills are called ___*craft*___ unions. A union of workers in a given industry, regardless of their different skills, is called a(n) ___*industry*___ union.

7. Originally, the Trades and Labour Congress in Canada was based on _____ _craft_ _____ unions, while the Canadian Congress of Labour was formed on the basis of _____ _industrial_ _____ unions. However, in 1956 the two groups amalgamated into a federation called _____.

8. It was easier for skilled than for unskilled workers to organize and get higher wages because the demand for skilled workers was more (elastic/inelastic); moreover, their numbers, and therefore total costs to the employer, were (larger/smaller).

9. If a union wishes to obtain higher wages without creating an increased amount of excess labour, it will usually have to limit the _____ _supply_ _____.

10. If a worker does not have to join the union at a plant in order to get or to keep his job, the firm is called a(n) _____ _open shop_ _____.

11. If a new employee must join the union within a certain period after starting a job, the firm is called an _____ _union shop_ _____.

12. Federal government legislation in 1944 guaranteed workers _____.

13. According to Table 21-1 in the text, the total number of union members in Canada is just over _____ million. Referring to Figure 21-4 in the text, this number represents over _____ percent of nonagricultural employment.

14. Unions find it easier to gain wage increases under which conditions?
    (a) The industry or firm is (profitable/unprofitable).
    (b) Labour costs are a (small/large) part of total costs.
    (c) Firms are (competitive/monopolistic).
    (d) Demand for the product is (increasing/decreasing).
    (e) Labour supply is (elastic/inelastic).

15. If unions push wages up, *ceteris paribus*, unemployment is apt to increase if the employer is able to substitute _____ _labor-saving equipment_ _____. Unions often try to protect their jobs from technological displacement by practices known as _____ _featherbedding_ _____.

16. When workers combine to refuse to work, it is a _____ _strike_ _____; when they combine to avoid buying the products of a particular firm, it is a _____ _boycott_ _____; when they form a line outside a plant to try to prevent the entry of strikebreakers and/or customers, it is a _____ _picket line_ _____.

_____

    If you have not answered all questions correctly, review the text in order to be sure that you have all of the important concepts clearly in mind before going on to the next chapter.

1. completely elastic or infinite 2. less; surplus 3. raise; all workers; higher; marginal revenue product; fewer; lower 4. bilateral; strength or power 5. higher 6. craft; industrial 7. craft; industrial; the Canadian Labour Congress 8. inelastic; smaller 9. supply of labour 10. open shop 11. union shop 12. the right to form a union and to elect an exclusive bargaining agent 13. 2; 30 14. profitable; small; monopolistic; increasing; inelastic 15. labour-saving equipment; featherbedding 16. strike; boycott; picket line

MULTIPLE-CHOICE QUESTIONS

1. For a given set of conditions in the product market, wages will be highest under
   (a) monopoly in the labour market
   (b) monopsony in the labour market
   (c) perfect competition in the labour market
   (d) bilateral monopoly in the labour market

2. If a group of workers or members of an occupation are able to reduce their numbers and prevent others from entering, in an otherwise competitive market,
   (a) it will still be necessary for them to bargain for any wage increases
   (b) the antitrust laws may be used against them
   (c) their wages will rise, *ceteris paribus*
   (d) the individual members will benefit only if the demand curve for their services is inelastic

3. Which of the following was *not* a general problem for U.S. union leadership during the 1950s and 1960s?
   (a) whether or not to strike for its demands
   (b) how to obtain legal recognition of the right of collective bargaining
   (c) what choice to make between higher wages and increased unemployment for its members
   (d) how to fight technological displacement of its members

4. The Canadian Union of Public Employees is an example of
   (a) a federation in Canada
   (b) an international union
   (c) a national union
   (d) a member of the Confederation of National Trade Unions

5. Pension rights for workers may help employers keep total costs down because
   (a) they are a form of incentive pay
   (b) many workers choose not to accept them
   (c) employers have ways of avoiding providing them
   (d) they may reduce labour turnover

6. An arrangement in which workers must join the union upon employment is called
   (a) a union shop
   (b) a closed shop
   (c) an open shop
   (d) a jurisdictional shop

7. Which best sums up the text analysis of the influence of unions on wage levels?
   (a) Union influence has been unimportant because, in the absence of unions, wages rise as labour productivity rises.
   (b) Labour's share of the national income has risen steadily since the 1930s because of union action.
   (c) The fact of higher wages in highly unionized industries such as steel and automobiles proves that unions have been the chief cause of higher wages.
   (d) Unions may have helped raise wages, but it is hard to tell by how much.

EXERCISE

Referring to the diagram, which represents the labour market in an industry, answer the questions below.

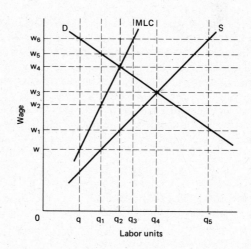

(a) If a completely competitive market prevailed, the equilibrium wage would be _____ W₂ _____ , and the amount of employment would be _____ q₄ _____ .

(b) If a wage-setting union enters this market and sets the wage at w_6, the amount of employment would be _____ q _____ , and the amount of surplus labour unemployed would be _____ qᵣ - q _____ . How would the labour-supply curve look?

_____

(c) Assume that this market consists of a single large firm hiring labour in a competitive labour market. If the firm hired q_1 workers, it would have to pay all workers the wage _____ w _____ , but the marginal-labour cost of the last man hired would be _____ W₂ _____ . Because the marginal-revenue product of the last man hired is equal to the amount _____ W₅ _____ , there is an incentive for the firm to continue hiring to the amount _____ q₂ _____ , at which the wage will be _____ W₁ _____ , the marginal-labour cost will be _____ W₄ _____ , and the marginal-revenue product will be _____ W₄ _____ . Compare this with the result in (a): _____ W↓ q↓ _____

_____

(d) Suppose a union now organizes and sets a wage at w_3. The amount of employment will be _____ q₄ _____ . But if the monopsonist firm feels that it is as strong as the monopoly union, what is probably the only prediction we can make about wages and employment? _____ W₂ → W₃   q₂ q₄ _____

_____

(e) Draw a new labour-supply curve showing what happens when a union organizes this labour market, but, instead of setting a high wage, excludes half the workers by a combination of stiff apprenticeship rules, high union dues, nepotism, and racial discrimination.

PROBLEM

TWO CASES ON MINIMUM WAGES

A. The Case of the Rural Mill Owner

A traditional argument was that unionization (and/or a legal minimum wage) was necessary to prevent exploitation of labour by the monopsonistic firm—the only employer in an area, a fairly common situation. Not only would wages be raised, it was contended, but also employment would be *increased*.

Take the hypothetical case of Mr. Alfred Newman, whose mill was the only major employer in a rural county. Everyone available locally was on his payroll at the profit-maximizing wage ($1.20 per hour). He had decided not to expand output because he would have had to offer higher wages to attract workers from the next county. Then the United Textile Workers won a representation election and negotiated $1.50 as the minimum wage in the mill.

Questions

1. Show on the diagram what happens to the supply curve of labour with the new minimum wage.

2. What happens to the marginal-cost-of-labour (MLC) curve?

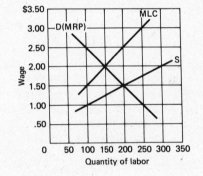

3. Where does the new MLC curve intersect the D curve for labour?

4. If Mr. Newman now wishes to maximize profits, how many people will he employ? _____

5. Assume that the union gets a further raise; at what level will it reduce employment below the original level? _____

B. The Case of Ontario's Minimum Wage Increase

In January 1969, the minimum hourly wage rate was raised from $1.00 to $1.30 by the Province of Ontario. This was done to increase the income of workers who have relatively little bargaining power. However, some economists are skeptical about the use of minimum-wage laws to alleviate poverty because of the possibility of higher unemployment for those workers who are directly affected by minimum wage laws.

A study was conducted by Fantl and Whittingham* for the Research Department of the Ontario Department of Labour in order to investigate, among other matters, the *initial* employment effect of the 30-cent rise in the minimum wage. Five low-wage industries which would be relatively sensitive to the change in the wage law were chosen for this investigation.

Questions

1. Assuming that these industries can exert no monopoly power in buying labour, discuss the theoretical implications for the employment of workers of the 30-cent-per-hour increase.

2. If we assume that decreases in employment are likely, discuss the actions that firms might pursue to avoid layoffs.

*The Short-Run Impact of the Thirty Cent Revision in Ontario's Minimum Wage on Five Industries, Ontario Department of Labour, Research Branch, September 1970.

3. During the period from November 1968 (just before the increase) to early January 1969, employers reported, only 25 workers (less than 10 percent of total layoffs) were dismissed because of the increase in the minimum wage.

      (a) According to marginal-productivity theory, what type of workers would be affected by the increase?

      (b) Consider the following information below, taken directly from the report. Given that females comprise about one-half of the labour force in these industries, what would your predictions be as to incidence of layoffs? Males or females?

Percentage Distribution of Non-Supervisory Employees by Sex and Wage Class for Selected Industries, Ontario, November 1968

Wage Class	Shoe Factories			Luggage, Handbags, Small Leather Goods			Hosiery Mills		
	Male	Female	Total	Male	Female	Total	Male	Female	Total
Under $1.10	0.5	4.3	3.0	1.0	2.9	2.2	0.8	4.6	3.8
1.10 - 1.19	1.4	7.5	5.4	0.6	9.0	6.2	1.6	11.6	9.4
1.20 - 1.29	2.3	13.2	9.4	2.6	13.0	9.5	3.5	14.9	12.4
1.30 - 1.39	2.6	11.9	8.6	1.3	6.7	11.5	2.6	13.6	11.2

Wage Class	Children's Clothing			Foundation Garments		
	Male	Female	Total	Male	Female	Total
Under $1.10	2.1	11.3	10.4	—	4.5	4.0
1.10 - 1.19	2.1	10.7	9.8	—	9.1	8.0
1.20 - 1.29	5.7	12.7	12.0	1.6	17.6	15.7
1.30 - 1.39	2.1	11.1	10.2	1.0	10.1	9.0

Source: Ontario Department of Labour, Research Branch, 1970.

Chapter Twenty-two
Interest and the
Return on Capital

<table>
<tr><td>CHECKLIST</td><td>Make certain that you understand the following concepts: productivity of capital; gross return to capita; pure return on capital; capital stock; marginal efficiency of capital (MEC); marginal-efficiency-of-capital schedule; capital deepening; capital widening; present value (PV); capitalized value; human capital; market rate of interest, money rate of interest; real rate of interest; credit rationing; money capital; real capital; equity capital; debt; stockholders; common stock; preferred stock; bondholders; bond; stock market; securities market; perpetuity; PE ratio (P/E).</td></tr>
</table>

REVIEW QUESTIONS

1. The difference between a flow of output in which part of a given amount of labour and raw materials is first used to produce capital goods and a flow in which the labour and raw materials are directly applied to producing consumption goods is a measure of the _____productivity_____ of capital.

2. In order to increase the production of capital goods, economic resources must be reallocated from the production of _____consumption_____ goods (assuming no unemployed resources exist). The current sacrifice should be more than offset by the future gain because of the (increase/decrease) in output.

3. Education may act as a source of _____human_____ capital. It is productive if the increase in the output of the trained worker over that of the untrained worker _____exceeds_____ the resources used in training him.

4. The gross return to capital is comprised of three elements: a _____risk_____ premium; the _____pure_____ rate of return on capital; and _____economic_____ profits, which may be negative.

5. The rate of return on the last dollar of capital employed is called the _____MEC_____. The marginal-efficiency-of-capital schedule relates the rate of return on each additional dollar of the capital stock to the size of the _____capital stock_____.

6. Increasing the quantity of capital without changing the proportions of factors used is called _____capital widening_____.

7. Since funds earned in future periods have opportunity costs, future incomes must be _____ *discount* _____.

8. Future funds are discounted more heavily the (greater/lower) is the market rate of interest (opportunity cost of money).

9. The interest rate will tend in equilibrium to _____ *equal* _____ the MEC at the amount invested.

10. In a world of static knowledge, the return on capital and the interest rate will _____ *decrease* _____ as capital is accumulated.

11. If the money rate of interest is 8 percent and the price level is rising at 5 percent a year, the real rate of interest is _____ *3* _____.

12. If you are willing to swap $100 now for not less than $110 a year from now, you are discounting that future amount of money at an interest rate of _____ *10%* _____ percent. If, in addition, you were not very sure that you would get your money back at the end of the year, you would, no doubt, require another 1 percent or more to compensate for _____ *risk* _____. If you also would have to go to considerable trouble in correspondence, telephone calls, or personal visits to get your money back, you would add another few percentages to cover _____ *cost* _____. Thus, most interest rates charged on consumer borrowing consist of far more than what is called _____ *pure* _____ interest.

13. Important sources of financing for a firm are _____ *common* _____ or _____ *preferred* _____ stock, borrowing from banks or through sale of _____ *bonds* _____, and _____ *reinvested* _____ profits.

14. The capitalized value of a perpetuity is found by dividing the current appropriate interest rate into the _____ *annual income* _____.

15. If the market is paying 6 percent per year on similar alternate investments, then a building that brings in a net rental income of $3,000 per year should sell for about _____ *50,000* _____. If market interest rates now fall, the value of this building will (rise/fall). $\frac{3000}{6} = 100$

16. A rise in the rate of interest (raises/lowers) the capital value of any asset that yields a fixed future money income.

If you have not answered all questions correctly, review the text in order to be sure that you have all of the important concepts clearly in mind before going on to the next chapter.

1. productivity 2. consumption; increase 3. human; exceeds 4. risk, pure, economic 5. marginal efficiency of capital; capital stock 6. capital deepening 7. discounted 8. greater 9. equal 10. decrease 11. 3 percent 12. 10; risk; costs; pure 13. common, preferred, bonds, reinvested 14. annual income 15. $50,000; rise 16. lowers

---

MULTIPLE-CHOICE QUESTIONS

1. When a firm uses its own funds instead of borrowing for investment purposes,
    (a) its economic costs are lower because it does not have to pay interest
    (b) it should impute an interest rate to get a true picture of cost
    (c) it means it cannot get a loan at the bank
    (d) it does not have to worry about the rate of return on the investment

2. Capital earns income because
   (a) it is productive
   (b) it is expensive
   (c) it is always cheaper to substitute capital for labour
   (d) it is technically more efficient

3. Profits of a particular business could be at a rate less than the pure return on capital
   (a) if economic profits were negative
   (b) if risks were unusually low
   (c) never
   (d) if most income had been paid out as dividends

4. The present value of x dollars a year from now equals
   (a) xi
   (b) $x(1 + i)$
   (c) $x/(1 + i)$
   (d) $(1 + i)/x$

5. The higher the rate of interest, *ceteris paribus,*
   (a) the more investment opportunities will be profitable
   (b) the higher the necessary rate of return on any investment
   (c) the lower the amount of borrowing by the federal government
   (d) the greater the demand for investment funds

6. A rise in the interest rate on new debts is associated with
   (a) a fall in the price of old bonds
   (b) a fall in the income on old bonds
   (c) a rise in the price of old bonds
   (d) a rise in the income on old bonds

7. The value of an income-earning asset
   (a) is the sum of all its income payments
   (b) is the discounted present value of its expected income stream
   (c) is measured by its reproduction cost
   (d) rises as interest rates rise

8. Capital deepening occurs
   (a) whenever investment takes place
   (b) when a firm doubles output by replicating its existing facilities
   (c) when capital accumulation increases the proportion of capital to other factors
   (d) when a firm must go more deeply in debt

9. If you borrow $300 and pay it back in twelve equal monthly installments of $28, the true rate of interest is about
   (a) 12 percent
   (b) 6 percent
   (c) 24 percent
   (d) 10 percent

10. The MEC shifts to the right
    (a) as capital is accumulated
    (b) as the interest rate drops
    (c) as technical knowledge increases
    (d) as households save more

11. The advantage for shareholders of cumulative preferred stock over common stock is that
    (a) the dividends will be higher than those on common stock
    (b) the opportunity for capital gains is greater
    (c) the payment of dividends is certain
    (d) preferred dividends (including arrears) will be paid before common dividends

EXERCISES

1. Just for practice, fill in the following blanks using the present value (PV) table, Table 22-1, on page 141.

	This many $	in *t* years	has this PV	at *i* rate of interest
(a)	10	5	7.47	6%
(b)	100	50	$60.80	
(c)	1,000		3.00	12
(d)		6	4.56	14

2. More practice, this time with the annuity table, Table 22-2, on page 142.

	This many $	received each year for *t* years	has this PV	at *i* rate of interest
(a)	10	5		6%
(b)	100	50	$3,919.60	
(c)	1,000		8,304.00	12
(d)		6	38.89	14

3. *Present-Value Calculations*

(a) *Dropping out with Dad.* Business executive R. P. Squarehole, after a vigorous discussion with R. P., Jr., is considering whether he should drop out of the establishment. He is 50 years old and has $100,000 and adequate pension rights at age 60. Would a 6-percent, 10-year annuity yield him the $13,500 a year he feels would make it feasible? (Note that such an annuity would provide equal payments, pay 6 percent on the declining balance, and exhaust his capital at the end of 10 years.)

(b) *Calculating the net rate of return.* The Acme Machine Shop is analyzing a proposal to purchase labour-saving equipment estimated to save $15,000 a year less $1,000 maintenance. It calculated a 10-year life and $10,000 salvage value for the $75,000 machine. It wishes a return of 14 percent per year before taxes. Should it invest?

(c) *My son, the doctor, maybe.* The senior Schmidts were considering with son Hermann whether he should go on to medical school or enter the family business. They estimated that, if he went on to medical school (four years), internship (one year), and a residency for surgical training (four years), the opportunity cost would be $10,000 a year—mostly for reduced earnings for the nine years. It was estimated that, from the tenth to the fortieth year, his earnings in

Table 22-1   Present Value of $1.00

$$PV = \left(\frac{1}{1+i}\right)^t$$

Years hence (t)	1%	2%	4%	6%	8%	10%	12%	14%	15%	16%	18%	20%	22%	24%	25%	26%	28%	30%	35%	40%	45%	50%
1	0.990	0.980	0.962	0.943	0.926	0.909	0.893	0.877	0.870	0.862	0.847	0.833	0.820	0.806	0.800	0.794	0.781	0.769	0.741	0.714	0.690	0.667
2	0.980	0.961	0.925	0.890	0.857	0.826	0.797	0.769	0.756	0.743	0.718	0.694	0.672	0.650	0.640	0.630	0.610	0.592	0.549	0.510	0.476	0.444
3	0.971	0.942	0.889	0.840	0.794	0.751	0.712	0.675	0.658	0.641	0.609	0.579	0.551	0.524	0.512	0.500	0.477	0.455	0.406	0.364	0.328	0.296
4	0.961	0.924	0.855	0.792	0.735	0.683	0.636	0.592	0.572	0.552	0.516	0.482	0.451	0.423	0.410	0.397	0.373	0.350	0.301	0.260	0.226	0.198
5	0.951	0.906	0.822	0.747	0.681	0.621	0.567	0.519	0.497	0.476	0.437	0.402	0.370	0.341	0.328	0.315	0.291	0.269	0.223	0.186	0.156	0.132
6	0.942	0.888	0.790	0.705	0.630	0.564	0.507	0.456	0.432	0.410	0.370	0.335	0.303	0.275	0.262	0.250	0.227	0.207	0.165	0.133	0.108	0.088
7	0.933	0.871	0.760	0.665	0.583	0.513	0.452	0.400	0.376	0.354	0.314	0.279	0.249	0.222	0.210	0.198	0.178	0.159	0.122	0.095	0.074	0.059
8	0.923	0.853	0.731	0.627	0.540	0.467	0.404	0.351	0.327	0.305	0.266	0.233	0.204	0.179	0.168	0.157	0.139	0.123	0.091	0.068	0.051	0.039
9	0.914	0.837	0.703	0.592	0.500	0.424	0.361	0.308	0.284	0.263	0.225	0.194	0.167	0.144	0.134	0.125	0.108	0.094	0.067	0.048	0.035	0.026
10	0.905	0.820	0.676	0.558	0.463	0.386	0.322	0.270	0.247	0.227	0.191	0.162	0.137	0.116	0.107	0.099	0.085	0.073	0.050	0.035	0.024	0.017
11	0.896	0.804	0.650	0.527	0.429	0.350	0.287	0.237	0.215	0.195	0.162	0.135	0.112	0.094	0.086	0.079	0.066	0.056	0.037	0.025	0.017	0.012
12	0.887	0.788	0.625	0.497	0.397	0.319	0.257	0.208	0.187	0.168	0.137	0.112	0.092	0.076	0.069	0.062	0.052	0.043	0.027	0.018	0.012	0.008
13	0.879	0.773	0.601	0.469	0.368	0.290	0.229	0.182	0.163	0.145	0.116	0.093	0.075	0.061	0.055	0.050	0.040	0.033	0.020	0.013	0.008	0.005
14	0.870	0.758	0.577	0.442	0.340	0.263	0.205	0.160	0.141	0.125	0.099	0.078	0.062	0.049	0.044	0.039	0.032	0.025	0.015	0.009	0.006	0.003
15	0.861	0.743	0.555	0.417	0.315	0.239	0.183	0.140	0.123	0.108	0.084	0.065	0.051	0.040	0.035	0.031	0.025	0.020	0.011	0.006	0.004	0.002
16	0.853	0.728	0.534	0.394	0.292	0.218	0.163	0.123	0.107	0.093	0.071	0.054	0.042	0.032	0.028	0.025	0.019	0.015	0.008	0.005	0.003	0.002
17	0.844	0.714	0.513	0.371	0.270	0.198	0.146	0.108	0.093	0.080	0.060	0.045	0.034	0.026	0.023	0.020	0.015	0.012	0.006	0.003	0.002	0.001
18	0.836	0.700	0.494	0.350	0.250	0.180	0.130	0.095	0.081	0.069	0.051	0.038	0.028	0.021	0.018	0.016	0.012	0.009	0.005	0.002	0.001	0.001
19	0.828	0.686	0.475	0.331	0.232	0.164	0.116	0.083	0.070	0.060	0.043	0.031	0.023	0.017	0.014	0.012	0.009	0.007	0.003	0.002	0.001	
20	0.820	0.673	0.456	0.312	0.215	0.149	0.104	0.073	0.061	0.051	0.037	0.026	0.019	0.014	0.012	0.010	0.007	0.005	0.002	0.001	0.001	
21	0.811	0.660	0.439	0.294	0.199	0.135	0.093	0.064	0.053	0.044	0.031	0.022	0.015	0.011	0.009	0.008	0.006	0.004	0.002	0.001		
22	0.803	0.647	0.422	0.278	0.184	0.123	0.083	0.056	0.046	0.038	0.026	0.018	0.013	0.009	0.007	0.006	0.004	0.003	0.001	0.001		
23	0.795	0.634	0.406	0.262	0.170	0.112	0.074	0.049	0.040	0.033	0.022	0.015	0.010	0.007	0.006	0.005	0.003	0.002	0.001			
24	0.788	0.622	0.390	0.247	0.158	0.102	0.066	0.043	0.035	0.028	0.019	0.013	0.008	0.006	0.005	0.004	0.003	0.002	0.001			
25	0.780	0.610	0.375	0.233	0.146	0.092	0.059	0.038	0.030	0.024	0.016	0.010	0.007	0.005	0.004	0.003	0.002	0.001	0.001			
26	0.772	0.598	0.361	0.220	0.135	0.084	0.053	0.033	0.026	0.021	0.014	0.009	0.006	0.004	0.003	0.002	0.002	0.001				
27	0.764	0.586	0.347	0.207	0.125	0.076	0.047	0.029	0.023	0.018	0.011	0.007	0.005	0.003	0.002	0.002	0.001	0.001				
28	0.757	0.574	0.333	0.196	0.116	0.069	0.042	0.026	0.020	0.016	0.010	0.006	0.004	0.002	0.002	0.002	0.001	0.001				
29	0.749	0.563	0.321	0.185	0.107	0.063	0.037	0.022	0.017	0.014	0.008	0.005	0.003	0.002	0.002	0.001	0.001	0.001				
30	0.742	0.552	0.308	0.174	0.099	0.057	0.033	0.020	0.015	0.012	0.007	0.004	0.003	0.002	0.001	0.001	0.001	0.001				
40	0.672	0.453	0.208	0.097	0.046	0.022	0.011	0.005	0.004	0.003	0.001	0.001										
50	0.608	0.372	0.141	0.054	0.021	0.009	0.003	0.001	0.001	0.001												

Table 22-2 Present Value of $1.00 Received Annually for t Years

$$PV = \left(\frac{1}{1+i}\right)^1 + \left(\frac{1}{1+i}\right)^2 + \cdots + \left(\frac{1}{1+i}\right)^t$$

Years (t)	1%	2%	4%	6%	8%	10%	12%	14%	15%	16%	18%	20%	22%	24%	25%	26%	28%	30%	35%	40%	45%	50%
1	0.990	0.980	0.962	0.943	0.926	0.909	0.893	0.877	0.870	0.862	0.847	0.833	0.820	0.806	0.800	0.794	0.781	0.769	0.741	0.714	0.690	0.667
2	1.970	1.942	1.886	1.833	1.783	1.736	1.690	1.647	1.626	1.605	1.566	1.528	1.492	1.457	1.440	1.424	1.392	1.361	1.289	1.224	1.165	1.111
3	2.941	2.884	2.775	2.673	2.577	2.487	2.402	2.322	2.283	2.246	2.174	2.106	2.042	1.981	1.952	1.923	1.868	1.816	1.696	1.589	1.493	1.407
4	3.902	3.808	3.630	3.465	3.312	3.170	3.037	2.914	2.855	2.798	2.690	2.589	2.494	2.404	2.362	2.320	2.241	2.166	1.997	1.849	1.720	1.605
5	4.853	4.713	4.452	4.212	3.993	3.791	3.605	3.433	3.352	3.274	3.127	2.991	2.864	2.745	2.689	2.635	2.532	2.436	2.220	2.035	1.876	1.737
6	5.795	5.601	5.242	4.917	4.623	4.355	4.111	3.889	3.784	3.685	3.498	3.326	3.167	3.020	2.951	2.885	2.759	2.643	2.385	2.168	1.983	1.824
7	6.728	6.472	6.002	5.582	5.206	4.868	4.564	4.288	4.160	4.039	3.812	3.605	3.416	3.242	3.161	3.083	2.937	2.802	2.508	2.263	2.057	1.883
8	7.652	7.325	6.733	6.210	5.747	5.335	4.968	4.639	4.487	4.344	4.078	3.837	3.619	3.421	3.329	3.241	3.076	2.925	2.598	2.331	2.108	1.922
9	8.566	8.162	7.435	6.802	6.247	5.759	5.328	4.946	4.772	4.607	4.303	4.031	3.786	3.566	3.463	3.366	3.184	3.019	2.665	2.379	2.144	1.948
10	9.714	8.983	8.111	7.360	6.710	6.145	5.650	5.216	5.019	4.833	4.494	4.192	3.923	3.682	3.571	3.465	3.269	3.092	2.715	2.414	2.168	1.965
11	10.368	9.787	8.760	7.877	7.139	6.495	5.988	5.453	5.234	5.029	4.656	4.327	4.035	3.776	3.656	3.544	3.335	3.147	2.757	2.438	2.185	1.977
12	11.255	10.575	9.385	8.384	7.536	6.814	6.194	5.660	5.421	5.197	4.793	4.439	4.127	3.851	3.725	3.606	3.387	3.190	2.779	2.456	2.196	1.985
13	12.134	11.343	9.986	8.853	7.904	7.103	6.424	5.842	5.583	5.342	4.910	4.533	4.203	3.912	3.780	3.656	3.427	3.223	2.799	2.468	2.204	1.990
14	13.004	12.106	10.563	9.295	8.244	7.367	6.628	6.002	5.724	5.468	5.008	4.611	4.265	3.962	3.824	3.695	3.459	3.249	2.814	2.477	2.210	1.993
15	13.865	12.849	11.118	9.712	8.559	7.606	6.811	6.142	5.847	5.575	5.092	4.675	4.315	4.001	3.859	3.726	3.483	3.268	2.825	2.484	2.214	1.995
16	14.718	13.578	11.652	10.106	8.851	7.824	6.974	6.265	5.954	5.669	5.162	4.730	4.357	4.003	3.887	3.751	3.503	3.283	2.834	2.489	2.216	1.997
17	15.562	14.292	12.166	10.477	9.122	8.022	7.120	6.373	6.047	5.749	5.222	4.775	4.391	4.059	3.910	3.771	3.518	3.295	2.840	2.492	2.218	1.998
18	16.398	14.992	12.659	10.828	9.372	8.201	7.250	6.467	6.128	5.818	5.273	4.812	4.419	4.080	3.928	3.786	3.529	3.304	2.844	2.494	2.219	1.999
19	17.226	15.678	13.134	11.158	9.604	8.365	7.366	6.550	6.198	5.877	5.316	4.844	4.442	4.097	3.942	3.799	3.539	3.311	2.848	2.496	2.220	1.999
20	18.046	16.351	13.590	11.470	9.818	8.514	7.469	6.623	6.259	5.929	5.353	4.870	4.460	4.110	3.954	3.808	3.546	3.316	2.850	2.497	2.221	1.999
21	18.857	17.011	14.029	11.764	10.017	8.649	7.562	6.687	6.312	5.973	5.384	4.891	4.476	4.121	3.963	3.816	3.551	3.320	2.852	2.498	2.221	2.000
22	19.660	17.658	14.451	12.042	10.201	8.772	7.645	6.743	6.359	6.011	5.410	4.909	4.488	4.130	3.970	3.822	3.556	3.323	2.853	2.498	2.222	2.000
23	20.456	18.292	14.857	12.303	10.371	8.883	7.718	6.792	6.399	6.044	5.432	4.925	4.499	4.137	3.976	3.827	3.559	3.325	2.854	2.499	2.222	2.000
24	21.243	18.914	15.247	12.550	10.529	8.985	7.784	6.835	6.434	6.073	5.451	4.937	4.507	4.143	3.981	3.831	3.562	3.327	2.855	2.499	2.222	2.000
25	22.023	19.523	15.622	12.783	10.675	9.077	7.843	6.873	6.464	6.097	5.467	4.948	4.514	4.147	3.985	3.834	3.564	3.329	2.856	2.499	2.222	2.000
26	22.795	20.121	15.983	13.003	10.810	9.161	7.896	6.906	6.491	6.118	5.480	4.956	4.520	4.151	3.988	3.837	3.566	3.330	2.856	2.500	2.222	2.000
27	23.560	20.707	16.330	13.211	10.935	9.237	7.943	6.935	6.514	6.136	5.492	4.964	4.524	4.154	3.990	3.839	3.567	3.331	2.856	2.500	2.222	2.000
28	24.316	21.281	16.663	13.406	11.051	9.307	7.984	6.961	6.534	6.152	5.502	4.970	4.528	4.157	3.992	3.840	3.568	3.331	2.857	2.500	2.222	2.000
29	25.066	21.844	16.984	13.591	11.158	9.370	8.022	6.983	6.551	6.166	5.510	4.975	4.531	4.159	3.994	3.841	3.569	3.332	2.857	2.500	2.222	2.000
30	25.808	22.306	17.292	13.765	11.258	9.427	8.055	7.003	6.566	6.177	5.517	4.979	4.534	4.160	3.995	3.842	3.569	3.332	2.857	2.500	2.222	2.000
40	32.835	27.355	19.793	15.046	11.925	9.779	8.244	7.105	6.642	6.234	5.548	4.997	4.544	4.166	3.999	3.846	3.571	3.333	2.857	2.500	2.222	2.000
50	39.196	31.424	21.482	15.762	12.234	9.915	8.304	7.133	6.661	6.246	5.554	4.999	4.545	4.167	4.000	3.846	3.571	3.333	2.857	2.500	2.222	2.000

medicine would exceed his business earnings by $10,000 a year. Mother Schmidt argued for the prestige of the M.D., but father wanted assurance that this investment in Hermann capital would yield at least 6 percent. Would it? What is it estimated to yield?

(d) A. E. Ames & Co. report in their August 9, 1974, edition of *Money and World Markets* that the ask price of a Bell Canada bond maturing in June 1979 with a coupon rate of 9.75% was $99. Using the present-value tables, prove that the ask price is equal to the capitalized value of the bond.

PROBLEM

CASH BONUSES ON CANADA SAVINGS BONDS (CSB)

Canada savings bond have been one of the major sources of cash for the federal government for many years. They were first issued to the public in November 1946. They represent a contractual agreement between the government and the original buyer who must be a bona-fide Canadian resident. Canada savings bonds are not transferable; that is, the original buyer cannot sell his CSBs to anyone else. However, CSBs can be cashed in at any time.

There are at least three types of CSBs. The "coupon" variety is the most common. If a bond has a maturity of five years, there may be five coupons attached, which indicate the annual interest payment which is to be paid. One coupon is detached each November, and the holder receives a cash payment from the government. Often there will be additional coupons. These will be bonuses paid to the holder if he holds the bond to its maturity date.

During 1973 and 1974, the number of redemptions (the number of bonds sold back to the government) increased substantially and hence the cash position of the federal government became serious. Therefore, the Minister of Finance introduced a system of additional cash bonuses which would become effective on September 1, 1974. The bonuses depended on the date of purchase and the date of maturity of the CSB. For the bonds maturing on or before November 1, 1979, a cash bonus would be paid if they were held to maturity. There were two additional cash bonuses for bonds maturing after November 1, 1979; one in November 1979 and one at the date of maturity.

Some of the economic facts during this period are outlined in the table below.

Year	Average CSB Rate (December observation)*	Annual Inflation Rate	Rate of 5-Year Trust Company Investment Certificates (December observation)
1971	7.13%	2.85%	7.14%
1972	7.18	4.80	7.57
1973	7.58	7.58	8/61

*L. N. Christofides, *Aspects of the Canada Savings Bond Market*, Special Study for the Economic Council of Canada, September 1974.

Questions

1. Why do you think that the number of redemptions increased in 1973 and 1974 (the 1974 inflation rate was about 11 percent, and the CSB rate some time before September 1974 was probably less than 8 percent)?

2. Why was it necessary for the Minister of Finance to introduce the special cash bonus system? Why were bonuses paid only if the bond was held to maturity? What effect would this change have on the CSB rate?

Chapter Twenty-three
Inequality, Mobility, and Poverty

CHECKLIST	Make certain that you understand the following concepts: marginal-productivity theory of distribution (demand for factors); hypothesis of equal net advantage (supply of factors); functional and size distributions of income; poverty and poverty level; correlates of poverty; categorical assistance and social assistance.

REVIEW QUESTIONS

1. Marginal-productivity theory explains the (demand for/~~supply of~~) factors of production. Profit-maximizing firms will hire units of a factor to the point at which its marginal _____*revenue*_____ equals its _____*price*_____ .

2. The theory of supply of factors asserts that factors will move between uses in search of the _____*highest*_____ net advantage.

3. Labour markets differ from other factor markets in that they are often (~~more~~/less) competitive, and differences in money earnings alone (~~are~~/are not) enough to make factors move.

4. This chapter suggests that (~~lower~~/higher) wages or incomes and (lower/~~higher~~) unemployment rates may persuade labour to move from one region to another. The relative importance of one over the other is an empirical question.

5. In order to explain the (rise/fall) in the wages of coal miners in the face of (declining/rising) demand for their labour, the monopoly power of _____*union*_____ must be recognized. Employment, however, has _____*fallen*_____ in this industry.

6. Functional distribution of income refers to the distribution among such categories as rent, interest, profits, and _____*wages*_____ .

7. According to two studies by the Economic Council of Canada and Statistics Canada, the percentage of the population classified below the poverty standard of income is approximately ___*18-20*___ percent.

8. According to the data given in the text, the chances of being poor are greater for people who live in (rural/~~urban~~) areas and who work on a (~~full-time~~/part-time) basis.

_____

    If you have not answered all questions correctly, review the text in order to be sure that you have all of the important concepts clearly in mind before going on to the next chapter.

1. demand for; revenue product, price 2. highest 3. less; are not 4. higher; lower 5. rise, declining; unions; fallen 6. wages and salaries 7. 18 to 20 8. rural; part-time

_____

MULTIPLE-CHOICE QUESTIONS

1. The condition that firms equate a factor's marginal-revenue product to that factor's price
   (a) is true only in the short run
   (b) is true for all firms, industries, and market structures
   (c) is true only for monopolistic firms
   (d) assumes profit maximization and competition in factor markets

2. Which of the following statements is not true of the marginal-productivity theory?
   (a) It requires competition in all markets.
   (b) It requires that employees be numerous enough to be competitors in factor markets.
   (c) It permits employers to be monopolists.
   (d) It is a theory of demand.

3. To test the theory of distribution, one question which must be answered is
   (a) whether an employer knows the marginal-revenue product of a factor
   (b) whether factors do in fact move to other occupations in response to higher earnings
   (c) whether factor owners have complete knowledge of all opportunities
   (d) whether each factor is being paid the value of its own contribution to production

4. One reason why income differentials do not set up movements of the labour factor as readily as they stimulate movements of nonhuman factors is that
   (a) labour is made less mobile because of nonpecuniary considerations
   (b) people do not really care much about making money
   (c) nonhuman factors are typically small and easily shipped around the country
   (d) nonhuman factors are owned by profit-maximizing people

PROBLEMS

1. THE TREND OF DISTRIBUTIVE SHARES IN CANADA

    In what proportions is income distbibuted between the function of furnishing current labour services and the function of furnishing properties in Canada?
    Have these relative shares of income changed over time?
    The table below suggests some clues to the answer to these questions. However, the text makes the point that the traditional theory of distribution has not done well in explaining why the shares are as they are.
    We have grouped the various components of Net National Income at Factor Cost into three categories. *Employee Compensation* involves wages, salaries, and supplementary income. *Property Income* includes corporation profits before taxes (but net of dividends paid to nonresidents and inventory valuation adjustment) *plus* interest and miscellaneous investment income. *Entrepreneurial Income* includes net income of farm operators *plus* net income of nonincorporated businesses. This last group also includes rent income, which might more suitably be classified as property income, but we are unable to separate it out of entrepreneurial income.

Distributive Shares in Canada's National Income, 1926–1970, in Percentages*

Period	Employee Compensation	Property Income	Entrepreneurial Income
1926–1930	60.3	11.8	27.7
1931–1935	72.8	8.3	20.0
1936–1940	63.9	12.1	22.9
1941–1945	54.6	14.3	21.5
1946–1950	61.8	13.2	23.6
1951–1955	62.7	16.2	19.4
1956–1960	66.4	16.3	15.6
1961–1965	67.7	16.6	13.9
1965–1970	70.8	16.5	11.4

*Compiled from data in *Revised Estimates of Income and Expenditures*, Statistics Canada, 1972. Omitted are military salaries and allowances.

Questions

1. Check those generalizations that seem true from the table above.

_____ (a) The share of employee compensation in national income has remained stable since 1945.

_____ (b) The share of employee compensation rose drastically during the depression years, fell during war years, and since then has risen steadily.

_____ (c) The property share declined during depression years but has risen steadily since then.

_____ (d) The property share has remained relatively constant since the end of World War II.

_____ (e) The entrepreneurial income share has fallen steadily since the depression years.

2. Many factors have contributed to the fall in the entrepreneurial share of national income. However, given that a large majority of entrepreneurs have been farmers or small retailers, what is one obvious reason why the share of entrepreneurial income has declined?

3. If we neglect the element of rent included in entrepreneurial income, is it reasonable to argue that entrepreneurial income may itself be divided between labour and a return to capital (property income)? Explain.

2. THE INCIDENCE OF POVERTY ACCORDING TO OCCUPATIONS IN CANADA

Table 23-2 in the text illustrated some of the major characteristics of families whose income was below some cut-off point called the *poverty line*. We now consider an additional characteristic: the main occupation of the head of the family. In the table below we have shown the incidence of low income according to the main occupation of the head of the family. These figures give rough indications of the chances or "probabilities" of poverty according to various occupations. For example, we can say that there is about a 3-percent probability of being poor if you have a professional or technical occupation.

Incidence of Low Income, Canada, 1967*

Occupation of Head	Percentage
Managerial	6.7
Professional and technical	3.3
Clerical	5.6
Sales	7.2
Service and recreation	16.7
Transportation and communication	14.9
Farmers and farm workers	52.8
Loggers and fishermen	42.3
Miners	8.9
Craftsmen	9.6
Laborers	21.4

*Statistics on Low Income in Canada, 1967,
Statistics Canada, 1971.

Questions

1. In Chapter 22 you were introduced to the concept of investments in human capital. Specifically, academic and vocational education along with apprenticeship programs are examples of investments in human capital that improve individual skills and crafts. In turn, higher income is obtained for the improvement in skills. By inspecting the table above, select those occupations that most likely involve the greatest amounts of investments in human capital. Are the probabilities of poverty relatively high or low for these occupations?

2. If an individual finds himself continually unemployed and/or hired for particular seasons, his income is likely to be low. In your opinion, which of the above occupations tend to have the highest levels of unemployment and/or seasonality? Give reasons for your choices. What relationship exists between your choices and the incidence of poverty?

Chapter Twenty-four
The Price System: Market Success and Market Failure

> **CHECKLIST** Make certain that you understand the following concepts: laissez-faire; partial-equilibrium analysis; general-equilibrium analysis; collective consumption goods; net private benefit; net social benefit; internalization; effluent charge.

REVIEW QUESTIONS

1. One of the features of a market economy is that centralized planning is not necessary for allocating resources. Private enterprise responds to signals, such as _____ _price_ _____, _____ _cost_ _____, and _____ _profit_ _____ that result from the interaction of supply and demand.

2. A market that is working most efficiently is one where marginal net private benefits _____ _equal_ _____ marginal net social benefits.

3. The more efficient the market in allocating and producing, the (greater/less) the net social benefit.

4. A policy of least possible governmental interference in the market is called one of _____ _laissez-faire_ _____. Such a policy is apt to be abandoned if net social benefits are greatly (in excess of/exceeded by) net private benefits.

5. Because of the interdependence of markets, a change in one area of the economy produces a series of three effects: _____ _impact_ _____, _____ _spillout_ _____, and _____ _feedback_ _____. Where feedback is noticeable, _____ _general_ _____ equilibrium analysis is important.

6. Markets often fail to perform efficiently because of so-called market imperfections, such as (name several): _____ _factor immobility_ _____, _____ _ignorance_ _____, _____ _barriers to entry_ _____, _____ _monopoly_ _____.

7. Goods or services that, if provided at all, benefit simultaneously a large group of people are called _collective consumption good_. Local roads are financed by _____ _government_ _____ rather than by private enterprise, because there is generally no practical way to collect payment directly from users.

8. By *internalizing* externalities, we mean that the producer is required to _____ _pay the cost_ _____.

9. If a particular polluting activity is causing $1 million of damage to the environment and would cost $3 million to prevent, the economic cost of the pollution is _____ _1 million_ _____.

If you have not answered all questions correctly, review the text in order to be sure that you have all of the important concepts clearly in mind before going on to the next chapter.

1. prices, cost, profits 2. equal 3. greater 4. laissez-faire 5. impact, spillout, feedback; general 6. factor immobility, ignorance, barriers to entry, monopoly
7. collective consumption goods; government 8. pay their cost 9. $1 million

MULTIPLE-CHOICE QUESTIONS

1. A market is operating most efficiently if
   (a) total social cost is minimized
   (b) total private benefit is maximized
   (c) net social benefit is maximized
   (d) the excess of private benefits over social cost is maximized

2. General-equilibrium analysis as compared with partial-equilibrium analysis
   (a) is necessarily more comprehensive
   (b) is more dependent on *ceteris paribus* assumptions
   (c) is not concerned with relative prices
   (d) includes feedback effects

3. A collective consumption good is
   (a) the same as a free good
   (b) goods provided to union members
   (c) a good which is provided at all automatically is provided to many
   (d) a consumption good produced by a co-operative

4. A firm would have no incentive to internalize its externalities if
   (a) it is penalized by a fine
   (b) its pollution is subject to tax
   (c) its stockholders are environmentalists
   (d) the cost of the externalities is borne by others

5. From the point of view of those who favor a market economy, government intervention would be least justifiable to
   (a) protect the health and safety of the public
   (b) guarantee profits to businessmen
   (c) ensure correct information to consumers
   (d) provide needed public services that private enterprise finds unprofitable

6. All but which of the following are market imperfections that could be alleviated by government intervention?
   (a) nonmonetary preferences of labour that reduce mobility
   (b) lack of knowledge of the market by consumers and workers
   (c) monopoly power
   (d) artificial barriers to entry

EXERCISES

1. Suppose that installing an antipollution device adds $10 to the cost of making each unit of a product at every level of output. *Ceteris paribus:*
   (a) marginal cost will _____.
   (b) average cost will _____.
   (c) the supply curve will _____.
   (d) short-run equilibrium price will _____ but by less than _____.
   (e) short-run equilibrium output will _____.

2. Suppose that all firms in an industry must install an antipollution device at $10,000 regardless of the level of output. *Ceteris paribus:*
   (a) marginal cost will _____.
   (b) average cost will _____.
   (c) variable cost will _____.
   (d) short-run equilibrium price will _____.
   (e) short-run equilibrium output will _____.
   (f) long-run equilibrium price will _____.

3. The following are examples of possible government intervention in the economy. In a word or two, predict the effect on relative profitability of indicated industries or relative desirability of indicated activity.
   (a) The Province of Ontario passes new laws reducing allowed length and weight of trucks on provincial highways. Effect on:
       trucking _____
       railroads _____
   (b) The government of Canada imposes a tax on gasoline which applies only to individuals who use gasoline for noncommercial purposes. Effect on:
       private gasoline consumption _____
       trucking _____
       private transportation _____
   (c) The Federal Department of Transport announces a new policy of letting aviation pay its own way; federal aid to airport construction and air-traffic control will be financed from higher taxes on airline fares, aviation gasoline, and airport taxes, instead of from general taxation revenues. Effect on:
       airlines _____
       railroads _____
   (d) Parliament legislates new laws that disallow tax advantages which various U.S. magazines (*Reader's Digest* and *Time*) had in Canada and gives subsidies to Canadian publications. Effect on:
       foreign publishers _____
       Canadian publishers _____

Chapter Twenty-five
Public Finance and
Public Expenditure:
Tools of Microeconomic Policy

> | CHECKLIST | Make certain that you understand the following concepts: tax incidence; excise; progressivity of taxes; marginal tax rate; negative income tax; ad valorem tax; transfer payments; equalization payments; conditional grants. |
> |---|---|

REVIEW QUESTIONS

1. When a tax takes an increasing proportion of income as income increases, it is termed _____*progressive*_____. If it takes a decreasing proportion of income as income increases, it is termed _____*regressive*_____.

2. Sales taxes on such commodities as tobacco and gasoline are generally *regressive* _____. Most studies have shown property taxes to be somewhat _____*regressive*_____. The federal income tax is ____*progressive*____ both in structure and effect.

3. Negative income taxes are _____*payments*_____ to people whose income falls below a certain level.

4. Answering the question of who really bears the burden of a tax involves analysis of the _____*incidence*_____ of a tax.

5. As long as the demand curve for a commodity slopes downward and the supply curve upward, the incidence of an excise on that commodity falls on (the sellers/the buyers/both).

6. In general, the greater the *smaller* elasticity of demand with a given elasticity of supply, the (greater/less) the rise of price following the imposition of a specific excise.

7. In general, the greater the elasticity of supply with a given elasticity of demand, the (greater/less) the rise of price following the imposition of a specific excise.

8. A tax on pure profits (will/will not) affect price and output and thus the incidence will fall on (producers/consumers).

9. Payments by government to individuals for no productive service are called
   _____ *transfer* _____ payments. Such payments constitute about ___ *one-third* ___
   of total federal expenditures; the rest consists of purchases of ___ *goods and service* ___
   Federal conditional grants to provinces are primarily for two main purposes:
   _____ *health* _____ and _____ *education* _____.

10. Indicate the major source or sources of tax revenue for the following levels of
    government:
    (a) federal— _____ *income* _____
    (b) municipal— _____ *property* _____
    (c) provincial— _____ *sales and income* _____

11. Increasing tax rates and public expenditures in North American cities result primarily from a combination of circumstances:
    (a) (high/~~low~~) income elasticity of demand for certain public services
    (b) departures of the (wealthy/~~poor~~) to the suburbs
    (c) tax revenues that rise (more slowly/~~faster~~) than income
    (d) government pay that has risen (faster/~~more slowly~~) than productivity in these jobs
    (e) relocation of industry and jobs in the (cities/suburbs)

_____

     If you have not answered all questions correctly, review the text in order to be sure that you have all of the important concepts clearly in mind before going on to the next chapter.

1. progressive; regressive 2. regressive; regressive; progressive 3. payments
4. incidence 5. both 6. less 7. greater 8. will not, producers 9. transfer; one-third, goods and services; health, education 10. income, property, sales and income
11. high, wealthy, more slowly, faster, suburbs
_____

MULTIPLE-CHOICE QUESTIONS

1. A 10-percent surtax on income taxes all across the board raises the tax rate in each bracket by 10 percent of itself. This meant that the income tax
   (a) became slightly more progressive than before
   (b) became slightly closer to proportional than before
   (c) required an equal absolute increase from everyone
   (d) even affected those with no taxable income

2. A tax that takes the same amount from everyone, regardless of income, is
   (a) regressive
   (b) progressive
   (c) not fair at all
   (d) proportional to the benefit received

3. The text suggests that personal income taxes are progressive, while sales taxes are apt to be
   (a) proportional
   (b) intolerable
   (c) about the same as federal
   (d) regressive

4. A negative income tax of the type described in the text would have the advantage of
   (a) eliminating all need for welfare or relief programs
   (b) guaranteeing a minimum income to the poor with less red tape and with increased work incentives
   (c) penalizing those with large families ✗
   (d) keeping recipients out of the labour force where they would cause unemployment

5. The marginal rate (1972) of 50 percent on a taxable income of $24,000
   (a) meant that the average person with $24,000 of income paid $12,000 in taxes
   (b) had no effect whatever because of exemptions, deductions, and tax avoidance
   (c) signified the collection of 50 cents on each additional dollar of income
   (d) applied to capital gains as well as ordinary income

6. The more elastic the demand for a commodity on which a specific excise was levied, *ceteris paribus,*
   (a) the greater the after-tax price increase
   (b) the less the reduction in the quantity produced
   (c) the more elastic the associated supply curve
   (d) the less the after-tax price increase

   MTR

   50 %

   2<

7. Property taxes generally
   (a) fall entirely on the home-owner or landlord
   (b) are less likely to be shifted in the long run than in the short run
   (c) fall on renters as well as home-owners and landlords
   (d) are borne entirely by the occupant of a house

8. Which of the following has *not* been a significant reason for the financial difficulties of local overnments over the last decade?
   (a) tax revenues that do not respond relatively to growth in income
   (b) lower local tax rates
   (c) rising demands for government services
   (d) rising unit costs of providing government services

9. Decentralization of government economic activity can be justified by all but which of the following?
   (a) regional preferences
   (b) income redistribution
   (c) particular local needs for public expenditure
   (d) cultural differences within the country

10. Increasing amounts of tax revenue have been transferred to the provincial and municipal governments for all except which of the following reasons?
    (a) expenditure needs of urban areas are rapidly growing
    (b) municipal revenue sources have been growing slowly
    (c) provincial and municipal governments don't collect tax revenue
    (d) the federal government has access to the high-growth tax sources

EXERCISES

1. Assume that an excise of one-fifth of P is imposed on each of the commodities for which demand and supply curves are given below.

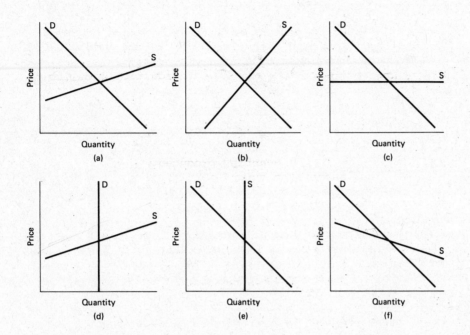

(a) In which cases is the price predicted to rise by at least the full amount of the tax? _____c_____ _____d_____ _____f_____ ℓ

(b) In which case is the price unaffected? _____ℓ_____

(c) Is the price rise greater in case a or case b? _____a_____ Why?

(d) Is the price rise greater in case a or case d? _____d_____ Why?

2. Below are five schedules for five different taxes, showing how much tax is paid at each indicated level of income. Identify whether each is regressive, proportional, or progressive.

Income	A	B	C	D	E
$1,000	0	100	100	100	100
2,000	0	200	250	180	200
3,000	0	300	450	250	300
4,000	0	400	700	320	400
5,000	200	500	1,000	380	500
6,000	500	600	1,350	440	500
7,000	900	700	1,750	480	500

A is _____ . B is _____ .
C is _____ . D is _____ .
E is _____ .

3. *Conditional Grants for Dimeland*

In the country of Utopia, the federal government is "concerned" that expenditures on education in the province of Dimeland are below those on a per capita basis in the rest of the country. The federal government is considering two policies: (1) an outright grant of one-half million dollars to Dimeland; (2) a conditional grant whereby the federal government will match, on a 50-50 basis, each additional dollar spent by Dimeland on education up to a cost of one-half million dollars to the federal government.

(a) Which policy do you think the government of Dimeland would prefer? Why?

(b) Given the "concern" of the federal government about education in Dimeland, what policy do you think should be adopted? Why?

PROBLEM

THE PROPERTY TAX IN ONTARIO

A study by the Province of Ontario in Guelph, Ontario, produced the following table illustrating the relationship between household income and property taxes in 1968.

Household Income (class)	Average Property Tax Paid
Less than $ 2,500	$268
$ 2,500- 2,999	276
3,000- 3,499	261
3,500- 3,999	276
4,000- 4,499	278
4,500- 4,999	285
5,000- 5,499	275
5,500- 5,999	268
6,000- 6,499	281
6,500- 6,999	290
7,000- 7,499	301
7,500- 7,999	302
8,000- 8,499	317
8,500- 8,999	319
9,000- 9,499	330
9,500- 9,999	342
10,000- 11,999	355
12,000- 14,999	417
15,000- 19,999	495
20,000- 24,999	581
25,000- 49,999	650
50,000- 99,999	836
100,000 and over	—

Source: Ministry of Treasury, Economics and Intergovernmental Relations. *Analysis of Property Taxes in Guelph,* October 1972.

Questions

1. Given these data, does the property tax appear to be regressive or progressive? Why?

2. To make the tax a proportional one, at a tax rate roughly equal to 8 percent, what kind of subsidies and additional taxes would the government need to impose at each household income level?

Chapter Twenty-six
National Income

> **CHECKLIST** Make certain that you understand the following concepts: national income; value added; intermediate products; final products; saving; investment; investment goods; gross investment; depreciation; net exports; gross national product (GNP); gross national expenditures (GNE); net national product; government transfer payments, disposable income; closed economies; open economies; GNP deflator; real national income.

REVIEW QUESTIONS

1. The total market value of all goods and services produced for final use in an economy in a given period of time is called the ___National income___ .

2. There are two approaches to measuring GNP: the ___Input – Income___ approach and the ___Output – Expenditure___ approach.

3. Adding up the value of output produced by *all* firms in the country would not give the correct value for GNP because of ___double accounting___ . To eliminate this problem it is necessary to arrive at a figure for the firm's ___intermediate goods___ in production. The firm's value added is found by subtracting from its total revenues ___the value of input___ .

4. The factor-income approach adds up four types of income: ___wages___ , ___rent___ , ___corporate profit___ , and ___interest___ .

5. The value of the factor-income approach must be ___equal___ to the value of output-expenditure approach.

6. Income not spent or paid in taxes is ___saving___ . Gross business savings are of two categories: ___depreciation___ and ___undistributed profit___ .

7. To the economist, *investment* means production of goods for ___future profit___ . Gross business investment falls into two general categories: ___machine___ and ___change in inventories___ .

8. Net investment equals gross investment minus ___depreciation___ .

9. In an economy without government or foreign trade, the sum of the values of consumption and investment is called the ___GNP___ .

10. The accounting definition of the sum of factor-income payments is the
_____GNP_____. Its value must be equal to the value of
GNE.

11. One type of government expenditure not included in GNE is _transfer payment_.
This is because such payments are not for _productive service_.

12. Total income received by households is less than national income not only because
of business savings but also because of _income tax_. The amount of
income remaining to households after payment of personal income taxes is called
disposable income; this includes not only earned income but also
transfer payment.

13. For an economy with international trade, calculating the value of total output produced domestically (or, alternatively, the value of expenditures on domestically
produced goods and services) requires subtracting _imports_ and adding
exports.

14. An economy which is engaged in foreign trade is called a(n) (closed/**open**) economy.

15. The equation for calculating national income by the expenditure approach is:
GNE = consumption + ____I____ + ____G____ + ____$X-M$____.

16. National income deflated for price-level changes is GNP or GNE expressed in
constant dollars; when not deflated, it is in _current_
dollars.

17. National income which has been deflated by a price index is called _real_
income.

18. GNP per capita is not a good measure of human welfare because it includes such
things as (give several) _arms cost of pollution illness_.
An approach to measuring household welfare emphasizes not production but
consumption. One way of valuing leisure time in measuring welfare
is by opportunity cost, which means valuing it according to _income sacrificed_ by not working.

Appendix

19. Which of the following expenditures by a firm would be termed a final good in the
definition of national income? (**a**) a new machine for production; (b) raw materials
for further processing; (c) the president's salary; (**d**) a newly constructed executive office; (e) indirect business taxes.

20. New housing construction is included under (consumption/**investment**) in the GNE.
Housing services provided by owner-occupied dwellings are (ignored/**given an imputed
value**).

21. The largest component of national income measured by the factor-income approach
or GNP is _wages_.

22. The largest component of national income measured by the expenditure approach or GNE
is _consumption_.

23. "Net change in inventories" for a period equals inventories at the (beginning/**end**)
minus inventories at the (**beginning**/end). This item will appear in the (GNP/GNE)
account.

24. Purchases of foreign cars by Canadians are considered (**imports**/exports). Spending by
foreign tourists in Canada is treated as an (**export**/import).

25. Transfer payments such as social insurance payments, _____unemployment insurance_____
    relief payments, and _____pensions_____ are excluded from national income.

26. Indirect business taxes are (included/excluded) in the measurement of (GNE/GNP).

27. Corporate profits before taxes are (included/excluded) in the measurement of
    (GNE/GNP).

_____

        If you have not answered all questions correctly, review the text in order to be
sure that you have all of the important concepts clearly in mind before going on to the
next chapter.

1. national income 2. output-expenditure, factor-income 3. double counting; intermediate goods; purchases of goods and services from other firms 4. rents, wages, interest, profits 5. equal 6. saving; depreciation, undistributed profits 7. future
production; machines and equipment, changes in inventories 8. depreciation or capital
consumption allowances 9. gross national expenditures (GNE) 10. gross national product (GNP) 11. transfer payments; productive services 12. income taxes; disposable,
transfer payments from the government 13. imports; exports 14. open 15. gross investment, government expenditures, net exports (X − M) 16. constant, current 17. real
18. arms, costs of illness, pollution, crime; consumption; income or commodities sacrificed by not working 19. (a), (d) 20. investment; given an imputed value 21. wages
and other labour income 22. consumption 23. beginning, end; GNE 23. imports; export
25. unemployment insurance, pensions 26. included, GNP 27. included, GNP

_____

MULTIPLE-CHOICE QUESTIONS

  1. We define the circular flow of income as
     (a) the sum of all the withdrawals from the system
     (b) the flow of income from domestic households to domestic firms and back again
     (c) the amount of money in the economy at any one point of time
     (d) all of the above

  2. Value added in production is equal to
     (a) purchases from other firms
     (b) profits
     (c) total sales revenue
     (d) total sales revenue minus purchases from other firms

  3. Which of the following about savings is *not* true?
     (a) It is the same as investing.
     (b) It is the result of not spending all of one's income.
     (c) It is often used to finance investment by business firms.
     (d) It is done by businesses as well as households.

  4. Mass marriages of men to housekeepers would
     (a) reduce national income as now measured
     (b) increase national income as now measured
     (c) leave national income the same
     (d) cannot tell the effect on GNP

  5. National income can be measured in all but which of the following ways?
     (a) by the flow of goods and services produced for final demand
     (b) by the payments made to purchase this flow of goods and services
     (c) by adding all money transactions in the economy
     (d) by the value of payments made to factors of production which have been
         used to produce final goods and services

6. Which of the following is *not* part of the total of final goods and services included in the national income?
   (a) transfer items
   (b) goods sold to government and foreign countries
   (c) increases in purchases of business equipment
   (d) additions to inventories

7. The difference between GNP and net national product is
   (a) depreciation or capital consumption allowances
   (b) total taxes paid to governments
   (c) net exports
   (d) personal savings

8. Personal disposable income is
   (a) the same as personal income
   (b) income that is used for consumption
   (c) income remaining after personal income taxes
   (d) exclusive of social insurance payments or welfare

9. If there is unintentional investment in inventory,
   (a) inventories have declined
   (b) the rate of sales is less than the rate of production
   (c) total investment falls
   (d) GNE will not be affected

10. If GNP in current pesetas in 1970 was 500 billion while GNP is constant (1960) pesetas was 200 billion in 1970
    (a) real GNP doubled over the decade 1960-1970
    (b) the price level more than doubled over the decade
    (c) real income declined slightly over the decade
    (d) it is impossible to estimate what happened to prices over the decade; more information is needed

11. If actual GNP rises from $100 billion to $115 billion and the GNP deflator rises from 125 to 150,
    (a) real GNP has risen
    (b) real GNP has fallen
    (c) real GNP is unchanged
    (d) it is impossible to tell the change in real GNP

EXERCISES

1. Suppose that the following items represent the expenditures and factor incomes for an economy in 1973. By selecting the appropriate items, calculate the values for GNP and GNE. Prove that GNE = GNP. (Figures are in billions of dollars.)

Government purchases of goods and services	$277.1
Wages and employee compensation	785.3
Net exports of goods and services	4.6
Income of proprietors	84.3
Indirect business taxes	117.8
Gross private investment	201.5
Capital consumption allowances	109.6
Corporate profits	126.4
Personal consumption expenditures	805.0
Rental and interest income	75.5
Adjustments on GNP account	-10.7

2. From the figures given, calculate the 1929 GNP in 1961 dollars and the implicit price deflator that converts current 1929 GNP to constant 1961 dollars.

Year	GNP, 1961 Dollars (billions)	GNP, Current Dollars (billions)	Implicit Price Deflator (1961 = 100)
1929	12.4	6.14	50.2
1961	39.65	39.65	100.0
1970	64.01	85.69	133.8
1974	79.20	139.49	176.1

(a) What was the percentage increase in current-dollar GNP between 1961 and 1970?

(b) What was the percentage increase in the price level, as measured by the implicit price deflator, between 1961 and 1970?

(c) What was the percentage change in real GNP between 1961 and 1970?

(d) What was the percentage change in real GNP between 1970 and 1974?

3. From 1950 to 1970, personal disposable income in Canada rose from $12.69 billion to $53.60 billion. Population increased from 13.71 million to 21.41 million in the same period. The consumer price index increased from approximately 100.0 to 142.2. What was the total percentage increase in the per capita standard of living as measured by per capita real personal disposable income from 1950 to 1970?

4. (a) Identify the items below according to the following code:

C	Consumption	S_p	Savings of persons or households
I	Investment	M	Imports
G	Government spending on goods and services	X	Exports
T	Taxes	F	Factor-income payments
S_b	Savings of business	N	None of the above

_C+F_ (1) A student gets a haircut from a self-employed barber.

_I_ (2) The barber buys some new clippers from the Short-Cut Clipper Company.

_Sp_ (3) Out of each day's revenue, the barber sets aside $5 in his piggy-bank.

_N_ (4) When he has enough set aside, he buys a share of Royal Bank of Canada stock.

_I_ (5) The Royal Bank expands its computer facilities in its head office.

_____I_____ (6) The Royal Bank pays municipal taxes to the City of Montreal.
_____F_____ (7) The Royal Bank sets aside some of its income as depreciation re-
serves.
_____ (8) The Short-Cut Clipper Company has profits of $50,000 after paying
provincial and municipal taxes.
_____I_____ (a) It pays $17,500 in corporate profits taxes to the
federal government.
_____F_____ (b) It pays dividends of $20,000.
_____Sb____ (c) It retains the rest and adds it to its surplus.
_____M_____ (9) Canadians go to London, England, and stay at the Savoy Hotel.
(Two answers.)
_____X_____ (10) Russia buys beef cattle from Ontario beef cattle farmers.
_____I_____ (11) Acme Construction Company builds 1,000 new houses to put on the
market.
_____G_____ (12) The Province of Saskatchewan builds a new highway.

(b) Which of the above would be included in the output-expenditure approach to
measuring national income?

PROBLEM

NATIONAL INCOME ACCOUNTING: EXPENDITURE OR INCOME APPROACH?

National income can, as we have seen, be measured by aggregating expenditures by
consumers, business, government, and foreigners or by aggregating the payments made to
the factors of production or resources used to produce goods and services.

Below is a list of items that may or may not enter national income. Place them
under the factor-payments-approach or expenditures-approach account, and justify your
reason for doing so. If you do not place them in one of the accounts, explain.

	Account		
	Factor Payment	Expen-diture	Reason
1. Increase in business inventory	____	____	_____
2. Purchases of steel by General Motors	____	____	_____
3. Rent received by apartment building owners	____	____	_____
4. Capital consumption allowances	____	____	_____
5. Wages received by doctors	____	____	_____
6. Sales of snowmobiles to foreigners	____	____	_____
7. Expenditures on school construction	____	____	_____

Chapter Twenty-seven
What Determines National Income?

REVIEW QUESTIONS

1. In terms of the aggregate-expenditure approach, equilibrium national income or GNP is where desired total spending equals _____. This is shown on the disgram where the _____ intersects the 45-degree line.

2. If desired total spending exceeds actual output, inventories will _____ unexpectedly. Given the assumptions of the chapter, businessmen will react by expanding production; therefore employment will _____ and income will _____. Diagrammatically this situation is shown where the level of desired spending (which is a point on the aggregate-expenditure function) is (above/below) the 45-degree line and to the (right/left) of the equilibrium level of national income.

3. If desired total spending is less than actual output, inventories will _____. With the assumption of constant prices, businessmen will react by cutting production; therefore employment will _____ and income will _____. Diagrammatically this situation is shown where the level of desired spending (which is a point on the aggregate-expenditure function) is (above/below) the 45-degree line and to the (right/left) of the equilibrium level of national income.

4. Total consumption spending is a function of _____. In the two situations depicted above, income changes will therefore affect the _____ component of aggregate expenditures.

5. The ratio of the change in consumption to the related change in income is called the _____.

6. The ratio of total level of consumption to the related level of income is called the _____.

7. The ratio of the change in savings to the related change in income is called the
_____.

8. Aggregate expenditures on GNP in an open, governed economy consist of the spending of four sectors: consumption, _____, _____, and _____.

9. Equilibrium national income is defined as an income level in which $C + I + G + (X - M)$ equals _____.

10. Withdrawals from the circular flow consist of _____, _____, and _____. They tend to rise and fall with _____.

11. Injections into the circular flow are the expenditures for _____, _____, and exports.

12. Other things being equal, an increase in injections causes national income to _____; a decrease causes it to _____.

13. In terms of the injections-withdrawals approach, equilibrium national income occurs where desired withdrawals equal _____. If net exports are zero and taxes equal government spending, an excess of investment over desired savings will cause national income to _____. As GNP rises, income and savings _____ until at equilibrium desired savings equal _____.

14. If net exports are zero and desired savings equals investment, an excess of government expenditures over taxes will cause GNP to _____.

15. Potential GNP is the total output that would be produced with _____. If the unemployment rate were 6 percent, potential GNP would be (less/greater) than actual GNP. In a dynamic fluctuating economy, potential, actual, and equilibrium GNP are (usually/rarely) the same.

_____
    If you have not answered all questions correctly, review the text in order to be sure that you have all of the important concepts clearly in mind before going on to the next chapter.

1. actual output; aggregate-expenditure line or function 2. decrease; increase, increase; above, left 3. increase; decrease, decrease; below, right 4. income (or disposable income); consumption 5. marginal propensity to consume (MPC) 6. average propensity to consume (APC) 7. marginal propensity to save (MPS) 8. investment, government, net exports $(X - M)$ 9. actual output 10. saving, imports, taxes; income 11. investment, government expenditures 12. rise, fall 13. desired injections; rise; rise, desired investment 14. rise 15. full employment (about 4 percent unemployment); greater; rarely

MULTIPLE-CHOICE QUESTIONS

1. Investment, government expenditures, and net exports are
   (a) withdrawals from the circular flow
   (b) of minor importance to the determination of income
   (c) too unpredictable to study usefully
   (d) injections of spending into the circular flow

2. If aggregate expenditures (demand) exceed actual output,
    (a) withdrawals must exceed injections
    (b) GNP is less than the equilibrium level and will tend to rise
    (c) inventories will rise and employment and income will fall
    (d) a rise in the price level is inevitable

3. The first symptom of a reduction in aggregate spending will probably be
    (a) a tendency for prices to rise as sellers try to make up for losses
    (b) an increase in overtime work as firms try to sell more to make up for losses
    (c) an increase in unintended inventory
    (d) a decrease in unintended inventory

4. Government expenditure and imports are, respectively,
    (a) an injection and a withdrawal
    (b) a withdrawal and an injection
    (c) both withdrawals
    (d) both injections

5. Which of the following is *not* an injection into the circular flow of income?
    (a) The Province of Saskatchewan builds a road.
    (b) Molson's Brewery sells beer to foreign customers.
    (c) Stelco builds a new plant in Quebec.
    (d) General Motors buys an already operating ball-bearing plant in Ontario.

6. The level of GNP will be in equilibrium
    (a) when prices are stable
    (b) when injections equal desired withdrawals
    (c) only when there is full employment
    (d) always since GNP = GNE

7. We hypothesize that consumption
    (a) is a function of income, like withdrawals
    (b) is exogenous, like injections
    (c) is an independent variable, so we cannot predict it
    (d) is a relatively unimportant fraction of aggregate expenditure

8. The aggregate-expenditure function has an upward slope because we assume that
    (a) government spending increases as employment and income rise
    (b) business investment is the main component of aggregate spending
    (c) prices are rising as full employment is approached
    (d) consumption changes with income

EXERCISES

1. Suppose we have the following hypothetical consumption schedule. You may assume that there are no business savings, no personal income taxes, and no government transfers.

Consumption Expenditures (constant dollars)	GNP (National Income) (constant dollars)
100	0
180	100
260	200
340	300
420	400
500	500
580	600
660	700
740	800

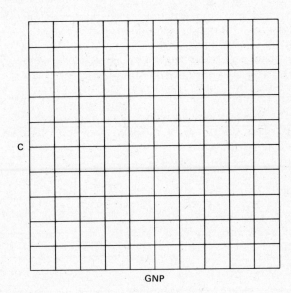

C

GNP

(a) Plot the consumption function on the graph.
(b) What is the "break-even" level of income?

(c) Calculate the marginal propensity to consume. Is it constant?

$$\frac{80}{100} = 0.8$$

(d) What happens to the value of the average propensity to consume as national income rises?

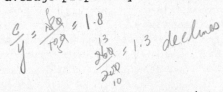

(e) Since savings are defined as national income minus consumption expenditure, calculate the saving schedule. Plot this function.

$$S = NI - C$$

(f) Prove that $S = 0$ at the break-even level of national income.

2. The aggregate-expenditure schedule below shows what the various components of intended spending would be at each income level. Fill in the blanks in the table and plot the data on the graph. Assume that all taxes are zero throughout and that all government expenditures are on goods and services.

Level of GNP = Y	C	I	G	(X – M)	Aggregate Expenditures	J	Y – C = W
0	90	10	30	10	140	50	-90
50	120	10	30	10	170	50	-70
100	150	10	30	10	200	50	-50
150	180	10	30	10	230	50	-30
200	210	10	30	10	260		-10
250	240	10	30	10	300		-30
300	270	10	30	10	320		30
350	300	10	30	10	380		60
400	330	10	30	10	380		70
450	360	10	30	10	410		90
500	390	10	30	10	440		110

(a) GNP is at equilibrium level at _____350_____.
    At this level, expenditures = _____350_____. W = _____50_____.
                                                J = _____50_____.

(b) Write the equation for the consumption schedule and for the W schedule.
    (*Hint:* These are linear equations of the form *a + bx*.)

$$W = -90 + 0.4Y$$

(c) The *C* and *W* equations added together should equal _____y_____.

(d) Calculate the value of the marginal propensity to consume. 0.6

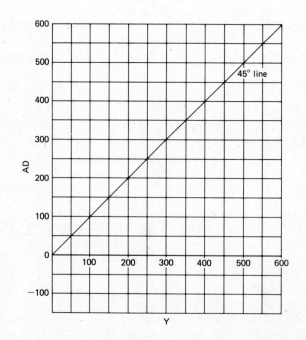

3. *Inventory Adjustment Model*

Suppose that the following diagram depicts the economic situation of a particular country.

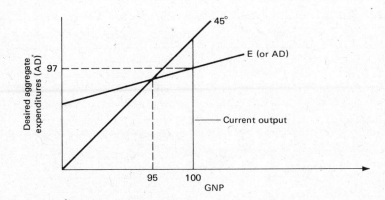

(a) Does this situation represent overproduction or underproduction? What is happening to inventory investment?

(b) Assuming that prices are constant, what changes in production would occur?

(c) As production is altered, employment and factor payments are affected. Would income rise or fall?

(d) Since consumption expenditures depend on the level of national income, would consumption rise or fall?

(e) Adjustment continues until aggregate expenditures equal _____.

PROBLEM

THE DETERMINATION OF EQUILIBRIUM INCOME

The purpose of this problem is to work through algebraically the determination of equilibrium income for a simple economy and then to work out a tabular and graphic representation similar to that in the text.

The households in this economy behave simply. They spend 90 percent of disposable income on consumption (one-thirtieth of this, or 3 percent of Y_d, goes for imports). The government (federal, provincial, and local) manages to collect 40 percent of GNP in taxes. It purchases $200 billion of goods and services including $15 billion of purchases abroad, the latter largely related to defense and peace-keeping operations. It also transfers $75 billion to persons for welfare, veterans benefits, and the like.

Gross private domestic investment is \$125 billion, of which \$5 billion is for foreign equipment and components. Much of the financing comes from gross business saving, capital consumption allowances, and retained earnings, which amount in total to 10 percent of GNP.

Exports are \$40 billion, but \$5 billion represents the materials and components that were initially purchased abroad.

Before striking a balance between J and W to see what the equilibrium GNP is, examine Y_d, which will determine consumption. Because business is keeping 0.1 GNP and the government gets 0.4 GNP, the amount of income at the disposal of the consumer is 0.5 GNP, or more briefly $0.5Y$, plus \$75 billion of transfers received from government. Consumption therefore equals $0.9(0.5Y + 75)$ or $0.45Y + 67.5$. Household savings would be equal to $Y_d - C$, or $0.05Y + 7.5$.

Gross injections and withdrawals can now be equated to determine equilibrium GNP.

$\underline{J}$		$\underline{W}$
$I = 125$		$S = S_p + S_b = 0.05Y + 7.5 + 0.1Y = 0.15Y + 7.5$
$G_E = G + Tr = 200 + 75$		$T = 0.4Y$
$X = 40$		$M = 25 + 0.03Y_d = 27.25 + 0.015Y$
———		———
440		$0.565Y + 34.75$

Note that all injections are assumed to be autonomous and that all withdrawals are rising functions of GNP, as was the case in text Table 27-3.

Finding equilibrium GNP is simply a matter of using the condition $J = W$ so that $0.565Y = 405.25$. To save you long division, GNP = 717 and C = 390.

The same result could be obtained by using adjusted injections, which are more theoretically satisfying because an injection composed of a withdrawal (imported goods) is not going to influence GNP directly. Then we would have:

Injections		Withdrawals
$I^* = 120$		$S = 0.15Y + 7.5$
$G_E^* = 260$		$T = 0.4Y$
$X^* = 35$		$M_C = 2.25 + 0.015Y$
——		———
415		$0.565Y + 9.75$

Note that all imports have been netted out except for imported consumption goods. Setting adj J = adj W and simplifying, we have exactly what we had before: $0.565Y = 405.25$. We should note that C^*, the consumption of domestic goods which constitutes the ongoing circular flow, is equal to $390 - M_C$, or 377. (Calculate to see why.)

In neither of these cases does C or C^* added to J fulfill the condition of equaling AD, which has been defined as equal to GNP at equilibrium. For diagrammatic simplicity we would like this condition to be true as well as $J = W$.

The problem is in the treatment of all government expenditures as injections, including transfers which go into the income stream (Y_d) instead of directly into production. In effect, most transfers have been counted twice, in the consumption for which they were used and as an injection.

Injections and withdrawals now look like this:

J^*		W^*
$I^* = 120$		$S = 0.15Y + 7.5$
$G^* = 185$	Net taxes $(t_n) = 0.4Y - 75$	
$X^* = \underline{35}$		$M_C = 2.25 + 0.015Y$
		————————
340		$0.065Y - 65.25$

The $J^* = W^*$ equation simplifies to the same numbers as before (check this for yourself). We also now can set AD = GNP (Y) and get the same results:

$$Y = AD = C^* + J^* = C^* + I^* + G^* + X^{*1}$$

$$Y = 0.45Y + 67.5 - 2.25 - 0.015Y + 340$$

which reduces to our old friend $0.565Y = 405.25$.

Next, the tabular and graphic presentation. First fill in the table below. The symbol headings have all been described in the material above. Then on the graph plot AD, C^*, J^*, and W^*.

GNP	J^*	S	T_n	M_C	W^*	C^* $(C - M_C)$	AD $(C^* + J^*)$
0	340	8	-75	2	-65	65.5	405.5
200	340						
400	340						
600	340						
717	340	115	212	13	340	377.0	717.0
800	340						
1,000	340						

Questions

1. At what level of GNP does AD intersect the 45-degree line of equality between AD and GNP?

2. What does the vertical distance between AD and C^* consist of? At equilibrium what other magnitude is also equal to this distance?

[1]The asterisks denote that the GNP components have been netted of imports. Since these magnitudes are not generally available this equation can be written $Y = AD = C + I + G + X - M$ with the imports netted from the total. Check to see that this equation is numerically equivalent.

3. Compute the multiplier using the formula, 1 minus the marginal propensity to withdraw. How does the multiplier show up on your graph?

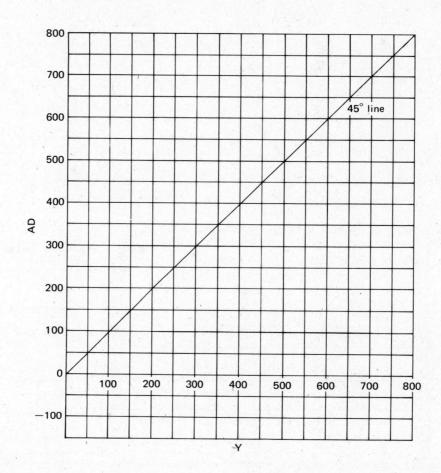

Chapter Twenty-eight
Changes in
National Income

REVIEW QUESTIONS

1. The response of any flow, such as consumption or saving, to a change in income is called a ___marginal propensity___.

2. The consumption function shows how desired consumption spending varies with ___income___. If the marginal propensity to consume is .60, a rise of $10 billion in incomes will cause consumption to rise by ___6 billion___. This describes a (movement along/a shift of) the consumption schedule.

3. If the marginal propensity to consume rises from .60 to .66, we would call it a (movement along/a shift of) the consumption schedule. This would have the same effect on equilibrium GNP as an increase in (injections/withdrawals).

4. If 60 percent of an increase in national income is respent, the marginal propensity to make withdrawals is ___0.4___. The marginal propensity to make withdrawals includes the marginal propensities to ___save___, ___pay tax___, and ___import___.

5. An increase in investment spending is an example of a(n) ___injection___. *Ceteris paribus*, this would cause total income to ___rise___, and desired and actual withdrawals would ___rise___ to equal ___injection___ at equilibrium GNP.

6. A rise in tax rates causes withdrawals to ___rise___, and causes spending to ___fall___; *ceteris paribus*, total output and income would ___fall___.

7. In addition to shifts in C and I schedules, the level of national income will be changed by changes in the amount of injections for ___investment___ and ___export___.

8. The level of national income will rise if there is a (fall/rise) in tax rates, savings, or import schedules, *ceteris paribus*.

9. An attempt to increase the rate of aggregate savings, *ceteris paribus*, will (raise/lower) the level of national income; this unexpected conclusion is called the _paradox of thrift_. The attempt to increase saving fails because _income falls_.

10. An increase in the rate of saving will *not* result in a fall in national income if offset by an increase in _investment_.

11. A rise in tax rates will not cause national income to fall if offset by an increase in government _spending_. If a government spends more than it collects in taxes, there is a budget _deficit_; if tax receipts exceed government spending, there is a budget _surplus_. The government finances a deficit by _borrowing_; it uses a surplus to _reduce tax rate_.

12. If government wishes to maintain a given level of income in the face of a fall in business investment, it can either increase its _expenditure_ or decrease _tax rate_.

13. The *multiplier* is the ratio of the change in _income_ to the change in _injection_. The formula is the reciprocal of the marginal propensity to _MPW $\frac{\Delta y}{\Delta w}$_.

14. If the marginal propensity to spend is .50, the marginal propensity to withdraw is _0.5_, and the multiplier is _2_. As long as part of all increase in income is respent, the multiplier is greater than (0/1).

15. If the multiplier is 3, an increase of injections of $10 billion will cause national income to rise by _30_.

16. Suppose that actual equilibrium GNP is $500 million and full-employment GNP is estimated to be $600 million, with a multiplier of 2.5; the size of the injection needed to reach full employment is _40_. The deflationary gap is _40_.

17. A country with heavy taxes and much saving will have a relatively (low/high) multiplier. A reduction in tax rates causes the multiplier to (rise/fall).

18. The L-shaped relation is the relation between output and _price level_. It assumes that, until full employment is reached, prices _are stable_.

19. Statistically, actual J equals actual _W_. In equilibrium, actual J equals _desired_ W. If actual X equals M, I plus G must equal actual _S + T_. If either I or G is increased, *ceteris paribus*, income will _↑_ so that both _S_ and _T_ will rise until actual J equals both desired and actual _W_.

20. Suppose that X equals M, G equals T, and I equals desired S, but there is considerable unemployment. The government therefore increases G. G is now greater than T, so there is a budget _deficit_. More G spending causes income to _rise_, and S to _rise_, so that the government can finance the deficit by _borrowing_. Because T will also rise with income, the final deficit will be (greater/less) than the original.

21. Remember that this analysis is based on increases and decreases in actual output responding to changes in desired _spending_; the changes in output cause similar changes in _employment_ and therefore in income.

If you have not answered all questions correctly, review the text in order to be sure that you have all of the important concepts clearly in mind before going on to the next chapter.

1. marginal propensity 2. income; $6 billion; movement along 3. shift of; injections 4. .40; save, pay taxes, import 5. injection; rise, rise, injections 6. rise, fall, fall 7. government, exports 8. fall 9. lower, paradox of thrift; income (and therefore the ability to save) falls 10. investment or other injections 11. spending; deficit, surplus; borrowing, reduce the national debt 12. spending, taxes 13. income, injections that caused the change in income; make withdrawals, or $\frac{1}{MPW}$ 14. .50, 2; 1

15. 30 16. $40 million ($100 million ÷ 2.5); $40 million 17. low; rise 18. *changes* in the price level; are stable 19. *W*; desired; *S* plus *T*; rise, *S*, *T*, *W* 20. deficit, rise, rise, borrowing the increased *S*; less 21. spending, employment

MULTIPLE-CHOICE QUESTIONS

1. Increases in national income are predicted to be caused by increases in all but which of the following, *ceteris paribus?*
   (a) consumption as a function of income
   (b) exports
   (c) government spending
   (d) investment spending

2. Increases in national income are predicted to be caused by decreases in all but which of the following, *ceteris paribus?*
   (a) consumption as a function of income
   (b) the savings schedule
   (c) tax rates
   (d) imports

3. If *G*, *I,* and *X* are not related to changes in *Y*, then
   (a) the AD schedule is horizontal
   (b) equilibrium income cannot be determined
   (c) the slope of AD will be the same as the consumption function
   (d) shifts in injections will not affect the AD schedule or *Y*

4. The effect on GNP of a fall in *I* could be offset by
   (a) a rise in taxes
   (b) a rise in savings
   (c) a rise in *G*
   (d) a fall in exports

5. A deflationary gap of $10 billion means that
   (a) actual GNP is $10 billion below full-employment GNP
   (b) prices will fall until GNP falls by $10 billion
   (c) an increase in injections of $10 billion is needed, which when multiplied will attain full-employment GNP
   (d) deflation is needed; spending must be reduced by $10 billion

6. The multiplier measures
   (a) the rise in injections resulting from an increase in income
   (b) the number of steps it takes to move from one equilibrium to another
   (c) the marginal propensity to invest or export
   (d) the extent by which income will change as a result of a shift in the aggregate-demand schedule

7. The size of the multiplier varies inversely with
   (a) the proportion of withdrawals from income
   (b) firms' attitudes toward investment
   (c) the level of unemployment
   (d) the level of government spending

8. If the withdrawals schedule has a slope of 0.33, the multiplier is
   (a) 1/3
   (b) 2/3
   (c) 3
   (d) 3/2

9. The message of the "paradox of thrift" is that
   (a) saving causes depressions
   (b) individuals who try to save cannot succeed
   (c) increased total saving may, *ceteris paribus,* have a contractionary effect on the economy
   (d) thrift is never a virtue

10. If all of any increase in income were saved, spent on imports, or taxed away, the multiplier would be
    (a) infinity
    (b) 1
    (c) 0
    (d) -1

11. Which of the following is basic to the hypothesis of the L-shaped aggregate-supply curve?
    (a) Output increases because the supply of labour is increasing along with population.
    (b) There is always full employment of resources.
    (c) As output increases, prices do not begin to rise until full employment is reached.
    (d) As output increases toward capacity, firms produce more efficiently.

12. One implication of the L-shaped aggregate-supply curve is that
    (a) output can be increased only with rising unit costs
    (b) output can be increased with no increase in the amount of inputs
    (c) changes in aggregate demand could affect the quantity of employment without affecting factor prices
    (d) unemployment cannot be reduced without prices beginning to rise gradually

EXERCISES

1. Suppose that there is a very simple economy in which only consumption expenditures and savings are influenced by the level of national income. Furthermore, business savings are zero and no government exists. The marginal propensity to consume is .8.

   We assume that the economy begins initially at an equilibrium level of 100 in period 0 but that in period 1 investment increases by 10 and stays at the level of 30 permanently.

   Furthermore, for expositional purposes, assume that consumption expenditures in period t depend on the income level one period in the past, e.g., $t - 1$. Fill in the table below.

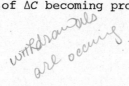

MPC = 0.8

Spending Period	Consumption	ΔC	Investment	ΔI	Income	ΔY (Δ in income)
0	80	0	20	0	100	0
1	80	0	30	10	110	10
2	88	8	30	0	118	8
3	94.4	6.4	30	0		
4			30	0		
5			30	0		
6			30	0		
7			30	0		
Total change or level			30	0		

(a) Why are the values of ΔC becoming progressively smaller?

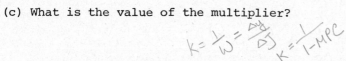

withdrawals are occuring.

(b) Will the economy reach a new equilibrium? Why?

(c) What is the value of the multiplier?

$$k = \frac{1}{w} = \frac{\Delta y}{\Delta J} \qquad k = \frac{1}{1 - MPC}$$

(d) What will the total change in savings be when the new equilibrium level is reached? Prove that total withdrawals are equal to 30 at the new equilibrium level.

2. Suppose that there is a more complicated economy than before. You may continue to assume that there is no business saving. The consumption function is given by the equation $C = .6Y_{t-1}$, with $.4Y_{t-1}$ going to S, T, and M. Fill in the following table to show the final effect on national income (Y) of a permanent decrease in exports of 6 millions. (Round off to one decimal place.)

Spending Round	ΔX	ΔC	ΔW	ΔY
0	-5	—	—	-5
1	—	-3.0	-2.0	-3
2		-1.8	-1.2	-1.8
3				
4				
5				
6				
Total change				

The multiplier $= \frac{\Delta Y}{\Delta J}$ _____; also it $= \frac{1}{\Delta W/\Delta Y} =$ _____.

Since w (the marginal propensity to withdraw) is .4, prove that the value of the multiplier is 2.5 by using the formula $1/w$.

3. You are told that the actual equilibrium value of national income of an economy is $90 billion but that potential income has been estimated at $98 billion. Economic advisors have estimated that the marginal propensity to withdraw for this economy has the value .5.

(a) Using an injection-withdrawal diagram, sketch the situation described above.

(b) What is the size of the multiplier for this economy?

$$4 \qquad gap = \frac{98-90}{2}$$

(c) What type of gap exists? What is its magnitude? Show this on your diagram.

(d) Would an increase in investment of $3.5 billion close the gap? Explain.

(e) Would an increase in government expenditure of $4 billion close the gap?

PROBLEM

MULTIPLIERS AND WITHDRAWALS

The multiplier can be defined in terms of withdrawals from the circular flow, or specifically as the reciprocal of $\Delta W/\Delta Y$, that is: $\Delta Y/\Delta W$. Students sometimes have difficulty with the discrepancy between a multiplier of 10 that is indicated by a consumer's marginal propensity to save of .1 and that of less than 2 which has been found to apply to many empirical studies of our complex economy. This problem seeks to show how the apparent multiplier of 10 is diminished to about 2 as the economic model takes on greater realism, with an increase in withdrawals related to income.

Economy A: Closed, Ungoverned, Without Business Savings

In this economy all income is disposable ($Y = Y_d$), and the only withdrawal is personal saving. Assuming that $.1Y_d$ is saved, then $S_p = .1Y_d = .1Y$. (Remember, $\Delta W/\Delta Y$ = the sum of the coefficients of Y in the various withdrawal functions.)
    $\Delta W/\Delta Y =$ _____, and the multiplier is _____.

Economy B: Closed, Ungoverned, with Business Savings

In this economy it is assumed that firms do not distribute all of their income. Assume that business savings (S_b) = .1Y and only .9Y is disposable income to households. Then S_p = $.1Y_d$ = (.1)(.9Y) = .09Y.

$\Delta W/\Delta Y$ = _____, and the multiplier is _____.

Economy C: Closed, Governed, with Business Savings

With government, another withdrawal in the form of taxes is introduced. It is conceivable that such taxes could be unrelated to Y, for example, head taxes so that T = $100 billion. Would the multiplier be affected in this case? Why?

It is more realistic to assume that taxes will be related to income and that the government will be concerned with transferring income to the old and the poor. With such transfers treated as negative taxes, assume T_n = .3Y - 75. Y_d now equals Y - .1Y - .3Y + 75, and S_p = .1(.6 Y+ 75).

$\Delta W/\Delta Y$ = _____, and the multiplier is _____.

Economy D: Open, Governed, with Business Savings

With trade opened up to foreign countries, not all expenditures will be made domestically and thus in the economy's circular flow. Assume that imports (M) = .04Y and that other withdrawals have the same relationship to Y as in economy C.

$\Delta W/\Delta Y$ = _____, and the multiplier is _____.

Chapter Twenty-nine
More on
Consumption

> **CHECKLIST** Make certain that you understand the following concepts: average propensity to consume; marginal propensity to consume; consumption; savings and withdrawals function; break-even level; cross-section data; time-series data; permanent-income hypothesis.

REVIEW QUESTIONS

1. In order to predict the effects on income of injections by government and investment spending, we need to know how consumption varies with ___income___.

2. Two measures of this function are C/Y, called the ___APC___, and $\Delta C/\Delta Y$, called the ___MPC___. By hypothesis, APC is expected to be (greater/less) than 1 below a break-even level of income; MPC is assumed to be between zero and ___1___ for all incomes.

3. If one is concerned about the behavior of households, consumption is best related to ___disposable income___. Disposable income minus consumption is equal to personal ___savings___.

4. The higher the MPC, the ___less___ the propensity to withdraw income from the circular flow, and the ___greater___ the multiplier.

5. A straight-line consumption function means that the marginal propensity to consume is (constant/increasing).

6. Cross-section consumption data relate consumption to income (at various income levels at one time/in the aggregate over a period of time). Cross-section consumption data show that as a household's income rises relative to others, (consumption rises as much as income/consumption rises, but not as much as income).

7. Time-series consumption data show how consumption varies (as incomes rise over time/at a given level of income).

8. Long-run consumption data indicate that APC is (larger than/smaller than/the same as) MPC. Both (rise/fall/remain constant) over the long run. Short-run data indicate that MPC is (less than/equal to) APC.

9. One of the hypotheses of the "permanent income" idea is that a household might have an MPC out of permanent income that was (higher/lower) than that out of temporary increases of income.

180

10. If high-income households have lower MPC than do low-income households, a more equal distribution of income would (increase/decrease/not affect) consumption. It would make the multiplier (larger/smaller), and it would (increase/decrease) the slope of the aggregate demand curve, *ceteris paribus*.

11. Greater difficulty in borrowing money for consumer purchases would, *ceteris paribus*, tend to shift the consumption function (upward/downward).

12. Expenditures on durable consumer goods are (less/more) variable than expenditures on nondurable goods. This is because they (can/cannot) be postponed.

13. The government can attempt to offset a decline in the consumption schedule by (reducing/increasing) taxes in order to maintain aggregate demand.

     If you have not answered all questions correctly, review the text in order to be sure that you have all of the important concepts clearly in mind before going on to the next chapter.

1. income 2. average propensity to consume, marginal propensity to consume; greater, 1 3. disposable income; savings 4. less; greater 5. constant 6. at various income levels at one time; consumption rises, but not as much as income 7. as incomes rise over time 8. the same as; remain constant; less than 9. higher 10. increase; larger; increase 11. downward 12. more; can 13. reducing

---

MULTIPLE-CHOICE QUESTIONS

1. If a consumption function is $30 + 0.9Y_d$, then the savings function
   (a) is $30 + 0.1Y_d$
   (b) is $70 + 0.9Y_d$
   (c) is $-30 + 0.1Y_d$
   (d) cannot be estimated

2. Assume that MPC out of disposable income is 80 percent and that disposable income is 75 percent of GNP; the multiplier is
   (a) about 5
   (b) about 1
   (c) about 2.5
   (d) impossible to estimate

3. Which statement is *not* true of studies of cross-section data on consumption related to income?
   (a) Many households have negative savings.
   (b) The break-even level of income was about $3,500 in 1967.
   (c) APC is rising over time.
   (d) C is closely related to Y_d at each level of income.

4. The short-run consumption function derived from time-series data
   (a) seems to confirm the hypotheses that MPC is constant and APC declines as income rises
   (b) seems to contradict the hypothesis on both counts
   (c) is not really valid because of frequent shifts in the function
   (d) suggests that a straight line cannot be used to represent it.

5. Studies of consumption functions over the long run have indicated that
   (a) both parts of the hypothesis are wrong
   (b) APC = MPC
   (c) negative savings a low income levels are considerably larger than had been expected
   (d) the relationship is not very close in the long run

6. The permanent-income hypothesis
   (a) predicts temporary income will be 100 percent spent
   (b) helps explain why long-run MPC is greater than short-run MPC
   (c) helps explain why long-run MPC is less than short-run MPC
   (d) is concerned with savings, not consumption

7. Changes in income distribution probably have not affected our measurements of the consumption function very much because
   (a) high-income households have just as high an APC as low-income households
   (b) we are dealing with aggregates, so that distribution does not matter
   (c) the changes have been limited and gradual
   (d) we can easily make allowances in our calculations for such changes

8. Which of the following would have the effect of shifting the consumption function upward?
   (a) Borrowing becomes more difficult.
   (b) Prices are expected to fall.
   (c) Tax rates on personal income are reduced.
   (d) The government launches a campaign to sell defense bonds through increased payroll deductions.

EXERCISES

1. Assume that line C on the graph is a household's consumption function.
   (a) The break-even level of income is at (use letters) _____H_____. APC = __$^e/_9$ $^4/_H$__.

   (b) At income OJ, APC = ___KJ/J___. This is equal to the slope of the line ___OK___. It is (more/less) than 1.

   (c) At income OG, APC = ___FG/G___. At this point, it is ___greater___ than 1.

   (d) MPC equals the slope of the line ___C___. It shows that in this case, the proportion of an increase in income spent on increased consumption is (increasing/constant/decreasing), while the APC is (falling/rising/constant).

   (e) At income OJ, savings = ___KM___; at OG, savings = ___-EF___.

2. In the consumption function described by the equation $C = 300 + 0.9Y_d$,

   (a) MPC = ___0.9___

   (b) at income of zero, C = ___300___

   (c) the APC is (rising/falling/constant) as income rises

   APC=1 (d) the break-even level of income is ___3000___

3. (a) If MPC out of disposable income is 0.90, and if disposable income is 60 percent of GNP, then MPC out of gross national income is ___0.14___.

   (b) The marginal propensity to make withdrawals is therefore ___1-0.14___.

   (c) The multiplier would be about ___1/0.46___.

PROBLEM

REGIONAL CONSUMPTION FUNCTIONS

A. The following consumption functions for regions of Canada have been estimated using annual data for 7 years between 1948 and 1964, where C represents personal consumption and Y represents personal disposable income. The subscripts refer to the region. (The constant term is ignored.)

Maritimes	$C_M = 0.994Y_M$
Quebec	$C_Q = 0.974Y_Q$
Ontario	$C_O = 0.909Y_O$
Prairies	$C_P = 0.917Y_P$
British Columbia	$C_{BC} = 0.901Y_{BC}$

Source: W. J. Gillen and A. Guccione, "The Estimation of Postwar Regional Consumption Functions in Canada," *The Canadian Journal of Economics,* May, 1970.

Questions

1. What are the corresponding regional savings functions?

2. Are these long-run or short-run consumption functions? Explain.

3. Do these results confirm any of the characteristics of the permanent-income hypothesis discussed in the text?

B. The same consumption function for all Canada from the same data is

$$C = 0.932Y$$

Questions

1. Given the income data in column 2 below, estimate consumption from the above equation for each year and record it in column 3.

2. Compare your result in column 3 with the actual consumption in column 4, and record the percentage error in column 5.

(1)	(2)	(3)	(4)	(5)
	Personal Disposable		Actual	
	Income	Estimated	Consumption	Percentage
Year	(1949 dollars)	Consumption	(1949 dollars)	Error
1959	$18,436 million		$17,392 million	
1960	19,112 million		17,945 million	
1961	19,652 million		18,501 million	
1962	20,982 million		19,220 million	
1963	21,973 million		20,046 million	

Source: Statistics Canada.

Chapter Thirty
Fluctuations in National Income: Business Cycles and Investment

<table>
<tr><td>CHECKLIST</td><td>Make certain that you understand the following concepts: business cycles; trough; depression; recovery; lower turning point; peak; upper turning point; accelerator; capital/output ratio; capital widening; capital deepening; inflation; recession; marginal efficiency of capital; marginal-efficiency-of-investment schedule.</td></tr>
</table>

REVIEW QUESTIONS

1. The condition of actual GNP below potential GNP is an example of (long-term/short-term) fluctuations of income.

2. Macroeconomic theory sees the primary cause of fluctuations of actual from potential GNP to be changes in _____AD_____. It is possible that output, employment, and income could also be depressed by shortages of important inputs such as _____energy_____.

3. That part of the business cycle characterized by substantial unemployment, losses for many firms, and downward trends in prices is called the _____trough_____. The last example of this occurred during _____.

4. In a severe depression, the amount of investment may be insufficient to replace worn-out capital, so that net investment is _____negative_____. This means that the total capital stock of the country is _____decreasing_____.

5. A period of labor and other shortages, rising costs, prices, interest rates, and investment suggests the part of the cycle called the _____peak_____.

6. In this century, large rapid increases in federal spending and resulting periods of boom and inflation have invariably resulted from events occurring during _____wars_____.

7. We distinguish three categories of investment: _____inventories_____, _____fixed investment_____, and _____residential construction_____. Of these three the smallest but most volatile is _____inventories_____.

8. Intended inventories are usually related to a firm's volume of _____sales_____. An increase in unintended inventories means that sales are (exceeding/less than) output; to correct the inventory/sales ratio, a firm would (reduce/increase) output. Firms may want to reduce their inventories if interest rates (rise/fall).

9. In addition to income changes, the main economic influence on investment in residential housing is the cost and availability of _____ *mortgage* _____. Thus housing construction tends to vary inversely with _____ *interest rate* _____.

10. Business fixed investment is influenced by several major variables: opportunities for new _____ *technique* _____, changes in aggregate _____ *expenditure* _____, expectations of _____ *profit* _____, rate of deterioration or obsolescence of _____ *old equipment* _____, and the rate of _____ *depreciation* _____. A firm that wishes to invest in new facilities or equipment without borrowing or selling shares may finance it out of either _____ *retained* _____ or _____ *lit* _____.

11. The act of investment is a *flow* of spending; the total amount of capital in existence is a _____ *stock* _____. Investment adds to the capital stock only if *net* investment is _____ *positive* _____. If gross investment is less than the amount estimated for depreciation in a period, net investment would be _____ *negative* _____.

12. It is predicted that, *ceteris paribus,* a fall in the rate of interest will (increase/decrease) the desired capital stock, and will therefore (increase/decrease) the amount of investment in a given period. However, regardless of the rate of interest and profit expectations, the amount of investment in a period is limited by _____ *capacity of capital-good industry* _____.

13. Suppose that, with a multiplier of 2 and some unemployed productive capacity, investment rises from $8 billion to $8½ billion per year, for one year: *ceteris paribus,* GNP would rise by _____ *1* _____. Suppose that the following year, after the desired amount of capital stock has been attained, investment returns to $8 billion; *ceteris paribus,* GNP will fall by _____ *1* _____.

14. The marginal-efficiency-of-investment schedule slopes downward to indicate that additional investment spending will be undertaken only if there is a fall in the _____ *rate of interest* _____. The steeper or less elastic the schedule, the (greater/smaller) the change in investment with a change in the _____ *rate of interest* _____.

15. The accelerator theory predicts that net investment is related also to changes in _____ *income* _____, expressed as I (net) $= a\Delta$ _____ *y* _____. The accelerator coefficient a represents the ratio of capital needed per unit of new _____ *output* _____. The theory points out that net investment occurs when desired capital stock differs from _____ *existing capital stock* _____.

16. The effect of the accelerator is to (widen/narrow) the amplitude of cyclical fluctuations in total spending. If the rate of increase in national income declines, the accelerator theory holds that investment spending will (decrease/remain constant/increase at a declining rate).

17. Peaks or ceilings to economic expansions are eventually reached because of _____ *no unused capacity to produce* _____. Floors and lower turning points of recessions or depressions are reached when there is a sufficient revival of spending for replacement of _____ *worn-out capital* _____.

If you have not answered all questions correctly, review the text in order to be sure that you have all of the important concepts clearly in mind before going on to the next chapter.

1. short-term 2. aggregate expenditure or demand; energy sources 3. trough; the depression of the 1930s 4. negative; decreasing 5. peak 6. wars 7. inventories, business fixed investment, residential construction; inventories 8. sales; less than; reduce; rise 9. mortgages, interest rates 10. products or techniques, expenditure, profit, old equipment, interest; depreciation reserves, retained profits 11. stock;

positive; negative 12. increase, increase; capacity of capital-goods industry 13. $1 billion; $1 billion 14. rate of interest; smaller, rate of interest 15. income, Y; output; existing capital stock 16. widen; decrease 17. bottlenecks, shortages, no unused capacity to produce; worn-out capital goods

---

MULTIPLE-CHOICE QUESTIONS

1. The demographic variable that most affects housing sales in a particular year is
   (a) the death rate
   (b) the birth rate
   (c) the marriage rate
   (d) the adjusted fertility rate

2. Investment in inventory in a year is measured by
   (a) the inventory/sales ratio
   (b) the level of inventory
   (c) year-end inventory minus beginning inventory
   (d) beginning inventory minus year-end inventory

3. If you were finding the total of investment spending, which would you *not* include?
   (a) changes in inventories
   (b) purchases of stocks and bonds
   (c) new residential construction
   (d) new plant and equipment

4. History shows that investment in Canada
   (a) has been quite a stable but small fraction of GNP
   (b) has fluctuated a great deal
   (c) has usually been about 30 percent of GNP
   (d) has never fallen below the amount needed for replacement

5. The marginal-efficiency-of-capital schedule relates
   (a) the amount of investment to GNP
   (b) the size of the capital stock to equipment prices
   (c) the size of the capital stock to the interest rate
   (d) the amount of investment to interest rates

6. Inventories tend to vary
   (a) directly with the level of sales, inversely with the rate of interest
   (b) inversely with sales, directly with interest rates
   (c) directly with sales and interest rates
   (d) inversely with sales and interest rates

7. The marginal-efficiency-of-investment schedule relates
   (a) the capital stock to interest rates
   (b) the amount of investment to the capitalized value of capital goods
   (c) the amount of investment to the rate of interest
   (d) the amount of investment to the accelerator

8. A shift of the MEI schedule upward implies
   (a) investment has become less profitable
   (b) interest rates have fallen
   (c) in general, firms are willing to pay higher interest rates for a given level of investment
   (d) the price of capital goods has risen

9. The amount of investment spending by firms
   (a) in influenced by profit expectations and interest rates
   (b) seems to be entirely random
   (c) has little effect on the economy
   (d) is quite stable and predictable

10. According to the accelerator theory, investment is a function of
    (a) the level of income
    (b) profits
    (c) changes in income
    (d) savings

11. The kind of borrowing most discouraged by high interest rates is
    (a) corporate borrowing
    (b) residential mortgages
    (c) consumer credit
    (d) government borrowing

12. The multiplier and accelerator effects operating together
    (a) tend to cancel out
    (b) help to explain why recoveries, once started, continue upward
    (c) make the amplitude of cycles less than they otherwise would be
    (d) tend to keep growth going perpetually

EXERCISES

1. *Illustrating the accelerator principle.* The table below shows the hypothetical situation for a firm that requires 1 machine for every 1,000 units of product it turns out annually. As it increases its output and sales in response to changing demand, show how its investment will be affected. Replacement for depreciation is 1 machine per year throughout.

Year	Annual Output (units)	Units of Capital Needed	New Machines Required	Replacement Machines	Total Machines to Be Purchased
1	10,000	10	0	1	1
2	10,000	10	0	1	1
3	11,000	11	1	1	2
4	12,000	12	1	1	2
5	15,000	15	3	1	4
6	17,000	17	2	1	3
7	18,000	18	1	1	2
8	18,000	18	0	1	1

   (a) Between year 2 and year 5, output increased by what percent? ___50%___
   (b) In the same period, total investment spending by this firm increased by what percent? ___300%___

2. A seller of shirts has had weekly sales of 100 and tries to keep inventory on his shelves equal to twice his weekly sales, adjusting his weekly orders from the jobber according to the current week's sales. Fill out the rest of the table, showing how his actual inventory and orders from his supplier would change as his weekly sales change.

Week	Weekly Sales	Actual Inventory, End of Week	Inventory/ Sales Ratio	Desired Inventory	Desired Inventory plus Expected Sales	Weekly Orders for Next Week
1	100	200	2	200	300	100
2	100	200	2	200	300	100
3	110	190	___	220	330	140
4	110	220	___	___	___	110
5	120	___	___	___	___	___
6	120	___	___	___	___	___
7	110	___	___	___	___	___
8	110	___	___	___	___	___
9	100	___	___	___	___	___

(a) The range of weekly sales was from _____ to _____.
(b) The range of weekly orders was from _____ to _____.

3. *MEC and MEI*
You are given the following MEC and MEI schedules.

Marginal Efficiency of Capital		Marginal Efficiency of Investment	
Capital Stock	MEC (%)	Investment	MEI (%)
100	20	0	14
200	18	60	8
300	14	100	6
400	8	145	2
500	1		

(a) Suppose that the interest rate was 14% and the economy had reached its desired level of capital stock. From the schedules above, determine the magnitude of the capital stock and the level of investment.

(b) If the rate of interest fell to 8%, what is the new level of desired capital stock? What is the desired level of investment?

(c) By inspecting the MEI schedule, determine the actual quantity of investment in the economy.

PROBLEM

POTENTIAL VERSUS ACTUAL GNP

Earlier you were introduced to the idea of deflationary and inflationary gaps, the amount by which aggregate demand differs from the amount necessary to produce a full-employment equilibrium. The GNP gap differs from this in two respects:

1. It is the difference between "potential," or full-employment, GNP and actual GNP. As indicated in Figure 30-1, it is measured horizontally along the axis rather than vertically. (When, as in Figure 30-2, the horizontal axis is time, then the difference between potential and actual GNP is measured vertically.)
2. The actual GNP may differ from the equilibrium GNP discussed in earlier chapters.

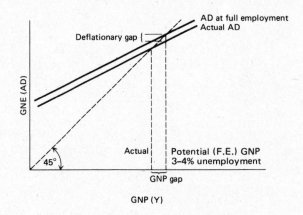

Figure 30-1

You are asked in this problem to investigate the relationship of changes in investment (as measured by GPDI expressed in constant 1958 dollars) and changes in the GNP gap. Because investment is an important injection, the hypothesis to be tested is that substantial year-to-year increases in investment will reduce the gap of potential minus actual GNP, whereas reductions will increase the gap.

First, examine the problem of measuring the gap, which is primarily a problem of measuring potential GNP.

In its report, *Performance and Potential, mid-1950s to mid-1970s,* the Economic Council of Canada defined the concept of potential GNP as the volume of goods and services that the economy would ordinarily produce at an unemployment rate of 3.8 percent. The measurement of potential GNP incorporates the effects of higher productivity, a larger labor force, and a fuller work schedule. As a consequence, potential GNP does not stand still. Over time, population trends add to the number of persons in the labor force. Furthermore, increases in the quantity and quality of capital, advances in technology, and improvements in the quality of labor raise the potential productivity of the labor force.

In Canada, between 1956 and 1969, the increase in the labor force was about 41 percent. In addition, between 1956 and 1961, real output per employed person grew at 1.3 percent per year; from 1961 to 1966 at the rate of 3.1 percent per year; and from 1966 to 1969 at 1.6 percent per year. Taking all of these factors into consideration, the annual growth rate in potential GNP was about 5.2 percent.

Comparing actual and potential output, the Council computed that in 1971 the Canadian economy was operating about 3 to 4 percent *below* its potential, or at about a $3 billion loss on an annual basis. This is a considerable loss to Canadian society.

The size of the GNP "gap" between actual and potential output between 1956 and 1974 is shown below.

ACTUAL AND POTENTIAL LEVELS OF
REAL GROSS NATIONAL PRODUCT

(Billions of 1961 dollars)

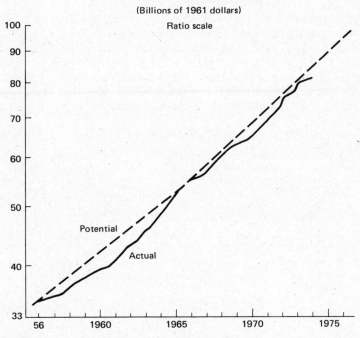

Figure 30-2

Sources: The Tenth Annual Review, Economic Council of Canada, p. 78; *Economic Review,* Department of Finance, pp. 29-30.

Questions

1. What relationship exists between the size of the "gap" and the percentage change in real output per employed worker?

2. We have displayed data on the percentage change in real private investment (excluding residential construction) expenditures in Canada between the years 1956 and 1974:

1956-1961	- 1.5% per year	1966-1974	+ 7.5% per year
1961-1966	+13.9% per year	1966-1971	+ 1.3% per year
1966-1969	- 0.5% per year	1971-1974	+ 9.1% per year

What relationship exists between the size of the gap and investment expenditures? Why would you expect this?

3. What effect might the size of the GNP gap in the United States have on the size of Canada's GNP gap? Explain.

Chapter Thirty-one
Theories and
Tools of
Fiscal Policy

| CHECKLIST | Make certain that you understand the following concepts: fiscal policy; balanced budget; budget surplus; budget deficit; treasury bill; crowding-out; pump priming; built-in or automatic stabilizer; fiscal drag; full-employment budget result; balanced budget multiplier. |

REVIEW QUESTIONS

1. The use of taxing and spending by government to promote certain macroeconomic goals is called _____ *fiscal policy* _____.

2. When government expenditures exceed taxes, the government has a (deficit/surplus). When the government has a deficit, it gets the money it needs by _____ *borrowing* _____ _____. If the money it borrows would not otherwise have been spent, the budget deficit will cause aggregate demand to _____ *rise* _____.

3. Government can close a deflationary gap and move the economy toward the full-employment level by (cutting/raising) tax rates or (decreasing/increasing) expenditures, or a combination of the two. When the government spends money on goods and services, (all of it/only part of it) is added to aggregate demand on the first round of spending. If the multiplier is 2, $1 million of government spending not financed by additional taxes will, *ceteris paribus*, increase GNP by _____ *$2* _____. If the government lowers tax rates in order to reduce personal income tax payments by $1 million, disposable income will rise by _____ *1* _____. If MPC out of Y_d = 0.9, first-round spending out of the tax cut will amount to _____ *0.9* _____. If the multiplier is 2, GNP will rise, *ceteris paribus*, by _____ *1.8* _____. Thus, to achieve an equivalent change in GNP with one method or the other, a (smaller/larger) change in tax revenues is required than in government spending.

4. A rise in GNP can thus be caused by a deliberate initial increase in the government deficit or a reduction in the _____ *surplus* _____. The initial rise in the deficit will be (reduced/increased) as income rises and tax collections (rise/fall).

5. If the economy is booming in an inflationary manner, the government can reduce aggregate demand by raising _____ *tax* _____ and/or lowering _____ *gov't exp.* _____. The cut in *G* spending necessary to remove a given inflationary gap will be (more/less) than the rise in tax revenue necessary to do the same job.

6. At given tax rates, rising incomes produce ___*rising*___ tax revenues. Thus, if the government has a deficit, *ceteris paribus*, it will grow (smaller/larger) as incomes rise. For given tax rates and a constant level of government spending, the surplus or deficit which it is calculated that the government would experience at full employment is called the ___*full employment surplus*___ ___*deficit balance*___. It is (possible/not possible) for a government to have simultaneously an actual budget deficit and a full-employment surplus. The analysis suggests that to reach full employment in this case, taxes should be (cut/raised) and/or government expenditures (reduced/increased).

7. If the government increases its expenditures and increases its taxes by the same amount, there will be (an increase/no increase) in aggregate demand and therefore (also/not) in income. This is because (all/not all) of the increased taxes would otherwise have been spent on domestic goods. Part of them would have been used for ___*saving*___ and ___*import*___. If 10 percent of the increased personal income taxes of $1 million had been saved or spent on imports, and if government had spent all of the increased tax revenues at home, aggregate demand would have increased initially by $ ___*0.1*___. If the multiplier is 2, $w =$ ___*$\frac{1}{2}$*___; the increase in GNP would be $ ___*0.2*___, and the balanced budget multiplier would be 10 percent/w, or ___*0.2*___. We would thus expect that a reduction in government spending of $2 million, matched by an equal reduction in taxes, would usually have, *ceteris paribus*, a total effect of reducing income by (the same or a lesser amount/a greater amount).

8. "Stabilizing" the economy means (narrowing/widening) the range of fluctuations in production, employment, and prices.

9. A built-in stabilizer is any feature of the government's fiscal structure that automatically in booms tends to (decrease/increase) taxes relative to government spending, and in slumps tends to (decrease/increase) them relative to government spending. Such a stabilizer makes withdrawals (rise/fall) in good times and (rise/fall) in poor times, relative to injections.

10. The higher and more progressive the tax structure, the (more/less) stabilizing its effects will be, *ceteris paribus*.

11. Government expenditures will have a greater stabilizing effect the (less/more) they fall as income rises and the (less/more) they rise as incomes fall.

12. Fiscal drag occurs when the tax structure is overstabilizing and thus prevents an upswing in the economy from reaching ___*full-employment level*___

13. The chief built-in stabilizers are agricultural support policies, social security and unemployment insurance, and above all ___*tax*___. The original purpose of these measures (was/was not) to stabilize the economy. Since World War II, they have been (partially/entirely) successful in limiting economic fluctuations.

14. The choice of what fiscal policy "mix" to adopt is (affected/not affected) by attitudes toward government. If expansion in the economy is needed, those who wish to limit the growth of the government would usually favor ___*tax cuts*___.

15. The decisions lag in Canada is ___*shorter*___ than in the United States. In both countries, however, these lags make it (easy/difficult) to time tax changes and government spending in order to counteract the business cycle rather than to intensify it.

16. The 10 percent reduction in income taxes voted in 1965 by Parliament is an example of a(n) (automatic/discretionary) tool of fiscal policy.

If you have not answered all questions correctly, review the text in order to be sure that you have all of the important concepts clearly in mind before going on to the next chapter.

1. fiscal policy 2. deficit; borrowing; rise 3. cutting, increasing; all of it; $2 million; $1 million; $0.9 million; $1.8 million; larger 4. surplus; reduced, rise 5. tax rates, expenditures; less 6. rising; smaller; full-employment surplus, deficit, or balance; possible; cut, increased 7. an increase, also; not all; saving, imports; $0.1 million; 0.5; $0.2 million; 0.2; the same or a lesser amount 8. narrowing 9. increase; decrease; rise; fall 10. more 11. more; more 12. full-employment levels 13. taxes, especially on income; was not; partially 14. affected; tax cuts 15. shorter; shorter; difficult 16. discretionary

---

MULTIPLE-CHOICE QUESTIONS

1. Government spending will increase incomes only if
   (a) it is spent on capital goods
   (b) it is spent on transfer payments
   (c) it is in addition to what would otherwise have been spent by households and firms
   (d) it is spent out of taxation

2. It is possible that government spending, even if financed wholly out of taxes, will increase incomes if
   (a) taxpayers would have saved some of the money they had to pay in taxes
   (b) only high-income levels are taxed
   (c) prices rise as a result
   (d) investment declines by an equivalent amount

3. If the government spends more than it receives in taxes and other revenues,
   (a) it is obviously spending too much
   (b) national income will surely rise
   (c) there will be a surplus in the budget
   (d) there will be a deficit in the budget

4. A budget deficit will increase GNP only if
   (a) the government borrows money that otherwise would have been spent on investment
   (b) the government borrows money that otherwise would not have been spent at all
   (c) the government borrows from households money that otherwise would have been lent to firms
   (d) the government spends the money abroad rather than at home

5. Which of the following is not a built-in stabilizer?
   (a) a change in tax rates
   (b) unemployment insurance payments
   (c) the corporate income tax
   (d) agricultural subsidies

6. A "full-employment surplus" means that
   (a) a countercyclical fiscal policy is being followed
   (b) the budget will be in surplus at all levels of GNP
   (c) government spending must have declined
   (d) there may be fiscal drag in the tax structure

7. The balanced-budget multiplier
   (a) applies only when government expenditures are equal to taxes
   (b) is larger than the multiplier for government expenditures
   (c) applies when additional tax receipts are equal to additional government expenditures
   (d) is the same as the multiplier for government expenditures

8. With a multiplier of 2, a personal income tax cut of $2 million will raise GNP
   (a) by $4 million
   (b) by $2 million only
   (c) by somewhat less than $4 million, depending on the MPC out of Y_d
   (d) totally by less than $2 million because of withdrawals

9. All but which one of the following are practical problems connected with successful use of fiscal policy to stabilize the economy?
   (a) It is hard politically to get rapid action on proposed tax changes.
   (b) Forecasting is sometimes inaccurate, so the right policy measures may not be taken, or taken soon enough.
   (c) Time lags are too great both in decision making and action taking.
   (d) There is no evidence that lower taxes will actually increase consumption.

EXERCISES

1. Say that, for all levels of income, G will be $100 million and net taxes (taxes minus transfer payments) will be 0.25Y. Plot G and T_n on the graph below, and answer the questions. Suppose that the full-employment level of GNP is $500 million.

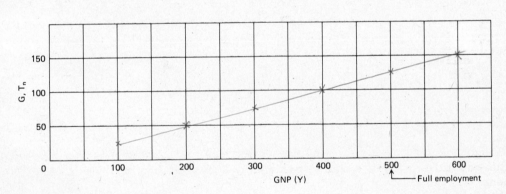

(a) The budget will be balanced at a GNP of ____400____.

(b) At GNP of $200 million, the budget will show a (deficit/surplus) of ___50___.

(c) At full-employment GNP, the budget will show a (deficit/surplus) of ___25___.

(d) Suppose that at full-employment GNP, I equals S and X equals M. Can this economy ever reach full employment with the fiscal policy depicted here? _____no_____

(e) Show on the graph what two moves fiscal policy could make in this situation if full employment were the goal, and explain briefly.

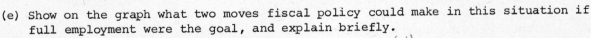
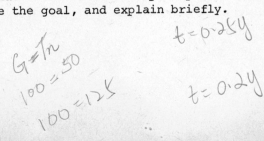

2. Below is a graph of an aggregate-demand schedule for a hypothetical economy, showing an estimated full-employment level of 40 GNP.

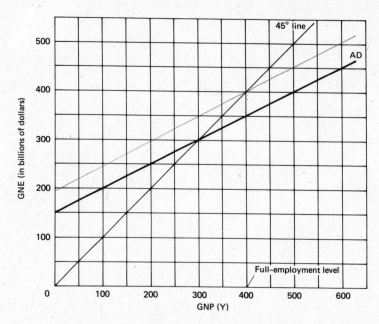

(a) What will be the *actual* GNP level in equilibrium? ___300___

(b) How big is the gap between actual and potential, or full-employment, GNP?
(*Hint:* Measure along the horizontal axis.) ___100___

(c) How much of an increase in aggregate demand would be needed to move GNP from
actual to full-employment GNP? (*Hint:* Measure along the vertical axis.)
___150___

(d) Explain in a few words why your answer to (c) is different from your answer
to (b).

X 2 by subsequent rounds of spending

(e) What fiscal policy measures would be appropriate in this situation?

↑G

(f) Draw in the new AD curve, showing the elimination of the deflationary gap
(assuming no change in slope).

3. Suppose that the government increases total spending by $10 million per year and
at the same time increases taxes so that it collects $10 million more in tax
revenues. Assume that $C = 0.60Y$ and $K = 2.5$.

(a) The G spending increases aggregate demand by $10 million and, via the multi-
plier, *increases* GNP by ___25___.

(b) The tax increase reduces Y by $10 million and thus reduces consumption spending
by $0.60Y$, or $6 million. This reduction in C, multiplied through the economy
reduces GNP by _6 × 2.5 = 15_.

(c) *Net change* in GNP is ___10___. (This exercise illustrates, but does
not prove, the idea of the balanced-budget multiplier.)

4. The following relationships are assumed to characterize a hypothetical economy:

$C = 5 + 0.80(Y - T)$
$I = 5$
$G = 5$
$Y = C + I + G$

where C = consumer expenditure; Y = national income; I = planned investment; G = planned government expenditure, and T = tax revenue, all in billions of dollars.

(a) What is the equilibrium level of national income, assuming that the government budget is balanced?

$$5 + 0.8y - 0.8T + 5 + 5 = y$$
$$0.2y = 15 - 4$$
$$= 11 \quad \$55$$

(b) If the full-employment level of national income is $65 billion, what income tax policy is needed to achieve the full-employment income level? (Indicate both the direction and the magnitude of the policy.)

$$65 = 5 - 0.8T + 52 + 10$$
$$0.8T = 2$$
$$T = \frac{20}{8} = \frac{5}{2} = 2.5$$

(c) What will happen to the original balanced budget position after the execution of the tax policy in (b)?

$$G > T$$
$$5 > 2.5$$
$$\text{deficit}$$

PROBLEM

THE FULL-EMPLOYMENT BUDGET SURPLUS AND CANADIAN FISCAL POLICY

The concept of the full-employment budget surplus (FEBS) is one of the tools that can be used to analyze fiscal policy. In the chart below, the actual federal deficit/surplus and the FEBS result for the recession period 1957-1963 are shown.

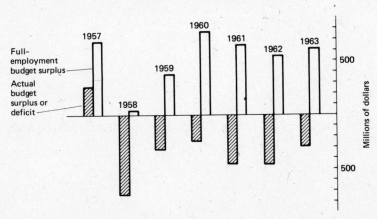

Source: R. M. Will, *Canadian Fiscal Policy, 1945-63,* Study no. 17, Royal Commission on Taxation, Queen's Printer, Ottawa, 1967.

Questions

    1. From this chart, what can you suggest about the adequacy of fiscal policy during this period?

    2. Following a substantial increase in federal spending in 1958, tax revenue increased the following year without there being any major tax changes. The economy was still performing below its potential. Describe what was occurring and its probable effect on unemployment in the absence of any discretionary policy changes.

Chapter Thirty-two
Fiscal Policy
in Action

CHECKLIST	Make certain that you understand the following concepts: secular stagnation; secular boom.

REVIEW QUESTIONS

1. In relying on pump priming in the 1930s, the government used deficits that proved too (small/large) to bring the economy close to full employment. The depression was finally ended with enormous _____ expenditures.

2. The milestone legislation for conscious use of fiscal policy to influence the Canadian economy was the _____.

3. Fiscal policy was not really used as a means of achieving full employment in the United States until _____.

4. One method of offsetting "fiscal drag" (as in 1965) is to _____ taxes.

5. A cyclically balanced budget implies (surpluses/deficits) in booms and (surpluses/deficits) in recessions. It will not work if there is a chronic tendency for saving to exceed _____ at full-employment levels. The appropriate response to this situation, which is called secular _____, is a policy of continuing budget _____.

6. The opposite situation of secular boom in which full-employment investment exceeds full-employment _____ would call for a continuing _____ in the federal budget.

7. The opportunity cost of a given government expenditure (is the same regardless of/varies according to) how it is financed. If government expenditures take resources away from consumer-goods production, the opportunity cost is borne in the (present/future). If government expenditures take resources from capital-goods production, the opportunity costs will be borne in the _____, in the form of (fewer/more) consumer goods produced than otherwise. If government expenditures used unemployed resources, the opportunity cost would be _____.

8. If the government borrows from the private sector to finance expenditures, the opportunity cost is borne by the _____. The latter will be rewarded by _____ paid by the taxpayers. When the government pays interest to domestic holders of the debt, it usually pays it with money raised by _____;

this is called a _____ payment and does not affect total income. Government debt can be a burden to future generations if it is owed to _____.

9. Referring to Figure 32-3 in the text, in what year was the national debt actually larger than the GNP? _____ Since 1949, the debt as a percentage of GNP has been (falling steadily/rising steadily).

10. As measured by the ratio of debt to GNP, the national debt since 1950 has been a(n) (increasing/constant/declining) burden. As measured by the ratios of interest on debt to GNP or to taxes, the burden has for the most part been (increasing/constant/declining).

If you have not answered all questions correctly, review the text in order to be sure that you have all of the important concepts clearly in mind before going on to the next chapter.

1. small, war 2. White Paper of 1945 3. 1964 4. lower 5. surpluses, deficits; investment; stagnation, deficits 6. savings; surplus 7. varies according to; present; future, fewer; zero 8. lenders; interest; taxes, transfer; foreigners 9. 1944-1947; falling steadily 10. declining; constant

---

MULTIPLE-CHOICE QUESTIONS

1. The hypothesis of secular stagnation
   (a) was proved to be true by the Great Depression
   (b) implies government deficits if employment is to be maintained at high level
   (c) depends upon an excess of private investment over savings
   (d) assumes a secular rise in the marginal propensity to consume

2. Interest on the federal debt
   (a) has risen in relation to GNP since 1945
   (b) represents a transfer from taxpayers to bondholders
   (c) is less of a burden when paid to foreigners
   (d) is included in our aggregate of government purchases of goods and services

3. The burden of the economic cost of a war
   (a) is borne mainly by future generations
   (b) is the current and future consumption that is forgone
   (c) is borne only by the losers
   (d) is almost always less than the economic benefits

4. Fiscal policy in the 1930s was one of
   (a) pump priming
   (b) compensatory fiscal policy
   (c) cyclically balanced budgets
   (d) annually balanced budgets

5. The Finance Minister stated in the February 1973 Budget Speech that by concentrating the personal income tax reduction in the lower income strata the most expansion would be attained. This implies
   (a) that high income earners don't know how to spend their money wisely
   (b) a belief that the marginal propensity to consume rises as incomes fall
   (c) a value judgment about income redistribution
   (d) none of the above

PROBLEMS

1. WAS THE 1965 TAX CUT INFLATIONARY?

In the text, it is suggested that fiscal policy makers, in retrospect, misjudged the situation in 1965 when they reduced taxes. What evidence, however, did the government have at that time with respect to the overall economic situation?

In the table below, some basic statistics, taken from the *Budget Papers* that accompanied the 1965 Budget, are shown. Given this information, the Minister of Finance, the Hon. Walter Gordon, announced a reduction in federal tax payable equal to 10 percent of the basic tax payable subject to a maximum reduction of $600 per year.

In making this tax cut, the Minister said, "I believe this budget should be an expansionary one."

Selected Economic Indicators	1963-1964	1963	1964
Percentage change in consumer price index	1.8%		
Unemployment (percent of labor force)		5.5%	4.7%
Percentage change in real GNP	5.0		
Percentage change in average weekly wages and salaries	3.7		
Gross private investment (real 1957 dollars)		$6.97	$7.85

Source: Statistics Canada.

Questions

1. Would this tax proposal be expansionary? If so, how would it generate increases in income and employment?

2. In view of the statistics and goals of economic policy, do you think that this policy was the right one for the time? Justify your answer with reference to the information given in the table.

2. A TURNING POINT IN FISCAL POLICY

In the Budget Speech of February 19, 1973, the Hon. John Turner proposed a reduction in personal income taxes, higher personal exemptions, and a reduction in sales taxes and tariffs on certain consumer goods. Mr. Turner stated, "We shall be attacked in some quarters for still not doing enough to stimulate the economy. Others will say that we are doing too much and that by overshooting the target we will aggravate inflation. We recognize that we are running a risk, and . . . that is a risk worth taking at this time in the interests of dealing more effectively with unemployment." Regarding the sales tax reductions specifically, he said, "This action should help to moderate prices. . . ."

Quarterly Period and Year	GNP (real 1961 dollars)	Gross Private Fixed Investment (real 1961 dollars)	Consumer Price Index (1961 = 100.0)	Unemployment Rate	Average Weekly Wages in Industry
1971					
Q1	$65.8 billion	$15.5 billion			$134.75
Q2	66.6 billion	16.3 billion			138.06
Q3	68.4 billion	16.8 billion	134.7	6.9%	140.99
Q4	68.9 billion	17.2 billion	136.3	6.3	140.90
1972					
Q1	69.6 billion	17.8 billion	137.4	6.0	145.88
Q2	71.0 billion	18.3 billion	138.5	6.2	148.03
Q3	70.5 billion	18.5 billion	141.8	7.1	152.61
Q4			142.8	6.8	

Source: Statistics Canada.

Questions

1. Explain how Mr. Turner's proposals are expected to operate to reduce unemployment and moderate price inflation.

2. On February 20, the spending estimates were tabled in the House of Commons. These estimates called for a 17-percent rise in federal spending which, when coupled with the tax revenues, would result in a deficit of almost a billion dollars.

(a) Given these spending estimates, tax proposals, and other budgetary changes such as increased old-age pensions, do you think the federal government was running a risk of overstimulating the economy? (Some key economic statistics are presented in the table above.)

(b) Traditional antiinflationary policy calls for higher taxes. Why do you think that the government is reducing taxes to combat inflation?

Chapter Thirty-three
The Nature
and History
of Money

REVIEW QUESTIONS

1. The function served by money in making possible specialization and the division of labor is its use as a _____ *medium of exchange*. If there were no form of money, trade in goods and services would have to be conducted by _____ *barter*.

2. The function served by money in making easier the saving of claims on someone else to use at a later date is its use as a _____ *store of value*. This use of money is not very satisfactory unless its value is _____ *stable*.

3. The function served by money in facilitating the recording of claims of members of society upon each other is its use as a _____ *unit of account*.

4. Before the days of paper money, debasing the coinage had the effect of (increasing/ decreasing) the money supply and causing prices to (rise/fall).

5. Originally, the earliest paper money usually represented a claim on a deposit of _____ *gold*. When a country's money is thus convertible into _____ *gold*, the country is said to be on a _____ *gold* standard.

6. In nineteenth-century Canada, private banks (were/were not) allowed to issue their own bank notes. These were promises to pay in _____ *gold*. Typically, banks kept enough gold on hand to pay off (all/only a fraction) of these claims at one time.

7. Fiat currency has value because it is (backed by gold/declared to be legal tender).

8. One aspect of the gold standard that was both an advantage and a disadvantage, depending on the circumstances, was that it (regulated/had little relation to) the quantity of money in circulation.

9. Our paper currency is now issued by the _____ *B of C*; the old-time bank note has been replaced by a claim on the bank in the form of a _____ *demand deposit*, convertible into _____ *cash*.

10. Only (demand/notice) deposits earn interest. Only (demand/notice) deposits are totally transferable by cheque.

11. As the authors of the text indicate, the distinction between money and near money is difficult in Canada. However, one type of near money is an account in a (trust/chartered bank).

12. The narrow definition of the term "supply of money" is _____ *Cash* _____ and _____ *demand deposit* _____. The broad definition is _____ *Cash* _____ and _____ *privately held deposit* _____

13. If the supply of money is completely determined by the needs and forces of the economy, it is called _____ *endogenous* _____. If it is wholly determined by the central bank, it is _____ *exogenous* _____.

    If you have not answered all questions correctly, review the text in order to be sure that you have all of the important concepts clearly in mind before going on to the next chapter.

1. medium of exchange; barter 2. store of wealth; stable 3. unit of account 4. increasing, rise 5. gold; gold; gold 6. were, gold; only a fraction 7. declared to be legal tender 8. regulated 9. central banks, demand deposit, cash 10. notice; demand 11. trust 12. currency, demand deposits at the banks; currency, privately held Canadian dollar deposits at the banks 13. endogenous; exogenous

MULTIPLE-CHOICE QUESTIONS

1. For money to serve as an efficient medium of exchange, it must have all but which one of the following characteristics:
   (a) general acceptability
   (b) convertibility into gold
   (c) high value for its weight
   (d) divisibility

2. Bank deposits constitute about what percent of the Canadian money supply?
   (a) 50
   (b) 25
   (c) 80
   (d) 10

3. One way that notice deposits differ from demand deposits is that
   (a) it is in practice always necessary to give advance warning before withdrawing money from notice deposits
   (b) notice deposits are not considered very liquid assets
   (c) demand deposits earn interest; notice deposits do not
   (d) notice deposits cannot always be drawn on by personal cheque

4. "Debasing the coinage" by adding less precious metals to gold coins had the effect of
   (a) increasing the money supply
   (b) reducing the price level
   (c) increasing what could be bought with each coin
   (d) reducing aggregate demand

5. The value of money depends primarily on
   (a) the gold backing of the currency
   (b) the gold backing of both currency and deposits
   (c) what it will buy
   (d) government decree that it is legal tender

6. A requirement for a gold standard was that
   (a) the price level should be stable
   (b) there should be no paper money
   (c) the paper money should be convertible into gold
   (d) gold reserves should be 100 percent of the money supply

7. At present, deposits are convertible by their owner into
   (a) currency
   (b) gold
   (c) nothing
   (d) loans

8. An asset is, to a person or bank or business,
   (a) a debt owed to someone else
   (b) a liability
   (c) the same as income
   (d) owned property or a claim on someone else

9. A government bond could fill one function of money by acting as
   (a) a medium of exchange
   (b) a store of wealth
   (c) a unit of account
   (d) a hedge against inflation

EXERCISES

1. Indicate which of the three functions of money is demonstrated in each of the following transactions. Use the appropriate letter: (a) medium of exchange; (b) store
   of wealth; (c) unit of account; (d) none.

   _____ 1. Farmer Brown puts cash in his mattress.
   _____ 2. Storekeeper Brown adds up his total sales for the day.
   _____ 3. Banker Brown uses some of his bank's reserves to buy government bonds.
   _____ 4. Traveling salesman Brown uses his credit card to buy gas for his car.
   _____ 5. Mrs. Brown buys a good oriental rug with the thought that it will keep
           its value for a long time.

2. From the data below, calculate the magnitudes of the narrow definition of the
   supply of money (M_1) and the broad definition of the supply of money (M_2).

Financial Statistics, December 1973 (in millions of dollars)	
Coins	581
Bank of Canada notes held by the public	4,559
Chartered bank deposits	
Demand	9,308
Personal savings	24,278
Nonpersonal term and notice	9,686
Government of Canada	2,200

   Source: Bank of Canada Review, July
   1974, Table 15.

   M_1 = _____. M_2 = _____.

PROBLEM

OLYMPIC COINS

The Olympic Committee announced early in 1973 that they intended to finance the 1976 Olympic Games in Montreal partly by the sale of about $240 million in special Olympic coins. A similar scheme had been successfully used by the Munich Olympic Committee in 1972.

The federal government has agreed to instruct the Mint in Ottawa to produce the coins in various face values. The coins will be sold to the Olympic Committee at cost, which is well below the total face value of the coins. The Olympic Committee will then sell the coins to the public at their *face value*.

Furthermore, the coins have been declared legal tender by the federal government.

Questions

1. If the Olympic Committee sold all of the coins, would the money supply increase? Explain.

2. According to the details you have been given, does it appear that the value of the coins depends on the value of their metallic content? What does their value depend upon?

3. Suppose that these coins became valuable collector items so that their market price (the price determined on the coin collectors' market) doubled. Would the money supply double?

4. Suppose that the price of the metals used to produce these coins increased tenfold, so that the metallic price of the coins became greater than their face value. How do you think the holders of these coins would react?

Chapter Thirty-four
The Importance of Money

CHECKLIST — Make certain that you understand the following concepts: neutrality of money; quantity theory of money; transactions demand; precautionary balances; speculative balances; income velocity of circulation; liquidity-preference schedule; demand for money.

REVIEW QUESTIONS

1. The nineteenth-century quantity-of-money theorists held that the price level changed proportionally with changes in the ___*quantity of money*___; relative prices were (not affected/also changed), according to the doctrine of the ___*neutrality*___ of money.

2. Actually in inflationary periods, individual prices rise by (similar/differing) percentages. Those most seriously hurt by inflation are people with ___*fixed*___ incomes.

3. Borrowers are (better/worse) off than lenders during inflation. If A lends B $100 at 5% and the price level rises by 8%, the effective interest rate earned by A is ___*3%*___.

4. The opportunity cost of holding money balances is equal to the ___*possible income given up*___. This cost is higher, the (lower/higher) the rate of interest.

5. Households and firms find it necessary to hold money balances for two motives: ___*precautionary*___ and ___*transactions*___. Other things being equal, these money balances will be a fairly steady fraction of ___*income*___. If the rate of interest rises, there will be an incentive to (reduce/increase) money balances if possible.

6. According to the modified quantity theory, a fall in the supply of money, *ceteris paribus*, results in a (rise/fall) in desired money balances, so that firms and households spend (more/less) in order to restore their cash position. Thus aggregate demand (falls/rises), and, if prices are rigid downward as in the L-shaped relationship, output, employment, and real income (rise/fall).

7. Likewise, the quantity theory holds that, since a rise in the money supply will cause a (rise/fall) in cash balances from desired levels, the difference will be used for (saving/spending). If the economy is at full employment, prices will

_____*rise*_____. At less than full employment, there will be instead an increase in _____*employment*_____ , _____*income*_____ , and _____*output*_____.

8. To summarize the quantity theory's basic prediction, actual GNP—what the book calls the money value of national income—will change in proportion to a change in the _____*supply of money*_____ . The effect occurs directly by changing _____*aggregate demand*_____ .

9. The more generally accepted monetary theory is that excess cash balances are used for the purchase of _____*securities*_____ . An increased demand for securities causes their price to _____*rise*_____ and yields and interest rates to _____*fall*_____ . This effect on interest rates will have some effect on interest-sensitive components of aggregate demand, especially _____*investment*_____ .

10. According to this theory, the desire for cash balances is referred to as "liquidity _____*preference*_____" and is related directly to the level of _____*income*_____ and inversely to the _____*interest rate*_____ . A third motive for liquidity is introduced, dependent only on the rate of interest, and is known as the _____*speculative*_____ motive.

11. There will be an increased preference for holding cash if interest rates are expected to _____*rise*_____ and securities prices are expected to _____*fall*_____ in the future. This speculative motive for liquidity emphasizes money's role not as a medium of exchange but as a _____*store of value*_____ .

12. The liquidity-preference schedule relates the demand for money to the _____*rate of interest*_____ . Its slope is (negative/positive) because the relationship is (direct/inverse). If the slope is steep, a fall in the rate of interest will cause a (small/large) rise in the demand for money; a given increase in the supply of money will cause a (small/large) drop in the rate of interest.

13. Keynes's insight in the Great Depression was that the liquidity-preference schedule was then almost flat, so a very large increase in the supply of money causes a very (small/large) fall in the rate of interest; thus investment (did/did not) respond sufficiently.

14. To summarize, the predicted process is: An increase in the supply of money causes interest rates to _____*fall*_____ ; this change in interest rates causes real investment spending (an injection) to _____*rise*_____ ; thus the GNP will rise by an amount depending on the size of the _____*multiplier*_____ .

15. In the view of this theory, an increase in the supply of money will increase aggregate demand and GNP only if investment and other spending responds to changes in _____*interest rate*_____ .

16. If either monetary theory is correct, one weapon against recession would be to (increase/decrease) the supply of _____*money*_____ ; a weapon against inflation would be to (increase/decrease) the supply of _____*money*_____ .

_____

    If you have not answered all questions correctly, review the text in order to be sure that you have all of the important concepts clearly in mind before going on to the next chapter.

1. quantity of money, not affected, neutrality 2. differing; fixed 3. better; -3
4. possible income given up; higher 5. transactions, precautionary; income; reduce
6. fall, less; falls, fall 7. rise, spending; rise; output, employment, income
8. supply of money; aggregate demand 9. securities; rise, fall; investment

10. preference, income, rate of interest; speculative 11. rise, fall; store of value
12. rate of interest; negative, inverse; small, large 13. small, did not 14. fall,
rise, multiplier 15. interest rates 16. increase, money, decrease, money

MULTIPLE-CHOICE QUESTIONS

1. Which one of the following is *not* an assumption of the simple quantity theory of
   money?
   (a) The economy is at full employment except for very temporary lapses.
   (b) People try to hold a fairly constant fraction of their income in money form.
   (c) Changes in this fraction caused by changes in the supply of money result in
       changes in spending.
   (d) The supply of money is a function of the price level.

2. The amount of money held for transactions balances
   (a) will vary in the same direction as income
   (b) will vary in the same direction as interest rates
   (c) will be larger the shorter the interval between paydays
   (d) none of the above

3. If the public finds ways of making the same amount of money achieve a larger
   amount of transactions than before
   (a) *K* must have risen
   (b) velocity must have risen
   (c) incomes and prices must have fallen
   (d) interest rates will rise

4. All but which one of the following are hypotheses of modern money theory?
   (a) The demand for money for some purposes varies inversely with the rate of in-
       terest.
   (b) Excess cash balances will be spent buying securities.
   (c) Changes in the supply of money affect aggregate demand via the rate of in-
       terest.
   (d) Changes in interest rates affect cash balances but not investment.

5. Liquidity preference for speculative motives
   (a) means that more cash will be held if bond prices are expected to rise in the
       future
   (b) means that more cash will be held if interest rates are expected to be lower
       in the future
   (c) varies directly with income
   (d) is greater the lower the rate of interest

6. According to modern theory, an increase in the supply of money will bring about a
   rise in income and employment only if
   (a) the business cycle is already in recovery
   (b) investment responds sufficiently to a reduction in interest rates
   (c) people buy goods instead of bonds
   (d) the velocity of money increases

7. One reason that inflation is undesirable is that
   (a) it causes loss to some lenders and savers
   (b) it benefits buyers, not sellers
   (c) wages rise faster than profits and prices
   (d) it puts an extra burden on debtors

8. Precautionary balances would be expected to increase
   (a) only if business conditions were to become much more uncertain
   (b) if interest rates increased
   (c) if people were expecting securities prices to rise
   (d) if prices and incomes rose

9. If incomes and GNP rise, and the supply of money is not increased, monetary theory would predict, *ceteris paribus,*
   (a) a rise in the demand for cash balances, and therefore in interest rates
   (b) a fall in the need for borrowing, and therefore in interest rates
   (c) a rise in bond prices, and therefore a fall in interest rates
   (d) a fall in the velocity of money

EXERCISES

1. If K = .20, and if Y = \$100 billion, what will be the desired or equilibrium amount of M? _____ 20 _____ What is the income velocity of money? ___ 5 ___
   Suppose that the actual money supply is \$25 billion. Outline the expected order of effects according to the quantity theory and the contemporary theory described in the chapter.

$$MV = P \cdot y$$
$$M \cdot \frac{1}{0.2} = 100$$
$$20$$

2. Below are graphed three hypothetical curves representing the demand for money balances at various rates of interest, *ceteris paribus.*

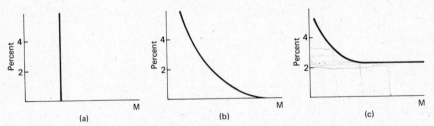

   (a)   (b)   (c)

   (a) Which curve could best represent the transactions demand for money? __b__ __a__
   (b) Which curve could best represent a very ready willingness to convert cash into securities at small increases in interest rates (assume i > 2%)? __b__ __c__
   (c) Which curve could best represent a rapidly increasing preference for liquidity at only slightly lower rates of interest? __c__

(d) Which curve shows no apparent relationship to the rate of interest? ___*a*___
   What do we assume that this curve is related to? ___*income*___

(e) If the central authorities wish to force interest rates higher, Which curve,
   (b) or (c), would require the smaller contraction in the money supply? ___*b*___

(f) Suppose that in the depths of a depression no investment appears profitable at
   any interest rate above 2 percent. Which curve, (b) or (c), would appear to
   make it impossible for the central authorities to achieve a sufficient reduction in interest rates through an expansion in the money supply? ___*c*___
   Why?

3. Here graphed are two hypothetical schedules of the
   marginal efficiency of investment.
   (a) With which schedule, I_1 or I_2, would a reduction in
      rates of interest encourage a greater amount of addi-
      tional investment? ___*I₁*___
   (b) Which schedule would better represent the views of
      those who believe the amount of investment is not
      affected very much by changes in rates of interest?
      ___*I₂*___

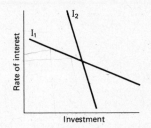

PROBLEM

CANADA'S INCOME VELOCITY OF MONEY

Below are some relevant data for recent years. M_1 is a narrow measure of the money
supply: currency and demand deposits. M_2 is the definition of the money supply as suggested by the authors of the text: currency plus private dollar deposits in the chartered banks. The velocity here is *income velocity* (GNP/M).

Year	M_1	M_2	GNP	V_{M_1}	V_{M_2}
	(billions of dollars)				
1950	4.0	8.5	18.5	4.6	2.2
1955	4.8	10.8	28.5	5.9	2.6
1960	5.5	13.2	38.4	7.0	2.9
1961	5.9	14.4	39.6	6.7	2.8
1962	6.1	14.9	42.9	7.0	2.9
1963	6.3	15.9	46.0	7.3	2.9
1964	6.7	17.0	50.3	7.5	3.0
1965	7.2	19.1	55.4	7.7	2.9
1966	7.7	20.3	61.8	8.0	3.0
1967	8.3	23.6	66.4	8.0	2.8
1968	8.9	26.7	72.7	___	___
1969	9.2	27.7	79.7	___	___
1970	9.7	30.7	85.7	___	___
1971	11.4	35.3	93.3	___	___
1972	12.9	40.9	103.5	___	___
1973	14.4	48.4	118.9	___	___
1974	15.3	56.5	139.5	___	___

Source: Statistics Canada, *Canadian Statistical Review,* various
issues.

Questions

   1. Which concept of the supply of money generally gives a more stable value for velocity?

   2. For a velocity of 3, what is the fraction of income held in money balances, on the average?

   3. Do the figures seem to suggest a substantial change over the last twenty years in the desire to hold balances in the form of cash or demand deposits?

   4. What role might higher interest rates on notice deposits, wider use of credit cards, and price inflation in the late 1960s and early 1970s have played in the higher V_{M_1}?

Chapter Thirty-five
The Banking System and Money Supply

REVIEW QUESTIONS

1. Chartered banks are unique in that they hold ___*demand*___ deposits, transferable by ___*cheque*___.

2. As contrasted to the U.S. banking system, Canada's banking system is characterized by a (large/small) number of banks which have (many/few) branches throughout Canada.

3. Most of a bank's income comes from ___*interest on loans and securities*___

4. *Assets* are property or claims (owned by/owed to) a person or firm.

5. A bank's reserves are listed as (assets/liabilities). But the major part of total bank assets consists of ___*loans*___. Most of a bank's liabilities consist of ___*deposits*___. The larger these are, the (larger/smaller) the amount of loans a bank can make.

6. The fraction of total deposits that a bank keeps in reserves is called the ___*reserve ratio*___. If the cash reserve ratio required by the Bank of Canada is 0.12, a bank with demand deposits of $12 million must have reserves of at least ___*1.44 mill.*___. These reserves must be in the form of either ___*cash*___ or ___*deposit in Big C*___.

7. Bank reserves beyond the amount legally required are called ___*excess cash*___ reserves.

8. If a bank gains deposits from another bank, the first bank's reserves will ___*rise*___ and the other bank's reserves and deposits will ___*fall*___. If banks gain deposits from outside the system, total reserves and deposits will ___*rise*___.

9. *Ceteris paribus*, banks will want to keep their excess reserves low if possible because reserves do not ___*earn interest*___. So they will prefer to change these assets into another form, namely ___*loans*___.

10. (a) When a bank makes a loan, the borrower takes the money in the form of either _____cash_____ or a _____cheque_____. Thus, the money supply is immediately _____increase_____; the bank has created _____money_____.

(b) When the borrower spends the borrowed money, and the recipient puts it in his bank account elsewhere, the second bank gains deposits and excess reserves from the first bank; it now has excess reserves and will similarly wish to _____make loans_____.

11. Thus, an increase in total bank reserves can result in a much (larger/smaller) increase in the _____money supply_____.

12. (a) An equal reduction in a bank's reserves and deposits when the bank has no excess reserves will leave the bank short of _____required reserve_____. To restore them it may temporarily borrow reserves, but in the longer run it will have to sell _____securities_____ or reduce its _____loans_____.

(b) This, in turn, draws deposits and reserves from other banks. The process causes the money supply to _____fall_____ by (more/less) than the original loss of reserves; the banks have destroyed _____money_____.

13. As bank loans increase, deposits _____increase_____; as loans decrease, deposits _____decrease_____.

14. The size of the change in the money supply associated with a change in bank reserves depends on the _____reserve ratio_____. If r = 1/5, the effect on the money supply of an increase in bank reserves could be _____5_____ times the change in reserves.

15. There are two main reasons why the expansion of the money supply for a given increase in reserves will probably not be as large as the maximum amount indicated by the reciprocal of the required reserve ratio:
(a) Some of an increase in bank reserves may be needed by the public as _____cash_____.
(b) The banks may not find a sufficient amount of worthy _____borrowers_____.

If you have not answered all questions correctly, review the text in order to be sure that you have all of the important concepts clearly in mind before going on to the next chapter.

1. demand; cheque 2. small; many 3. interest on loans and securities 4. owned by 5. assets; loans and securities; deposits; larger 6. cash reserve ratio; $1.44 million; currency, deposits in the Bank of Canada 7. excess 8. rise, fall; rise 9. earn interest; loans and securities 10. currency, deposit; increased, money; make loans or buy securities 11. larger; money supply 12. required reserves; securities, loans; fall, more, money 13. increase; decrease 14. cash reserve ratio; five 15. cash; borrowers

---

MULTIPLE-CHOICE QUESTIONS

1. The chartered banking system is distinct from trust and mortgage loan companies in that
(a) it lends the savings of the public to borrowers
(b) it pays interest on savings accounts
(c) it creates and destroys money
(d) none of the above

2. A bank is able to create money
(a) by printing it
(b) by creating a deposit as it extends a new loan
(c) by maintaining reserves
(d) by issuing cheques to its depositors

3. The required reserves of a bank
   (a) are listed among its liabilities
   (b) consist of currency
   (c) are kept at other banks
   (d) consist of currency and its deposits at the Bank of Canada

4. The process of creation of deposit money by banks
   (a) is possible because of the fractional-reserve requirement
   (b) is consciously undertaken by each bank
   (c) always occurs if there are excess reserves
   (d) permits only small, gradual changes in the supply of money

5. A reduction in bank reserves, say, by payments to foreigners,
   (a) will always cause a multiple contraction in deposits
   (b) will cause a multiple contraction in deposits only if there are no excess reserves
   (c) will not affect domestic deposits
   (d) will not affect the availability of domestic credit

6. If you withdraw $100 at your bank,
   (a) deposits fall by a multiple of $100
   (b) deposits and bank reserves fall by $100
   (c) currency in circulation is unaffected
   (d) the money supply is increased

7. A bank that has insufficient reserves
   (a) may borrow from the Bank of Canada
   (b) may stop making new loans
   (c) may sell securities to other banks or to the public
   (d) may do all of the above

8. The amount of currency in circulation is determined primarily by
   (a) the amount of gold backing
   (b) how much people need
   (c) the Board of Governors of the Bank of Canada
   (d) the individual banks

9. An increase in reserves will not cause a multiple increase in the money supply if
   (a) the public does not want more cash than before
   (b) the banks are unwilling to increase their loans and investments
   (c) full employment has been reached
   (d) the banks buy bonds instead of making loans

EXERCISES

1. Arrange the following items on the proper side of a bank's balance sheet.
   - (a) Demand deposits $5,000,000
   - (b) Notice deposits   1,000,000
   - (c) Currency in vaults   60,000
   - (d) Deposits in the Bank of Canada   1,000,000
   - (e) Loans to public   4,000,000
   - (f) Security holdings, Canadian government,
             provincial, municipal, and other   1,500,000
   - (g) Banking building and fixtures   360,000
   - (h) Capital and surplus   920,000

Assets	Liabilities
c c c g f	a b d e

2. We use "T-accounts," abbreviated balance sheets, for a bank to show changes in bank reserves, loans, and deposits. Make the entries on the T-accounts below, using + and - signs to show increase or decrease, for each of the following independent events. (Remember that all changes must balance.)

	Assets	Liabilities
(a) You deposit your pay cheque of $100 at your bank.	Reserves: +100 Loans and Securities:	Deposits: +100
(b) A bank sells $10,000 of government bonds in the market to replenish its reserves.	Reserves: +10000 Loans and Securities: -10000	Deposits: -
(c) A bank makes a loan of $5,000 to a local businessman and credits it to his chequing account.	Reserves: Loans and Securities: 5000	Deposits: 5000
(d) A bank sells $50,000 of securities to the Bank of Canada and receives deposits in the Bank of Canada.	Reserves: 50000 Loans and Securities: +50000	Deposits:
(e) A businessman uses $5,000 of his demand deposit to pay off a loan from the same bank.	Reserves: Loans and +5000 Securities:	Deposits: -5000
(f) A bank orders $5,000 in currency from the Bank of Canada.	Reserves: -5000 Loans and Securities:	Deposits: +5000

3. Suppose that bank A, a Canadian bank, begins with the following T-account. The cash reserve ratio is assumed to be 10 percent. Joe Doe, a holder of a deposit in bank A, withdraws $1000 and deposits this amount in a commercial bank in a foreign country. Thus, $1000 has been taken out of the Canadian banking system.

	Bank A (initial situation)		Bank A (after the withdrawal)
Reserves: $ 10,000	Deposits: $100,000	Reserves: $ 9900	Deposits: $ 99000
Loans: 990,000		Loans: 99100 / 99000	

(a) What were bank A's required reserves? What it "loaned up" to begin with?

10000

(b) Show the immediate effect of the withdrawal from bank A.

(c) What is the magnitude of bank A's reserve deficiency?

(d) Bank A reacts by calling in a loan, equal to the amount of its reserve deficiency, which it had made to Mary Smith. Mary repays the loan by writing a cheque on her account in bank B, another Canadian bank. Bank B's initial T-account is shown below. Fill in the T-accounts below for the effects of bank A's receiving the payment from Mary and of bank B's losing Mary's deposit.

	Bank B (initial situation)		Bank B (after losing Mary's deposit)
Reserves: $ 5,000	Deposits: $50,000	Reserves: $ 4910	Deposits: $ 49100
Loans: 45,000		Loans: 3690	

	Bank A (after receiving loan repayment)
Reserves: $ 10800	Deposits: $108000
Loans: 99200	

(e) After this transaction, is bank A "loaned up"? Bank B?

(f) In fact, bank B has a deficiency of reserves. It reacts by calling in a loan, equal to the amount of the deficiency, made to Peter Piper. Peter cashes in a savings deposit that he held in bank C; that is, bank C loses a deposit and Peter repays bank B. Bank C's initial situation is shown below. Fill in the T-accounts for the effects of bank B's receiving the loan repayment and bank C's losing Peter's savings deposit.

Bank C (initial situation)	
Reserves: $ 7,000	Deposits: $70,000
Loans: 63,000	

Bank C (after loss of deposit)	
Reserves: $	Deposits: $
Loans:	

Bank B (after receiving loan repayment)	
Reserves: $	Deposits: $
Loans:	

(g) After this transaction, is bank B "loaned up"? Bank C?

(h) After this transaction, the reduction in the money supply has been Joe's original withdrawal plus $_____ in other deposits. Loans have been reduced by $_____.

(i) The process will continue until the total reduction in the money supply will be $_____. The total reduction in loans will be $_____.

PROBLEM

PENNIES FROM HEAVEN

Suppose that a shower of Mint-fresh Canadian pennies falls from the sky onto the property of Joe Farmer. Joe, bewildered but delighted, collects all of them, worth the sum of $100, and takes them to his branch of the Bank of Nova Scotia. The manager of the bank, also bewildered, is skeptical. After making several calls to other bank managers, the manager of Joe's bank is convinced that the pennies have not been withdrawn from any other bank. In addition, the Mint in Ottawa cannot explain the shower of pennies, but assures the manager that the pennies are not counterfeit.

Asking no further questions, the manager accepts the $100 worth of pennies and Joe is given a deposit of $100.

Questions

1. Show the effect of this transaction on the balance sheet of the Bank of Nova Scotia.

Assets	Liabilities
(reserves) currency _____	deposits _____

2. If the cash reserve ratio is .2, what is the magnitude of the new loans that can be created by the Bank of Nova Scotia?

3. Fill in the table below for the various other generation banks.

Bank	New Deposits	Additions to Reserves	New Loans
Second generation	_____	_____	_____
Third generation	_____	_____	_____
Fourth generation	_____	_____	_____

4. What is your prediction for the *final* change in the money supply as a result of the shower of pennies? State the necessary assumptions.

Chapter Thirty-six
Monetary Policy

CHECKLIST	Make certain that you understand the following concepts: open-market operations; monetary policy; purchase and resale agreements (PRA); day-to-day loans; bank rate; discount rate; policy variables; policy instruments; target variables.

REVIEW QUESTIONS

1. The central bank of Canada is the ___Bank of Canada___. Its three major functions are: to serve as a bank for ___bank___; to perform banking services for the ___gov't___; and to control the supply of ___money___ and influence rates of ___interest___, for certain policy goals.

2. As banker for banks, it holds chartered banks' deposits of ___reserve___; it also lends to member banks, for which borrowings they pay an interest rate called the ___bank___ rate.

3. The two largest and most important liabilities of the Bank of Canada are ___bank reserve___ and ___B of C Notes issued___. The amount of currency in circulation depends on the amount (of gold backing/that people need for use).

4. Bank reserves and currency in circulation (used to be/are) required to be backed by gold reserves. The major asset item on the Bank of Canada's balance sheet is ___gov't securities___.

5. The federal government can make payments to the public out of deposits at the ___B of C___.

6. When the Bank of Canada buys bonds in the open market, the deposits of the sellers at the chartered banks (rise/fall) and the reserves of the banks (rise/fall) as the payment is cleared. If the banks now have excess reserves, they can buy assets and create ___deposit___. It becomes (easier/harder) to get a loan. Also, as the price of bonds rises as a result, interest rates will (fall/rise).

7. When the central bank sells government bonds from its holdings to the public, deposits and reserves will (rise/fall), and interest rates will tend to (rise/fall). The ratio of reserves to deposits will also have (risen/fallen); if it has (fallen too much/risen enough), the banks will (have to reduce/be able to increase) their loans and investments.

8. Required minimum cash reserve ratios for the member banks are decreed by the
    _____ Bank Act _____. The cash reserve ratio for notice deposits
    is (lower/higher) than that for demand deposits.

9. As an example, by reducing the required cash reserve ratio, the Bank of Canada
    could create (additional reserves/excess reserves).

10. Raising the required cash reserve ratio could reduce (total reserves/excess re-
    serves) or cause a deficiency of reserves. In the latter case, the banks may be
    forced to _____ reduce _____ loans and deposits, and the money supply would
    (fall/rise). The expansion ratio for deposit creation will be (increased/decreased)
    by a rise in the required reserve ratio.

11. Bank borrowing from the Bank of Canada is on a (short/long)-term basis and is
    supposedly used as a last _____ resort _____. A rise in the bank rate is
    usually taken as a signal of (tighter/easier) credit conditions to come.

12. Banks compute the value of the case reserve ratio every (day/two weeks) based upon
    the average volume of deposits during the (current/preceding) month.

13. The Bank of Canada has the authority to impose a secondary reserve ratio. Today,
    it is ____ 8 ____ percent. This means that a bank must hold this percentage of its
    deposits in the form of short-term liquid assets such as treasury bills, day-to-day
    loans, and short-term government securities. If the Bank of Canada increased the
    secondary reserve ratio, chartered banks would find that their ability to expand
    loans had _____ decrease _____.

14. Moral suasion between the Bank of Canada and the chartered banks is made easier in
    Canada because of the (small/large) number of banks.

15. An expansionary monetary policy would be one that (increases/reduces) the total re-
    serves or the excess reserves of the banks, (reduces/increases) interest rates, and
    makes it (easier/harder) for business and households to borrow money.

16. An expansionary monetary policy would be one, therefore, that makes (sales/pur-
    chases) of government securities in the open market, decrees a (decrease/increase)
    in the secondary reserve requirements, or announces a (higher/lower) bank rate.

17. An easy money policy may not result in stimulating aggregate demand if a strong
    preference for liquidity by the public keeps interest rates from (falling/rising),
    or if investment is very (elastic/inelastic) with respect to interest rates.

18. Aggregate demand may be reduced or a rise in it may be slowed up by a(n) (tighter/
    easier) monetary policy that makes borrowing (more difficult/easier) and (more/less)
    expensive.

19. If the Bank of Canada's open-market purchases are used to support the government's
    attempts to sell large amounts of new bonds, it will have difficulty in also trying
    to follow a(n) (tight/easy) money policy at the same time.

20. In the view of monetarist theorists, changes in the money supply have a(n) (direct/
    indirect) effect on national income, an effect that is (predictable and immediate/
    not well understood and delayed). They feel that the central bank tends to (under-
    react and do too little/overreact and do too much) in trying to influence money
    and credit conditions.

    If you have not answered all questions correctly, review the text in order to be
sure that you have all of the important concepts clearly in mind before going on to the
next chapter.

1. Bank of Canada; banks, government, money and credit, interest 2. reserves; bank
3. Bank of Canada Notes issued, bank reserves; that people need for use 4. used to be;
government securities 5. Bank of Canada 6. rise, rise; deposits; easier; fall
7. fall, rise; fallen, fallen too much, have to reduce 8. Bank Act; lower 9. excess
reserves 10. excess reserves, reduce, fall; decreased 11. short, resort; tighter
12. two weeks; preceding 13. eight; decreased 14. small 15. increases, reduces,
easier 16. purchases, decrease, lower 17. falling, inelastic 18. a tighter, more
difficult, more 19. tight 20. direct, not well understood and delayed; overreact
and do too much

MULTIPLE-CHOICE QUESTIONS

1. Which one of the following is *not* one of the functions of a central bank?
    (a) to provide banking services for the government
    (b) to act as lender of last resort to banks
    (c) to lend to business
    (d) to control the supply of money and credit

2. Which one of the following is an important function of chartered bank deposits in
   the Bank of Canada?
    (a) to settle accounts with foreign banks
    (b) to use for loans
    (c) to provide an easy way for banks to transfer funds among themselves
    (d) to earn interest for the banks

3. Purchase and Resale Agreements involve
    (a) sales and purchases of securities between the chartered banks
    (b) sales and purchases of securities between the chartered banks and the Bank of
        Canada
    (c) sales of securities by investment dealers to the Bank of Canada
    (d) sales of securities by investment dealers to the Bank of Canada with agreement
        of repurchase at a later date

4. Open-market operations are
    (a) used by the Bank of Canada regularly to meet seasonal, cyclical, and erratic
        fluctuations in the banks' need for reserves
    (b) used only sparingly by the Bank of Canada in order not to upset the government
        bond market
    (c) conducted primarily in order to make a profit for the Bank of Canada
    (d) not very effective as a means of influencing the supply of money and credit

5. Which one of the following is *not* a tool of monetary policy?
    (a) open-market operations
    (b) changes in the bank rate
    (c) changes in the required secondary reserve ratio
    (d) changes in tax rates

6. Open-market purchases of securities will tend to
    (a) lower the price of bonds
    (b) lower interest rates
    (c) raise interest rates
    (d) reduce bank reserves and deposits

7. Generally recognized as a sign of policy favoring tighter money is
   (a) a reduction of the required reserve ratio
   (b) a rise in the government bond market
   (c) a rise in the money supply
   (d) a rise in the bank rate

8. Monetary policy deliberately tries to influence the course of the economy by
   (a) acting as a good example to the private sector
   (b) making it harder or easier to borrow money
   (c) changing the velocity of money
   (d) directly affecting the price level

9. Monetary policy will affect the level of economic activity if
   (a) investment responds appreciably to changes in interest rates
   (b) investment is not much deterred by increases in interest rates so long as profits possibilities are rising more
   (c) velocity changes occur when the money supply changes
   (d) expansion, rather than contraction, is needed

10. Monetary policy will affect the level of economic activity if
    (a) it affects aggregate demand
    (b) the banks have lots of excess reserves
    (c) liquidity preference is very great
    (d) changes in the supply of money do not affect interest rates much

EXERCISES

1. Indicate on which side of the Bank of Canada's balance sheet the following items should go.
   (a) Chartered bank reserves
   (b) Currency in circulation
   (c) Canadian government deposits
   (d) Government securities
   (e) Foreign currency assets
   (f) Advances to chartered banks

Bank of Canada

Assets	Liabilities
	a
	b
	c

2. The Bank of Canada decides to purchase $100 million of Canadian government securities from the public for open-market account. Show the effect on the banking system of this first step. (Be sure to use + and - to indicate changes, not totals.)

(a)

Bank of Canada		All Banks	
Securities: 100	Bank reserves: 100	Reserves:	Demand deposits:

(b) If the reserve ratio is 20 percent, it now is possible for deposits to increase by a total of _____ (including the original increase).

3. Suppose the chartered banks sell government securities in the amount of $5 million in the bond market. Show the changes that would occur on the T-accounts involved if (a) the bonds are bought by the public; (b) the bonds are bought by the Bank of Canada in open-market operations.

(a)

All Banks		Bank of Canada	
Reserves:	Deposits:	Securities:	Deposits of banks:
Securities:			

(b)

All Banks		Bank of Canada	
Reserves:	Deposits:	Securities:	Deposits of banks:
Securities:			

(c) Which process, (a) or (b), would have an expansionary effect on the economy, *ceteris paribus*? _____ Why?

4. At holiday times the public's need for currency rises.
   (a) As the banks request more currency from the Bank of Canada and put it into circulation, what happens to their reserves?

   Show on the T-accounts below the changes that result from the public's conversion of $50 million of deposits into cash, met by the issue of an additional $50 million of Bank of Canada Notes.

All Banks		Bank of Canada	
Reserves:	Deposits:	Chartered bank deposits:	
		Bank of Canada Notes outstanding:	

   (b) How can the Bank of Canada prevent this temporary demand for cash from causing reserve difficulties for the banks?

   (c) What would you expect to happen after the holiday is over?

5. Suppose, with a cash reserve ratio of .10, that a bank has reserves of $4.8 million and demand deposits of $24 million.

(a) Excess reserves are _____.

Now suppose that the Bank of Canada is allowed to increase the reserve ratio to .20.

(b) Total reserves are _____.

(c) Excess reserves are _____.

6. Suppose that the economy is experiencing inflationary tendencies and the Bank of Canada decides to conduct open-market operations. It possesses new $100 Government of Canada one-year bonds with a coupon rate of 5%. Suppose also that the current market rate of interest is 7%.

(a) If the Bank of Canada wishes to maintain the current rate of interest, at what price should it sell the bonds to the public and to the banks? (Check the present-value table in Chapter 22.)

(b) If the Bank of Canada announced a selling price of $92.60 per bond, what is the effective rate of interest for these bonds?

(c) What might the effect of this policy change have on the level of all interest rates?

PROBLEM

THE EFFECTIVENESS OF MONETARY POLICY

The general conclusion we draw from our research is that the effect of monetary policy on the Canadian economy is *imprecise, slow,* and *variable;* there is a relationship present, but it is extremely hazy. This conclusion has important implications for the use of monetary policy as a short-run stabilizing instrument.*

This was the comment of Professor H. G. Johnson upon the results of research that he and Professor John Winder conducted for the Canadian Royal Commission on Banking and Finance. In their investigation, they distinguished between *inside* and *outside* lags. The inside lag was defined to be the lag between the appearance of a need for a change in monetary policy in the economy and the corresponding change in policy; the outside lag was the lag between the change in monetary policy and the appearance of a response in the economy. Both lags were found to be quantitatively large.

*H. G. Johnson, *The Canadian Quandary* (Toronto: McGraw-Hill, 1963), p. 187.

The impreciseness and variability of monetary policy stems from the fact that it is difficult to predict the behavior of businessmen, banks, and consumers. If individuals react differently from what has been assumed in a model, then the predictions of the model are no longer likely to hold. Slowness of monetary policy may result if individuals and firms do not react immediately to changes in economic variables. For example, the uncertainty about future events, the costs of adjusting plans, and various institutional constraints might outweigh the effects of changes in the money supply and the market rate of interest.

Let us suppose that the Bank of Canada wishes to counteract rising unemployment. We shall use a Keynesian approach (described in Chapter 34) to explain the course of events of the change in monetary policy and the change in employment and putput. Hence we concentrate on the *outside lag*. If a link in a chain is weak, then the chain is weak. Similarly, if the assumptions about behavior do not hold, then the effectiveness of monetary policy is reduced.

Questions

1. Should the Bank of Canada buy or sell bonds in the open market in order to counteract unemployment?

2. Because of the policy outlined in Question 1, the banks will find that reserves have (increased/decreased). As a result, a multiple (expansion/reduction) in the money supply is possible. Whether this multiple change in the money supply *actually* occurs depends on the behavior of the banks and the public. Explain the behavior that must exist in order for there to be a multiple change in the money supply. Why might banks or the public not react immediately?

3. If the money supply does change, the interest rate may be affected. What would be your prediction about the direction of the change in the interest rate as a result of the change in monetary policy? Whether the interest rate *actually* changes depends on events in the loanable funds market. In particular, the behavior of holders of cash balances with respect to the interest rate is critical (see Chapter 5). Under what conditions would the interest rate not change?

4. (a) If the interest rate does change, economic theory tells us that investment expenditures (and possibly consumption) might change. Discuss some factors that
might cause businessmen not to invest in new machines and equipment in the current
time period even though the interest rate changed. In your analysis distinguish between movements along and shifts in the marginal-efficiency-of-capital schedule.

        (b) What effect might the existence of excess capacity have on the decision
to invest?

5. (a) If investment changes, national income should change by a multiple. However, what assumption concerning the marginal propensity to spend does the multiplier
analysis depend upon?

        (b) If individuals did not spend immediately on each round of expenditures in
the multiplier process, what implications would this have for the time taken to change
national income by a multiple?

Chapter Thirty-seven
Exchange Rates

> | CHECKLIST | Make certain that you understand the following concepts: foreign exchange; exchange rate; arbitrage; balance-of-payments accounts; visibles; invisibles; balance-of-merchandise trade; balance-of-payments surplus; balance-of-payments deficit; fluctuating exchange rates; fixed exchange rates; appreciation; depreciation; revaluation; devaluation; |
> |---|---|

REVIEW QUESTIONS

1. The exchange rate is the _____*price*_____ at which purchases and sales of foreign currency (or claims on it) take place. The foreign currency traded, or claims on it, is called ___*foreign exchange*___.

2. When one dollar exchanges for £.41-2/3 pounds, one pound exchanges for _____ dollars.

3. Sales and purchases of foreign exchange to keep several exchange rates at mutually consistent ratios are called ___*arbitrage*___ operations.

4. The record of transactions between a nation and foreign countries is called its ___*balance-o payment*___. A transaction that typically leads to the purchase of a foreign currency is recorded as a _____*debit*_____, and a transaction that typically gives rise to the sale of a foreign currency is recorded as a ___*credit*___. Canadian exports, therefore, are ___*credit*___, and Canadian imports are ___*debit*___. A debit transaction for Canada is a ___*credit*___ transaction for the foreign country.

5. The balance of payments always balances, but particular categories may show a deficit if ___*debit*___ are greater than ___*credit*___. Similarly, a surplus may result if ___*credit*___ are greater than ___*debit*___. The most important division in the balance-of-payments account is between the ___*current*___ account and the ___*capital*___ account.

6. A deficit on the current account must be matched either by a ___*surplus*___ in the capital account, which means borrowing from abroad, or by a ___*reduction*___ in the foreign exchange and gold held by domestic central authorities, or by a combination of both.

7. A surplus on the current account must be matched either by a ___deficit___ on the capital account, which means loans or gifts to foreigners, or by a reduction of the ___reserve___ of gold and foreign exchange held by the foreign central authorities, or by a combination of both.

8. The current account is usually divided into visibles and invisibles, a distinction corresponding to the division of commodities into ___goods___ and ___service___.

9. Classify the following transactions by Canadians as debits (−) or credits (+) in the current account:
   (a) the importation of a Volkswagen ___−___
   (b) the purchase of insurance from Lloyds of London ___−___
   (c) the hotel bill of a Canadian tourist in Fort Lauderdale, Florida ___−___
   (d) dividends received from foreign stocks ___+___

10. The capital account consists of long- and short-term ___capital___. Purchases of foreign securities would appear as a (debit/credit) in the balance of payments. Shifts of bank deposits from Canadian to foreign banks in other countries would appear as a (debit/credit). Both of these transactions create a (demand for/supply of) foreign currencies or a (demand for/supply of) Canadian dollars.

11. A balance-of-payments surplus or deficit refers to the balance of the current account plus the capital account. A deficit in the Canadian balance of payments means that the total amount Canadians are trying to pay to foreigners (exceeds/is less than) the amount foreigners are trying to pay Canadians; the difference is financed by reductions in gold and ___foreign-exchange___ reserves.

12. An overall surplus on the balance of payments will result in a (reduction/increase) in a country's ___foreign exchange___ ·reserve.

13. If a country's foreign-exchange reserves and gold stock fall too low in the face of persisting balance-of-payments deficits, and it has a fixed exchange rate, the country can ___devalue___ its currency.

14. With fixed exchange rates, a continuing surplus in the balance of payments results in a (rise/fall) in a country's exchange reserves and gold holdings. The central authorities must be either willing to accumulate (claims on/debts to) foreigners in exchange for their own currency or ___revalue___ their currency. On the other hand, with exchange rates that are allowed to fluctuate, the country's currency would (appreciate/depreciate) with a continuing surplus in the balance of payments.

15. When Canadians import goods and services and securities, they supply ___$C___ and demand foreign currencies. When foreigners buy Canadian goods and services and securities, they (buy/sell) dollars and (buy/sell) their own currency.

16. An increase in the Canadian demand for German-made cars shifts the demand curve for marks to the ___right___ and the supply curve of dollars to the ___right___; with freely fluctuating exchange rates, the dollar price of marks will ___rise___ while the mark price of dollars will ___fall___.

17. An increase in the rate of return in Canadian manufacturing, compared with the rest of the world, would make it (more/less) attractive for foreigners to invest in Canadian manufacturing. With freely fluctuating exchange rates, the increase in the rate of return would be to cause the foreign price of Canadian dollars to (rise/fall).

18. If prices and incomes in country A rise relatively to those in countries B to Z, A's imports will probably ___rise___ and its exports will ___fall___. This effect could be offset by allowing A's currency to (appreciate/depreciate).

19. When the American dollar depreciates, American exports become (cheaper/more expensive) to foreigners and exports will (rise/fall). Imports into the United States become (more/less) expensive to Americans and will (rise/fall). It becomes (more/less) expensive for Americans to travel in Canada. An existing U.S. import surplus would be expected to (increase/decrease), and its deficit on current account would (fall/rise).

Appendix

20. If the demand for imported goods in both of two countries in a model is very inelastic, currency devaluation (will/will not) help the deficit country. It can be shown that this perverse case occurs only if the sum of the elasticities of demand for imported goods in the two countries is less than _____one_____.

21. Short-term capital may be attracted to a country by a rise in its ___interest rate___ _____. This will increase the (demand for/supply of) the country's currency in the exchange markets.

22. If a person in country A makes a loan to an entrepreneur in country B, he transfers to the citizen of B a claim to the ___output___ of A's ___resources___ .

_____

     If you have not answered all questions correctly, review the text in order to be sure that you have all of the important concepts clearly in mind before going on to the next chapter.

1. price; foreign exchange 2. 2.40 3. arbitrage 4. balance of payments; debit, credit; credits, debits; credit 5. debits, credits; credits, debits; current, capital 6. surplus, reduction 7. deficit, reserves 8. goods, services 9. -, -, -, + 10. capital; debit; debit; demand for, supply of 11. exceeds, foreign exchange 12. increase, gold and foreign-exchange reserves 13. devalue 14. rise; claims on, revalue; appreciate 15. dollars, buy, sell 16. right, right, rise, fall 17. more; rise 18. rise, fall; depreciate 19. cheaper, rise; more, fall; more; decrease, fall 20. will not; one 21. interest rates; demand for 22. output, resources

_____

MULTIPLE-CHOICE QUESTIONS

1. In the exchange market between dollars and sterling, a demander of dollars is also
   (a) a supplier of dollars
   (b) a supplier of pounds
   (c) a demander of pounds
   (d) everyone is always all these simultaneously

2. If, in a free market between Canadian and American dollars in which the rate is allowed to fluctuate, the number of Canadians withins to buy American goods falls (all other things staying the same),
   (a) at the new equilibrium, it will take more Canadian dollars to buy an American dollar than before
   (b) at the new equilibrium, it will take the same number of Canadian dollars to buy an American dollar as before
   (c) at the new equilibrium, it will take fewer American dollars to buy a Canadian dollar than before
   (d) at the new equilibrium, it will take more American dollars to buy a Canadian dollar than before

3. Which of the following statements is true about the balance of payments?
   (a) Current-account debits must equal current-account credits.
   (b) Visibles must equal invisibles.
   (c) Total debits must equal total credits.
   (d) Desired payments must equal actual payments.

4. Exports of Canadian goods are on the same side (credit) of the Canadian accounts as
    (a) Canadian investment abroad
    (b) Canadian government aid to underdeveloped countries
    (c) the money spent on travel in Europe by Canadians
    (d) investment by British people in Canadian stocks

5. Fixed exchange rates
    (a) need no government intervention in the currency market, whereas fluctuating rates do
    (b) usually result in balance-of-payments deficits and surpluses
    (c) have been demonstrated by experience to be inferior to fluctuating rates to everyone's satisfaction
    (d) have been demonstrated by experience to be superior to fluctuating rates to everyone's satisfaction

6. A dollar price of 25 cents for marks can be expressed as a mark price for dollars of
    (a) 4
    (b) 1/4
    (c) an indeterminant amount
    (d) 2.40

7. Arbitrage operations in the foreign-exchange markets are
    (a) any transactions in foreign exchanges
    (b) transactions involving currencies other than dollars or pounds
    (c) transactions between the central banking authorities
    (d) foreign-exchange transactions that seek gains from discrepancies in exchange rates

8. Suppose that the American demand for Canadian dollars is 5 billion Canadian dollars per year at an exchange rate of 93 U.S. cents for a Canadian dollar. It is estimated as 4 billion Canadian dollars a year at an exchange rate of $1 (U.S.). The elasticity of demand can be estimated as
    (a) inelastic (<1)
    (b) approximately of unitary elasticity
    (c) moderately elastic ($\approx$1.5)
    (d) very elastic (>2)

9. If the demand of nonresidents for a country's money is elastic and the country is running a deficit in its balance of payments, *ceteris paribus*,
    (a) a revaluation upward of its exchange rate would reduce the deficit
    (b) a change in the exchange rate would be inappropriate
    (c) a devaluation would reduce the deficit
    (d) a devaluation would increase the deficit

10. A loan and delivery by Canada of $2 million in agricultural equipment to India leads to the following in the balance of payments:
    (a) a $2 million credit in the current account
    (b) a $2 million debit in the capital account
    (c) both (a) and (b)
    (d) no record because the transaction was of agricultural equipment

EXERCISES (parts of Exercise 2 are on the Appendix)

1. Assume that the Bank of England is trying to maintain a fixed rate of about £1 = $2.40. Given demand and supply curves as on the graph at the right, will it have to be prepared to buy or to sell pounds to maintain the price? _____buy_____ About how much? _____ɔ̃ʰˢ_____

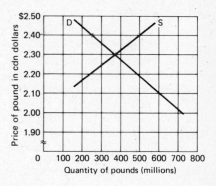

2. What policies are appropriate to the reduction of the payments deficit in question 1 (regardless of their desirability on other grounds)? A sentence or two on each subject is sufficient.
   (a) Exports of merchandise

   (b) Imports of merchandise

   (c) Tourism abroad

   (d) Interest rates

   (e) Government expenditures to stimulate domestic employment

   (f) Tax treatment of investment income (of foreigners in England and of English investment abroad)

3. Arrange the following balance-of-payments items into current-account, capital-account, and official-reserve-account groupings. Compute the balance-of-payments deficit, surplus, or equilibrium position. (Figures are in millions of dollars.)

(a) Long-term capital receipts $ 1,305
(b) Merchandise exports   17,785
(c) Freight and shipping receipts   1,170
(d) Freight and shipping payments   1,147
(e) Short-term capital receipts   1,182
(f) Changes in official reserves   + 777
(g) Merchandise imports   15,556
(h) Long-term capital payments   814
(i) Short-term capital payments   1,158
(j) Interest and dividend receipts   545
(k) Interest and dividend payments   1,613
(l) Other current-account payments   721
(m) Net travel payments   201

4. Suppose that Canada has adopted a flexible exchange-rate system and that the current price of a Canadian dollar in terms of American dollars is .98. That is, 98 U.S. cents equal 1 Canadian dollar. The diagram below depicts this situation.

   Various factors that will shift the demand curve or supply curve of Canadian dollars are listed below. Indicate how each factor will affect the appropriate curve by inserting a check mark in the correct column. Then decide how each factor will affect the price of Canadian dollars. (For example, if you anticipate the price to rise above 98 U.S. cents, insert a + sign.)

(a) an increase in U.S. income
(b) a reduction in the Canadian interest rate
(c) increased oil imports into the United States from Canada
(d) more inflation in Canada than in the United States
(e) increased tariffs on U.S. goods coming into Canada

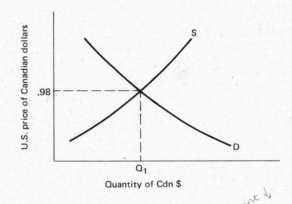

import ↓

Factor	Demand Curve	Supply Curve	Increases (+) in Price Decreases (−) in Price
(a)	+		+
(b)		+	−
(c)	+		+
(d)	−		+

PROBLEM

MR. COYNE AND THE EXCHANGE RATE

During the period between 1958 and 1961, a serious conflict of policies existed between the Bank of Canada and the federal government. The Diefenbaker government faced a serious unemployment problem. The unemployment rate was at a post-war high of about 6 to 7 percent during this period. On the other hand, even though the annual rate of increase in prices was less than 2 percent, Mr. Coyne, the Governor of the Bank of Canada, was worried about inflation, or perhaps future inflation. Hence, a basic difference in opinions existed.

Under Mr. Coyne's direction, the Bank pursued an extremely tight money policy by allowing exceptionally small increases in the money supply and unusually large increases in the interest rate. The highest increase occurred during 1958 and 1959 as a result of the Conversion Loan, which induced holders of war bonds to hold new bonds at higher rates of interest. As a consequence, the Canadian-United States long-term bond differential increased significantly.

During this period, Canada had a flexible exchange rate with the rest of the world. During most of the period, the price of Canadian dollars rose steadily, selling at a premium relative to the American dollar. In addition, large surpluses on the capital account occurred.

The situation became completely untenable. The government dismissed Mr. Coyne in June 1961. Soon afterward, in his budget speech, the Minister of Finance announced in the Commons that the government felt the exchange rate was too high and intended to use the Exchange Fund to reduce it. The price of the dollar immediately crashed and the government was finally forced to peg the dollar at 92.5 U.S. cents in May 1962. It was not until 1970 that the dollar was freed again.

Questions

1. Why do you think Canada was receiving large amounts of capital inflows during 1958-1961?

2. Why do you think the price of Canadian dollars was rising steadily? Use a diagram in your analysis.

3. What effect would you predict on Canada's exports as a result of the increased price of Canadian dollars? Show this in your diagram in question 2.

4. What would you predict the effect to be on imports into Canada as a result of the increased price of Canadian dollars? Show this in your diagram in question 2.

5. If you had been an exchange-rate speculator in 1961, would you have bought or sold Canadian dollars after hearing the Minister of Finance's speech in the Commons? If all other speculators had acted like you, would this have corresponded with the fact that the Canadian dollar crashed downward between 1961 and 1962?

Chapter Thirty-eight
The Gains
from Trade

CHECKLIST | Make certain that you understand the following concepts: gains from trade; absolute advantage; comparative advantage; learning by doing; terms of trade.

REVIEW QUESTIONS

1. Gains from trade between nations are (unlike/similar) to those from trade between individuals and regions. Trade allows _____ *specialization* _____ to occur; otherwise a nation, a region, or an individual must be _____ *self-sufficient* _____. Trade (raises/lowers) living standards, because a (greater/smaller) total output may thus be produced.

2. If an equal quantity of resources can produce more of product X in country A than in country B, A is said to have a(n) _____ *absolute advantage* _____ advantage over B in the production of X. For trade to take place, it is a (necessary but not sufficient/sufficient but not necessary) condition for B to have an absolute advantage in the production of some other commodity.

3. The gains from specialization and trade depend on the existence of _____ *comparative* _____ _____ *advantage* _____. Gains from trade are (possible/impossible) if one country can produce all commodities more efficiently than the other.

4. Suppose that country A is 10 times more efficient than country B in producing watches, and 5 times more efficient than B in producing dairy products. A has a comparative advantage in _____ *watch* _____, and B in _____ *dairy product* _____. A should specialize in and export _____ *watch* _____ to B; B should specialize in and export _____ *dairy product* _____ to A.

5. Comparative advantage can be restated in terms of _____ *opportunity* _____ costs. This avoids the problem of comparing real resource costs, because it expresses costs in terms of the _____ *output that otherwise could be produced* _____.

6. Opportunity costs depend on (absolute/relative) costs. Differing opportunity costs in two countries result in (absolute/comparative) advantage for one country.

7. Specialization may permit further gains from trade to occur if it results in the producers of a product becoming more _____ *skilled* _____, or if there are economics of _____ *scale* _____. As production expands, opportunity costs will (rise/fall) and gains from trade will (rise/fall).

8. If expanding production of a good with a comparative advantage results in long-run increasing costs in a country, opportunity cost of that good will (rise/fall) and comparative advantage will (increase/decrease).

9. The division of the gains from trade between nations depends on the so-called terms of _____trade_____. These are defined as the quantity of ___domestic goods___ that must be given up to obtain a unit of _____imports_____, in other words, the _____opp._____ cost of obtaining imports. If the opportunity cost of obtaining imports is less than that of producing the same goods at home, it makes sense to (import them/produce them at home).

10. As with other prices, the terms of trade are determined by conditions of _____demand_____ and _____supply_____ in the markets of the products concerned.

_____

    If you have not answered all questions correctly, review the text in order to be sure that you have all of the important concepts clearly in mind before going on to the next chapter.

1. similar; specialization, self-sufficient; raises, greater 2. absolute; sufficient but not necessary 3. comparative advantage; possible 4. watches, dairy products; watches, dairy products 5. opportunity; output that otherwise could be produced 6. relative; comparative 7. skilled, scale; fall, rise 8. rise, decrease 9. trade; domestic goods, imports, opportunity; import them 10. demand, supply
_____

MULTIPLE-CHOICE QUESTIONS

1. The doctrine of comparative advantage says that there are gains from international trade
   (a) only if both comparative and absolute advantage are present
   (b) if opportunity costs are the same in the countries involved
   (c) only if there are economics of scale available
   (d) if countries specialize in the production of goods in which they are *relatively* more efficient

2. A country is relatively more efficient than another in producing a good if
   (a) it produces it more cheaply in terms of alternate goods not produced
   (b) it produces it at lower money cost
   (c) it has lower wage levels
   (d) there are economics of scale available

3. Inaugurating trade with nations whose wage levels are much lower
   (a) will lower the real wages in the high-wage nation
   (b) will probably raise per capita real income in both countries
   (c) may help political relationships but does not contribute economically
   (d) will lower the real wages in low-wage nations

4. Nations through trade
   (a) may consume at levels beyond their production-possibilities frontiers
   (b) will be limited in their consumption to points on the production-possibilities frontier
   (c) will not alter their previous production patterns
   (d) are more likely to be confined to choices inside their production-possibilities frontiers

5. Which of these statements represents the *least* appropriate use of the concept of opportunity cost?
   (a) Exports can be thought of as the opportunity cost of imports.
   (b) The opportunity cost of product B is the amount of product A that could be produced with the same resources.
   (c) The opportunity cost of increased output may be measured by leisure given up to produce the output.
   (d) The opportunity cost of producing C is the sum of its fixed and variable costs.

6. Tweedledum has a comparative advantage over Tweedledee in planting as compared with harvesting.
   (a) Tweedledum must have an absolute advantage over Tweedledee in planting.
   (b) Tweedledum must have a comparative advantage over Tweedledee in harvesting.
   (c) Tweedledee must have an absolute advantage over Tweedledum in planting.
   (d) Tweedledee must have a comparative advantage over Tweedledum in harvesting.

7. A country would welcome an improvement in its terms of trade because
   (a) it can then export more
   (b) its exchange rate will rise
   (c) the cost of its imports will fall in terms of what it must give up to get them
   (d) it now becomes cheaper to produce the same goods at home instead of importing them

8. In the case of a country with one important exported commodity (like oil) and fixed exchange rates
   (a) a rise in its price in international markets will improve the country's terms of trade
   (b) a fall in its price will improve the terms of trade
   (c) its terms of trade will be unaffected by a change in its price, because of fixed exchange rates
   (d) a rise in its price will be helpful to the terms of trade and balance of payments only if world demand for it is elastic

EXERCISES

1. Assume that Lichtenstein (L) and Andorra (A) with equal resources (very few) can produce the following (in addition to postage stamps):

	Grapes	or	Wool
Lichtenstein	100,000 kilos		100,000 kilos
Andorra	50,000 kilos		100,000

   (a) Before trade, L produces 50,000 kilos of each and A produced 25,000 of grapes and 50,000 of wool. Show that trade has the potential of increasing total consumption for the two countries.

(b) A has a comparative advantage in _____Wool_____ and L has a comparative advantage in _____grapes_____.

(c) The opportunity cost of grapes in terms of wool is _____2_____ in A and _____1_____ in L. Therefore, the terms of trade will be between _____ and _____1_____.

2. If country A gives up the opportunity to produce 100 pounds of dairy products for each watch it makes, and B could produce 1 watch for each 200 pounds of dairy products it produces:

   (a) the opportunity cost of making watches (in terms of dairy products) is lower in country _____A_____.

   (b) the opportunity cost of making dairy products (in terms of watches) is lower in country _____B_____.

   (c) So country B should specialize in _____dairy_____ and let country A produce _____watch_____.

   (d) The terms of trade (the price of one product in terms of the other) would be somewhere between _____100_____ and _____200_____ pounds of dairy products for 1 watch.

3. The *Economic Review* of the Department of Finance measures terms of trade by means of an index calculated by dividing the price index of exports by the price index of imports.

   (a) If the price index of Canadian exports in 1972 was 126.8 and the price index of imports was 127.9, what was the index of the terms of trade? _____
   In 1970, the index of the terms of trade was 100. Would 1972 or 1970 be considered more favorable for Canada? _____

   (b) In 1973 there was a sudden sharp rise in the price of agricultural products and raw materials, major export products. *Ceteris paribus,* would you expect the terms of trade to become more or less favorable? _____ In fact, in 1973 the export price index rose from 126.8 to 145.0 while the import index rose from 127.9 to 139.3, an increase in the terms of trade index from _____ to _____.

PROBLEM

BREAKING THROUGH THE PRODUCTION-POSSIBILITIES FRONTIER WITH TRADE

In each of the cases below, assume a two-nation, two-product model in which no trade is taking place. The two nations, Austerity and Bacchanalia, henceforth referred to as A and B, make their production and consumption choices between products X and Y. Assume that both nations have identical patterns of tastes and preferences and that they are such that, when the products are equal in price, equal quantities will be consumed. In each case, after trade commences, assume that the prices are equal and that the consumption of X and the consumption of Y will be equal in each country. Perfect competition is assumed in product markets.

In each of the graphs below, you are given the production-possibilities frontier and the price and quantity produced and consumed before trade (indicated by the dots). The before-trade relative prices (P_X/P_Y) are given by the slope of the production-possibilities curve. Show the amount that will be produced and consumed by each after trade when $P_X = P_Y$. Note that when trade does take place, each nation in its consumption will have broken through its production-possibilities frontier. For questions on absolute advantage you should assume the same quantities of factors in each country.

Complete the table below on the before-trade conditions as you work with each case.

Before-Trade Conditions	1	2 (and 2a)	3	4	5
Opportunity cost of X (in terms of Y) in country A[a]	_____	_____	_____	_____	25/36
Opportunity cost of X (in terms of Y) in country B[a]	_____	_____	_____	_____	36/25
P_X/P_Y in country A	_____	_____	_____	_____	_____
P_X/P_Y in country B	_____	_____	_____	_____	_____

[a]At existing production levels.

Case 1

(a) A has an absolute advantage in the production of _____. B has an absolute advantage in the production of _____. Therefore, A has a comparative advantage in the production of _____ and is at a comparative disadvantage in the production of _____.

(b) With the opening of trade, A will produce _____ of product _____; B will produce _____ of product _____. With $P_X = P_Y$, A will export _____ units of product _____ and import _____ units of product _____.

(c) Both countries will have gained because A can now consume _____ more units of _____ and B _____ more units of _____, each while maintaining its consumption of the other product. P_X/P_Y is greater than before in country _____ and less than before in country _____.

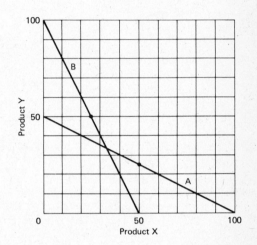

Cases 2 and 2a

(a) In case 2, there (is/is not) an absolute advantage for either; there (is/is not) a comparative advantage for either.

(b) In case 2a, country A has a(n) _____ advantage in both products. It has no _____ advantage because opportunity costs are the _____, as reflected in relative prices of the products, which are _____. There (will/will not) be trade.

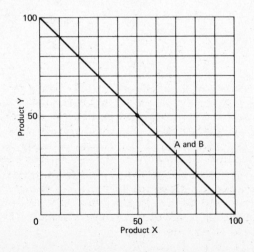

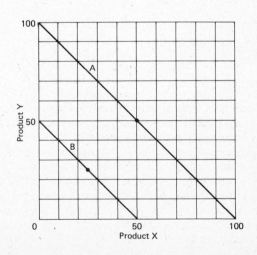

Case 3

Again, in this case there is apparently no absolute advantage or comparative advantage.

(a) This case differs from case 2, where opportunity costs were constant, since when either country expands its production of X or Y units it encounters _____ opportunity costs for that production in terms of the other. If trade is opened up, it therefore will pay one country, say A, to _____ in the output of X, and the other country, say, B, to _____ in the output of Y.

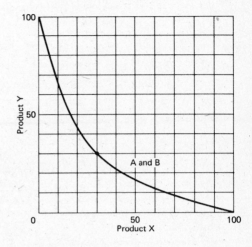

(b) With such specialization, A will establish a comparative advantage in X and B in Y, and with $P_X = P_Y$, A will export _____ of X in exchange for _____ of Y. Both countries will be at consumption levels beyond their _____ and will have gained by trade _____ units of each commodity.

Case 4

(a) A has _____ advantages in production of both X and Y, but B has a(n) _____ advantage in the production of Y.

(b) At an after-trade P_X/P_Y of 1, which is less than B's before-trade price ratio of 8/5 (reflecting the opportunity costs), the producers in B will choose to specialize in the production of _____. By exporting 40 units of Y in return for _____ units of X, B can consume _____ X and _____ Y, a gain of _____ X.

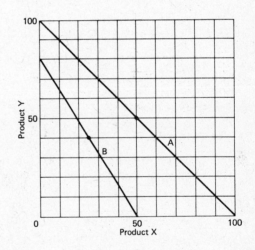

(c) If country A chooses to produce 90 of X and 10 of Y, it will be able to (increase/maintain) its before-trade consumption.

Note

You may be concerned about why the gains of trade go entirely to B. This reflects the assumption both of perfect competition and of the particular demand conditions that allowed P_Y to continue to equal P_X. For A to gain, it would be necessary that the after-trade price ratio be more favorable for product X, in which it has the comparative advantage. The complexities of this problem of price determination belong in a more advanced course in international trade, but the student should recognize this much: If country A can keep the price ratio of X:Y just below 8:5, B's producers will still find it profitable to offer Y in trade because trading for X will be cheaper than producing it. One way of accomplishing this would be for A to place a tariff on product Y of almost 60 percent ($37\frac{1}{2}/62\frac{1}{2}$). B could then get only $.62\frac{1}{2}X+$ instead of 1X for each unit of Y, and most of the gains of trade would go to A.

Case 5

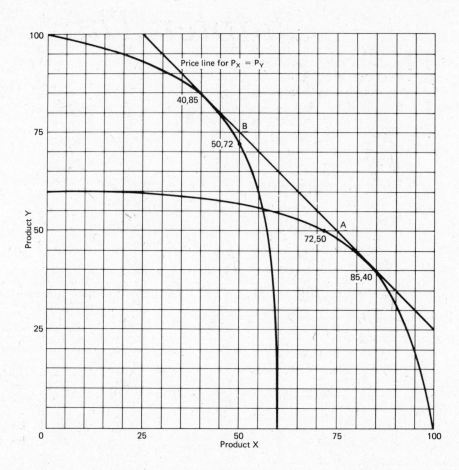

Price line for $P_X = P_Y$

40,85

B

50,72

A

72,50

85,40

Product Y

Product X

(a) In this case, the opportunity costs vary with the production level. In each country, the opportunity cost of each product becomes _____, the more that is produced. For any given production level, the opportunity costs in A are less for product _____ and in B for product _____. Thus, the comparative advantage in A is for product _____ and in B for product _____.

(b) Even with trade complete, specialization will not occur because the opportunity costs become very _____ as all resources are devoted to the output of one good. Cases 1, 2, and 4 can be termed as cases of constant costs, case 3 as one of decreasing costs, and this case as one of _____ costs.

(c) Trade can take place at $P_X = P_Y$ because in country A at before-trade consumption levels the opportunity cost of producing more X is _____ than 1Y, and in country B the opportunity cost of producing more Y is _____ than 1X. Thus, A will _____ its production of X from 72 to 85, where the opportunity cost is _____ Y, and B will increase its production of Y from 72 to 85, where the opportunity cost is _____ X.

(d) Total production of X for both countries together is now _____, instead of the before-trade _____. Total production of Y is likewise _____, instead of the before-trade _____.

(e) To achieve the equal consumption of both commodities called for by the demand assumptions, A will export _____ in return for _____. This new consumption point can be found on the graph on the price line with the slope of 1, which is _____ to the production-possibilities frontiers at the points of after-trade _____.

Chapter Thirty-nine
Tariffs

REVIEW QUESTIONS

1. Tariffs are used for two different and opposite purposes: _____ *protection* _____ and _____ *revenue* _____. A tariff makes imported goods (cheaper/more expensive).

2. If a country can produce all it needs of a product, there will be no demand for imports of it unless the price of the import is _____ *less* _____ than the price of the domestic product.

3. A domestic producer with costs 10 percent above foreign producers of the same item would be protected from foreign competition by a tariff of at least _____ *10%* _____ percent.

4. A nontariff barrier that allows only a limited quantity of imports of a good per year is called a _____ *quota* _____.

5. A country's government might rationally choose to use tariffs, if instead of complete specialization in only one commodity it preferred the goal of _____ *diversification* _____. Diversification might be preferable to specialization in one or two products, if the specialized product is one that suffers sharp fluctuations in *price or demand*.

6. National defense is used as an argument for a protectionist policy in such industries as _____ *shipping* _____ and _____ *oil* _____.

7. A developing country might justify tariffs to protect its _____ *infant industry*. This is a valid argument only if expanded production results in *economies of scales*

8. Judging from the amount of world trade, it is apparent that most tariffs at present are (very protective/not serious) barriers to trade.

9. Tariffs are usually used to protect industries that are (much less/only a little less) efficient than foreign producers.

If you have not answered all questions correctly, review the text in order to be sure that you have all of the important concepts clearly in mind before going on to the next chapter.

1. protection, revenue; more expensive 2. less 3. 10 4. quota 5. diversification; price or demand 6. shipping, oil 7. infant industries; economics of scale 8. not serious 9. only a little less

MULTIPLE-CHOICE QUESTIONS

1. From the point of view of the domestic standard of living, a country should
   (a) welcome cheap imports
   (b) try to expand exports
   (c) impose tariffs to keep out foreign competition
   (d) try to be self-sufficient

2. Lower wages in other countries than in Canada
   (a) create unfair competition for Canadian labour
   (b) mean that those countries cannot gain from trade with Canada
   (c) mean that Canadian costs are bound to be higher
   (d) may reflect lower labour productivity and higher unit costs abroad

3. Which of the following would *not* be a valid reason for imposing a tariff?
   (a) to protect an infant industry that will eventually be competitive
   (b) to diversify the economy
   (c) to maximize real income
   (d) to maintain a vital but high-cost defense industry

4. The principle of comparative costs indicates that
   (a) free trade is invariably best
   (b) free trade is hardly ever best
   (c) free trade is better than some trade
   (d) mutually advantageous trade is possible

5. The gains from the removal of tariff barriers within the Common Market have been estimated to be
   (a) very large
   (b) negative
   (c) significant but fairly small
   (d) zero

6. The infant-industry argument for tariffs
   (a) is recognized as wrong because protection often extends beyond infancy
   (b) is recognized as wrong because it is present and not future comparative advantage that should be considered
   (c) is recognized as theoretically sound if economies of scale exist
   (d) says that industries should be protected in poor countries to provide for the welfare of infants there

7. Canadians who feel that it is worth a cut in living standards for such purposes as national identity or independent cultural development are
   (a) irrational
   (b) irrational if the cut they are willing to take is very high
   (c) not aware of the principle of comparative costs
   (d) making value judgments that cannot be directly refuted by the classical case for trade

8. The "Buy Canadian" argument for tariffs
   (a) is economically valid
   (b) states that dollars spent on foreign goods will be used for Canadian exports
   (c) should be recognized as usually being fallacious
   (d) is a defense of tariffs as revenue-raising measures

9. A general increase of import duties by a nation during a time of unemployment
   (a) is unlikely to produce any short-run increase of income and employment
   (b) should prove a very substantial stimulus to employment
   (c) would have the same effect on the allocation of resources as an export subsidy
   (d) would have a mild expansionary effect on the economy provided others do not fully retaliate

10. If Japan became able to undersell Canada on all commodities at existing exchange rates,
   (a) Japan would continue to export to Canada but receive no imports
   (b) either the dollar would depreciate in terms of the yen or trade would very soon cease
   (c) Japan would continue to import from Canada but send no exports
   (d) Japan's exports to and imports from Canada would balance every year

EXERCISE

Listed below are short paraphrases of pro- or anti-tariff arguments that the text suggests are fallacious. Give a brief refutation. (Your choice may not necessarily be the same as the suggested answers.)

(a) Trade is exploitation.

(b) Buy Canadian and keep the money here.

(c) Protect Canadians against sweatshop labour.

(d) A tariff for infant industries is forever.

(e) Imports lower national income.

PROBLEM

DUMPING AND REQUESTS FOR ADDITIONAL EXCISE TAXES

The following excerpt is taken from the Toronto *Globe and Mail,* August 12, 1975.

Ottawa Finds Dumping of Color Television Sets
The Department of National Revenue has issued a preliminary finding of dumping involving color television sets made by about 20 companies in the United States, Japan, Taiwan, and Singapore.
Dumping is selling a foreign market at prices less than those charged in the home market.
The finding follows intensive lobbying by the Electronic Industries Association of Canada, which represents domestic producers, and likely will mean higher prices for consumers.
A department spokesman said that, effective July 31, importers of the television sets with screens 16 inches or larger must pay a provisional duty or post a bond to cover the amount by which the manufacturers are alleged to be dumping the televisions.
The federal Anti-dumping Tribunal now has started an inquiry to decide whether the dumping of imported TVs has harmed or may harm, the domestic industry. . . .
If it rules that no injury has occurred, then the importers' posted bonds or any additional duties paid will be refunded. If it decides the domestic industry has been harmed, the department will make a final ruling about the amount of extra duty to be paid.
The Electronic Industries Association asked the Government in May to restrict imports of color TVs claiming 46% of the one million sets with screens 16 inches or larger sold in Canada last year were imported.

Questions
1. Why would foreign producers "dump" in Canada?

2. In what sense does dumping harm the domestic industry? What might the Anti-dumping Tribunal look for?

3. If dumping is proven and a duty is imposed, how will the costs and benefits of this additional protection be distributed in Canada?

Chapter Forty
International
Economic
Experience

CHECKLIST	Make certain that you understand the following concepts: gold standard; competitive devaluation; reserve currencies; international liquidity; International Monetary Fund; special drawing rights; World Bank; Kennedy Round; Common Market; gold-exchange standard.

REVIEW QUESTIONS

1. The gold standard relied on _____fixed_____ exchange rates with adjustments brought about in domestic _____price level_____. If a country bought more goods from other countries than it sold to them, demand for _____foreign exchange_____ would exceed the supply at the fixed rates; the excess demand would be met by shipments of _____gold_____. The loss of gold in a deficit country would _____reduce_____ its money supply, while the gain in gold in the _____surplus_____ country would _____increase_____ its money supply. The changes in money supply would result in _____lower_____ prices in deficit countries and _____higher_____ prices in surplus countries. The change in price level would increase exports of _____deficit_____ countries and would _____reduce_____ exports of surplus countries, and thus move them both toward equilibrium in their _____balance of payment_____.

2. A difficult test for the gold standard came after World War I, when exchange rates were (close to/far from) equilibrium rates. Price levels adjusted slowly, and the gold standard was _____ in the 1930s when unemployment was widespread. Efforts made to _____ imports while maintaining exports (worked/did not work), and the volume of trade _____.

3. The Bretton Woods Conference in 1944 resulted in the creation of the _____ (IMF). The Fund could lend nations _____ in the face of temporary balance-of-payments deficits. It sought to prohibit the competitive devaluation of the 1930s by providing that changes in excess of _____ percent be made only after consultation with officials of the Fund.

4. The Bretton Woods Conference also provided for the establishment of the IBRD, usually called the _____. Its major concern is to facilitate _____ capital movements, particularly to developing countries. Offshoots of the World Bank are the _____ (IFC), which can make loans to firms, and the _____ (IDA), which makes loans on easier terms to less credit-worthy countries.

5. GATT, _____, encouraged bilateral negotiations
for concessions on _____ that would be extended to all member countries.
The _____ Round negotiations starting in 1964 resulted in substan-
tariff cuts which have been partly negated by quotas and other restrictions including the 10 percent surcharge announced by the United States in 1971.

6. The postwar grouping of the European Common Market (EEC) initially included, be-
sides the Benelux countries, _____, _____, and
_____. The entry of _____ was ratified in 1971.

7. The postwar gold exchange standard used dollars, convertible into _____
at approximately _____ an ounce, as international monetary reserves.
Other currencies, including the British pound, also used as a reserve currency,
were convertible into dollars, and therefore into _____, at
_____ rates.

8. After the heavy gold speculation in early 1968, the United States maintained the
$35 gold price for _____ only. The _____
market price for gold was allowed to fluctuate. In 1971, the United States sus-
pended the _____ of the dollar reserves into gold.

9. Three major problems confronted the gold-exchange standard: the provision of
_____ to iron out short-term fluctuations in international receipts and
payments, making adjustments to _____ trends in payments balances, and
meeting _____ crises. It seems likely that to meet short-
term fluctuations, _____ reserves will be needed as trade
grows.

10. A new form of exchange reserve was created in 1970, the _____
_____ (SDR) administered by the International Monetary Fund.
Creation of SDRs represents an alternative method of increasing reserves to that of
_____ the dollar price of the gold.

11. A solution to long-run disequilibria envisioned at Bretton Woods was the occasional
modification of _____. Two major rounds of devaluation,
in 1949–1950 and 1967–1968, were led by the _____. In
1971, after Germany and the Netherlands had allowed their currencies to float upward in value, the United States encouraged further upward revaluations by
_____ gold payments for dollars. One alternative to exchange-rate changes is changes in _____ price levels; such changes are
accomplished (easily/with difficulty). Restrictions on trade and foreign exchange
frequently have been used by nations to meet _____ in the balance of payments. In 1971, the United States inaugurated a temporary _____ surcharge of 10 percent.

12. Speculation is likely if expectations are high that there will be a change in
_____. In early 1968, many speculators expected that the offi-
cial dollar price of _____ would be raised, and the gold (inflow/outflow)
from the United States resulting from the speculation led to the two-tier system
of gold prices.

13. Flexible exchange rates are predicted to (reduce/increase) greatly the need for
international liquidity, or reserves. Instead of meeting the problem of long-run
disequilibria by delayed and politically difficult _____
revisions, difficult domestic price changes, or protectionism, a free market would
make gradual _____ adjustments.

14. Objections to flexible rates, particularly strong among the world's bankers, are that such a system will increase the _____ of exporters and importers and will thus _____ trade and lead to _____ speculation. Such speculation in the face of a depreciating exchange rate could lead to (a decrease/an increase) rather than (an increase/a decrease) in the quantity of that currency demanded and to (an increase/a decrease) rather than (a decrease/an increase) in the quantity supplied. Under such circumstances, the price of this currency would _____ further.

_____

        If you have not answered all questions correctly, review the text in order to be sure that you have all of the important concepts clearly in mind before going on to the next chapter.

1. fixed, price levels; foreign exchange, gold; reduce, surplus, increase; lower, higher; deficit, reduce, balance of payments 2. far from; abandoned; restrict, did not work, fell 3. International Monetary Fund; foreign exchange; 10 4. World Bank; long-term; International Finance Corporation, International Development Agency 5. the General Agreement on Tariffs and Trade, tariffs; Kennedy 6. France, Italy, West Germany; Great Britain 7. gold, $35; gold, fixed 8. official transactions (central banks); private or free; convertibility 9. reserves, long-term, speculative; increased 10. special drawing rights; increasing 11. exchange rates; British pound; suspending; domestic, with difficulty; deficits; import 12. exchange rates (gold price); gold, outflow 13. reduce; exchange-rate, price (exchange rate) 14. uncertainty, reduce, destabilizing; a decrease, an increase, an increase, a decrease; decline

_____

MULTIPLE-CHOICE QUESTIONS

1. Current Canadian loans and investments abroad
   (a) increase both current and future deficits in the balance of payments
   (b) increase current but reduce future deficits
   (c) reduce current but increase future deficits
   (d) reduce both current and future deficits in the balance of payments

2. Destabilizing speculation occurs
   (a) when lower exchange rates increase the quantity of a currency demanded
   (b) when higher exchange rates increase the quantity of a currency supplied
   (c) when there is no expectation that fixed exchange rates will be changed
   (d) when a change in exchange rates leads to expectation of further changes in the same direction

3. The major international agency making long-term development loans is
   (a) the IMF
   (b) the World Bank
   (c) GATT
   (d) the Export-Import Bank

4. Under the two-tier gold system, all but which one of the following took place?
   (a) monetary gold reserves continued to be valued at $35 an ounce
   (b) gold outside of the monetary reserve could be sold for more than $35 an ounce
   (c) industrial users continued to get gold from the U.S. Treasury for $35 an ounce
   (d) to keep prices down, governments no longer supplied gold reserves to free markets

5. Floating exchange rates
   (a) are the same as fixed rates
   (b) describe the fluctuations around fixed rates permitted by IMF rules
   (c) are necessarily destabilizing
   (d) are determined in international exchange markets

6. Under the gold standard
   (a) exchange rates fluctuated frequently
   (b) equilibrium was produced by changes in fixed exchange rates
   (c) crises of confidence were met quickly despite the small amount of gold relative to claims on it
   (d) equilibrium was supposed to be reached by changes in domestic price levels

7. Among postwar international developments were all except
   (a) the dollar shortage confronting war-torn countries which needed U.S. goods
   (b) the dollar surplus Europe and Japan accumulated as they recovered
   (c) prompt upward adjustments of undervalued currencies
   (d) considerable international cooperation to maintain stable exchange rates

8. The International Monetary Fund
   (a) is a fund for long-term development projects
   (b) was designed to assist in making exchange rates more readily flexible
   (c) was designed to help maintain fixed exchange rates in the face of short-term fluctuations
   (d) was abandoned after the dollar shortage of the early postwar years

9. Under the present international monetary arrangements,
   (a) currencies are all generally readily convertible into one another
   (b) currency exchange rates are quite flexible
   (c) it is very simple for all countries to solve their balance-of-payments problems
   (d) most major currencies are convertible, but many lesser ones are not

EXERCISE

Suppose that Canada is on a fixed exchange rate and has been experiencing a chronic balance-of-payments deficit with the United States, which is continually worsening. At the present time, the Canadian and U.S. dollars are fixed at par: C$1.00 = US$1.00.

(a) As a Canadian who is engaged in importing goods from the United States, what guarantees might you try to obtain concerning the goods which you are planning to buy during the next year? Why might you wish such guarantees?

(b) As a speculator in the foreign-exchange market, what activity might you become engaged in under the conditions described above? Explain why a speculator might undertake such activity.

(c) If the action in (b) were carried out, how would this affect the economic conditions that exist?

PROBLEM

RECYCLING OPEC DOLLARS

The foreign-exchange reserve position of a number of countries is shown below. (Figures are in billions of dollars.)

	1973	1974
Canada	$ 5.8	$ 5.8
United States	14.4	16.1
United Kingdom	6.5	6.9
Japan	12.2	13.5
OPEC (Organization of Petroleum-Exporting Countries)	4.5	14.7

Questions

1. Explain why the rise in the price of oil imposed by the OPEC countries in late 1973 contributed to the significant difference in the reserve position of the first four countries and the OPEC countries.

2. In the text, the authors point out that these reserves or "OPEC dollars" will eventually be recycled by way of trade and investment between the OPEC and other countries. Rumours have been heard that some OPEC countries are interested in investing hundreds of millions of dollars in Canada. If this were to occur, how might it affect:

(a) Canada's employment position?

(b) Canada's foreign-exchange reserve position?

3. In 1974, fixed exchange rates were in effect in many oil-importing countries. How would the foreign-exchange price of these countries' currencies have been affected if floating exchange rates had been in effect?

4. If Canada were to adopt a completely floating exchange-rate policy, how would the recycling suggested in question 2 affect:
   (a) the price of the Canadian dollar?

   (b) Canadian exports?

Chapter Forty-one
Stabilization Policy: Tools and Objectives

CHECKLIST	Make certain that you understand the following concepts: monetarists; neo-Keynesians; stabilization policy; underemployment equilibrium.

REVIEW QUESTIONS

1. By "stabilization policy" we mean trying to maintain the economy at satisfactory levels of ___employment___, without ___inflation___.

2. The monetarists believe that monetary policy is a very (weak/strong) tool of stabilization and that fiscal policy is usually (effective/ineffective).

3. That the economy has adequate self-correcting tendencies is believed by the ___monetarist___ group. That the economy probably cannot correct its tendencies toward unemployment unaided is the opinion of most ___neo-Keynesians___; they believe that fiscal policy is (more/less) potent than monetary policy.

4. Monetarists believe that changes in the money supply (cause/are caused by) changes in national income and, especially, inflation. Neo-Keynesians suggest instead that changes in the money supply are often the (result/cause) of changes in national income and inflation.

5. Neo-Keynesians believe that cyclical fluctuations are caused by changes in spending, especially for ___investment___. Keynes's theory was new in showing that the economy could be in equilibrium with a situation of ___underemployment___.

6. Neo-Keynesians argue that banks (increase/decrease) loans and therefore deposits (money supply) in response to good times, and (contract/expand) loans and deposits in response to depressed times. Thus changes in national income (cause/are caused by) changes in the money supply.

7. Monetarists believe that changes in interest rates affect the demand for and supply of money (much/little) but affect spending (much/little). But they believe that changes in the money supply have (much/little) effect on interest rates. Thus in their view monetary policy has a (powerful/weak) influence on spending.

8. Monetarists believe that fiscal policy is rather ineffective, because a rise in government spending causes interest rates to (rise/fall), thus "crowding out" ___private spending___. Also, the effect of government spending may be confused with the effect of increasing the money supply if it is financed indirectly by open-market (purchases/sales) of government bonds.

9. Neo-Keynesians believe that the demand for and the supply of money are (sensitive/insensitive) to changes in interest rates, but that aggregate expenditure is interest (elastic/inelastic). Thus monetary policy achieves (small/large) changes in interest rates and (small/large) changes in spending. The use of fiscal policy, in their view, causes (small/large) changes in interest rates and therefore a (small/large) "crowding out" effect.

10. The monetarists favor a neutral monetary policy in which the money supply is allowed to _____ *increase* _____ at about the same rate as _____ *real G.N.P* _____. Neo-Keynesians believe in using (only fiscal/only monetary/both fiscal and monetary) policy. They are, however, concerned about the uneven effect of _____ *monetary* _____ policy on small businesses and housing construction.

11. A decision to use monetary policy can be made (faster/more slowly) than a decision about fiscal policy, but the effects of the former operate with (more/less) uncertainly and (longer/shorter) time lags.

If you have not answered all questions correctly, review the text in order to be sure that you have all of the important concepts clearly in mind before going on to the next chapter.

1. employment, inflation 2. strong, ineffective 3. monetarist; neo-Keynesians, more 4. cause; result 5. investment; underemployment 6. increase, contract; cause 7. little, much; much; powerful 8. rise, private spending; purchases 9. sensitive, inelastic; small, small; small, small 10. increase, real GNP; both fiscal and monetary; monetary 11. faster, more, longer

---

MULTIPLE-CHOICE QUESTIONS

1. In the view of the monetarist group of economists,
   (a) changes in the money supply should be used often as a countercyclical tool
   (b) interest rates have very little effect on spending
   (c) the economy will not recover by itself from recessions
   (d) inflation is caused by excessive increases in the supply of money

2. The economists called neo-Keynesians in this chapter
   (a) do not agree with Keynes that investment spending is important in causing a rise in national income
   (b) believe that fiscal policy is a more effective stabilization tool than monetary policy
   (c) are opposed entirely to the use of monetary policy
   (d) believe that investment spending is very interest elastic

3. The monetary policy advocated by the monetarists
   (a) is one of growth in the money supply at about 3.5 percent per year
   (b) would use controls on and changes in interest rates to affect GNP
   (c) would be determined primarily by Parliament
   (d) includes the active use of fiscal policy as well

4. As compared with fiscal policy, monetary policy
   (a) can be decided quickly but may have a longer time lag in its effects
   (b) takes longer to put into operation, but the effects are quicker
   (c) is subject to more political obstacles in its formulation
   (d) is made by the Economic Council of Canada

Appendix
5. A shift to the right in the IS curve could be produced by
    (a) a cut in government expenditures
    (b) an increase in the reserve ratio
    (c) an increase in personal exemptions for the income tax
    (d) a decrease in personal exemptions for the income tax

6. A very flat IS curve would indicate
    (a) a high marginal propensity to consume
    (b) a balanced government budget
    (c) a low elasticity for the MEI
    (d) high sensitivity of investment to interest rates

7. A very flat LM curve would indicate
    (a) an interest-elastic demand for money
    (b) a tight monetary policy
    (c) a balanced federal government budget
    (d) unchanging reserve requirements

EXERCISE

Insert an M for monetarist or a K for neo-Keynesian after the statements below.

(a) The demand for money, especially for the speculative motive, is quite sensitive to interest rates. _K_
(b) The demand for money is quite insensitive to interest rates but depends mostly on income and transactions demand. _M_
(c) The cause of inflation and changes in national income is found primarily in changes in the supply of money. _M_
(d) Investment spending is much more responsive to profit expectations than to changes in interest rates. _K_
(e) Changes in the money supply may be a response to, rather than the cause of, changes in GNP and the price level. _K_
(f) Fiscal policy only works to the extent that it affects the supply of money. _M_
(g) Monetary policy is uncertain, variable, powerful, and lagged in its effects; therefore it should be as neutral as possible. _M_
(h) Fiscal policy has more general effects on the economy, whereas monetary policy affects primarily interest rates and therefore has too much effect on housing and small businesses. _K_

PROBLEM

INFLATION AND THE NOMINAL RATE OF INTEREST

The previous chapters have stressed the analysis that increases in the money supply should lead to decreases in the interest rate. However, monetarists stress that the nominal rate of interest depends positively on the real rate of interest and the rate of price inflation. Excessive expansion in the money supply, as is argued by the monetarists, is a key determinant of price inflation.

Canada's inflationary experience in the early 1970s has been an unhappy one, even though the inflation rates in most western European countries and Japan have been higher than that of Canada.

Professors Harry Johnson and Thomas Courchene have been critical of the Bank of Canada's overly expansionary monetary policy and its reluctance to allow the price of the Canadian dollar to appreciate on the world market.[1] It is argued that both of these policies have contributed significantly to the rate of inflation in Canada. The "dirty float" policy (the Bank of Canada's unwillingness to allow the dollar to appreciate) has meant that Canada "imports" more inflation from abroad than would be the case under a flexible exchange-rate policy.

The following table provides some of the evidence for Canada during the early 1970s.

Year	Percent Change in the Money Supply		Percent Change in the Consumer Price Index	Canadian Bond Rate (range)
	M_1	M_2		
1971	17.4	15.9	2.8	6.56 to 7.30
1972	13.6	16.5	4.8	7.12 to 7.46
1973	11.2	15.0	7.6	7.30 to 7.74
1974	7.2	19.9	10.9	8.19 to 8.77
1975 (first quarter)	25.8	21.6	11.7	8.47

Professor Courchene also stresses that the relevant money supply magnitude is M_2 rather than M_1. This is closely in tune with the monetarist's position.

Questions

1. From the evidence provided, is there a relationship between change in M_2 and changes in the price level?

2. What relationship exists between changes in the price index and the nominal rate of interest?

[1] Harry G. Johnson, "Inflation, Unemployment, and the Floating Rate," *Canadian Public Policy,* Spring 1975; Thomas Courchene, "Canadian Monetary Policy Under Fixed and Floating Exchange Rates: The 1969-74 Experience," unpublished monograph, delivered at the Conference on Canadian Monetary Issues, Queens University, August 1975.

3. Calculate the "real" rate of interest between 1971 and 1975. (See Chapter 22 for this discussion.)

4. If you have been a holder of bonds in 1974, what would you have done?

5. Why would allowing the price of Canadian dollars to appreciate help to prevent the importation of inflation from abroad?

Chapter Forty-two
Conflicts of Policy
in Developed
Countries

> **CHECKLIST** Make certain that you understand the following concepts: instrumental variables; policy variable (target variable); structural unemployment; demand-pull inflation; cost-push inflation; wage-price guidelines; Phillips curve; income policies; wage drift; expenditure-dampening policies; expenditure switching; X-inefficiency; technology gap.

REVIEW QUESTIONS

1. Four major macroeconomic goals studied here are _____ *no unemployment* _____, _____ *balance of payment equilb.* _____ *stable price level* _____, and _____ *economic growth* _____.

2. (a) When fiscal policy is used to increase employment, government spending and taxes would be the _____ *instrument* _____ variables, and the level of employment would be the _____ *policy* _____ variable.
   (b) When monetary policy is used to curb inflation, the money supply or the level of interest rates would be the _____ *instrument* _____ variables. What would be the policy variable? _____ *the price level* _____

3. Two major alleged causes of serious unemployment are _____ *recession unemployment* _____ and _____ *structural change* _____. A persistent pocket of high unemployment in a region or an industry is an example of _____ *structural* _____ unemployment.

4. Unemployment resulting from general recession can be reduced by government policy measures that increase _____ *AD* _____. Retraining or relocating workers is usually necessary to reduce _____ *structural* _____ unemployment.

5. The condition where the price level rises because of excessive total spending is termed _____ *demand-pull* _____ inflation. If the price level rises because unit costs rise for reasons unassociated with excess demand, and these rises are passed on to the public, it is termed _____ *cost-push* _____ inflation. If the price level rises because producers use wage increases as an excuse to raise prices, even though unit costs have not risen, it is termed _____ *price-push* _____ inflation. It is possible for the price level to rise because resources move (rapidly/slowly) from one use to another, so that excess (demand/supply) in a potentially expanding industry pushes price up. However, contracting industries may (reduce/not reduce) their price, so prices rise on the average; this is the theory of _____ *structural rigidity* _____.

6. Policies to reduce aggregate expenditure would be an appropriate weapon against (demand-pull/cost-push) inflation. An example of such a policy is ___*tax ↑*___ _____.

7. "Wage-price guidelines," "income policies," and appeals for restraint are weapons often used against ___*cost push*___ inflation. In inflation of this sort, price behavior reflects the existence of strong (competitive/monopolistic) elements.

8. It is generally felt that the adoption of (flexible/fixed) exchange rates will improve the effectiveness of domestic stabilization policy.

9. President Nixon's order in August 1971 to freeze wages and prices for three months was an example of the use of ___*income*___ policy, indicating that the situation was thought to be one of (demand-pull/cost-push) inflation.

10. Inflation can cause balance-of-payments problems by encouraging (exports/imports) and discouraging (exports/imports).

11. Expenditure-dampening policies to restrain inflation will tend to make balance-of-payments deficits (less/greater).

12. Fiscal policy measures to reduce unemployment through increases in aggregate demand will tend to make balance-of-payments deficits (less/greater).

13. A fall in interest rates at home relative to those abroad is likely to cause an (inflow/outflow) of capital and therefore make a balance-of-payments deficit (larger/smaller). Thus, an easy-money policy is (good/bad) for employment but (good/bad) for the balance of payments.

14. The worry that other nations will retaliate has sometimes limited the usefulness of expenditure-___*switching*___ policies for reducing a balance-of-payments deficit.

15. If a high rate of investment is important for economic growth, policies for increasing the rate of economic growth would be the (same as/reverse of) policies appropriate for reducing unemployment.

16. The L-shaped relation and the Phillips curve both relate the rate of unemployment to ___*change in price level*___.

17. The L-shaped relation assumes that prices (remain stable/rise) until full employment is reached; at that point, further increases in aggregate demand would cause ___*inflation*___. This relationship assumes that as unemployment increases, average prices (fall/remain the same).

18. The Phillips curve suggests that full employment without inflation is (possible/impossible). Prices begin to rise (before/not until) full employment is reached. The greater the rate of unemployment, the (greater/less) the rate of inflation. Accordingly, policy measures to stop inflation will cause ___*unemployment*___, whereas policies to achieve full employment will cause ___*inflation*___.

19. Because Canada has a high marginal propensity to import, any policy to increase employment and income will have a relatively (large/small) adverse effect on the balance of payments.

20. As incomes rise with long-run economic growth, the change in demand for various commodities will depend on their ___*income elasticities*___ of demand.

21. Demand for food has a relatively (low/high) income elasticity; demand for services such as hotels and medical care has a relatively (low/high) income elasticity. The proportion of Canadian workers employed in agriculture has (fallen/risen) and in services has (fallen/risen) greatly during this century.

22. If an industry's productivity rises by 5 percent and demand rises by 2 percent, employment in the industry will (rise/fall) and output will (rise/fall).

23. The evidence indicates that technological unemployment is a (temporary/permanent) problem, hitting (all/only some) industries. Thus, there (is/is not) a conflict between policies for growth and policies for reducing unemployment.

If you have not answered all questions correctly, review the text in order to be sure that you have all of the important concepts clearly in mind before going on to the next chapter.

1. full employment; price stability; balance of payments equilibrium; economic growth
2. instrumental, policy; instrumental, the price level 3. recession or insufficient aggregate demand, structural changes; structural 4. aggregate demand; structural
5. demand-pull; cost-push; price-push; slowly, demand; not reduce, structural rigidity
6. demand-pull; tax increase or high interest rates 7. cost-push; monopolistic
8. flexible 9. incomes; cost-push 10. imports; exports 11. less 12. greater
13. outflow, larger; good, bad 14. switching 15. same as 16. changes in price level
17. remain stable, inflation; remain the same 18. impossible; before; less; unemployment, inflation 19. large 20. income elasticities 21. low, high; fallen, risen
22. fall; rise 23. temporary, only some; is not

MULTIPLE-CHOICE QUESTIONS

1. A rise in interest rates would probably involve a conflict between the goals of
   (a) stable prices and balance-of-payments equilibrium
   (b) tighter money and reduction of aggregate expenditures
   (c) higher taxes and deflation
   (d) stable prices and increased residential home building

2. Expenditure-dampening policies would involve a conflict between the goals of
   (a) balance-of-payments equilibrium and freer world trade
   (b) more employment and faster growth
   (c) balance-of-payments equilibrium and stable prices
   (d) balance-of-payments equilibrium and more employment

3. A 3-percent wage increase, accompanied by a 3-percent rise in labour productivity,
   (a) will increase unit costs and therefore prices
   (b) will not increase unit labour costs
   (c) will reduce profits
   (d) leaves the worker no better off than before

4. The inflation in Canada during the 1968–1971 period
   (a) occurred while there was considerable unemployment and so resembled the cost-push type
   (b) is explained entirely by demand-pull
   (c) was apparently caused by a high rate of growth
   (d) resulted from shortages and bottlenecks

5. The inflation in the United States in the late 1960s
   (a) can best be explained by the structural-rigidity hypothesis
   (b) seems quite clearly the result of excessive aggregate demand
   (c) was successfully quenched by monetary and fiscal policy by 1968
   (d) was primarily the cost-push type

6. The rate of unemployment
   (a) is an instrumental variable with which we influence fiscal policy
   (b) is an intermediate variable with which we can affect the government deficit
   (c) is a policy variable that can be affected by the instrumental variable of
       aggregate expenditures
   (d) is unaffected by changes in aggregate demand

7. The rate of unemployment in the Maritimes is
   (a) higher than in Ontario
   (b) partly a problem of structural unemployment
   (c) unevenly distributed by industry
   (d) all of the above

8. Wage-price guidelines assume that
   (a) inflation is the demand-pull type
   (b) there is much competition in all markets
   (c) all firms behave in a way to maximize profits
   (d) many wage and price decisions are within the discretionary power of union
       leaders and monopolistic firms

9. Policies such as lower taxes and lower interest rates
   (a) will help the balance of payments but not investment
   (b) will help employment but possible have adverse effects on the balance of pay-
       ments
   (c) will help employment but not economic growth
   (d) will help the balance of payments but will cause inflation

10. Policy conflicts in the 1960s in Canada were
    (a) between guns and butter
    (b) between less unemployment and price stability
    (c) between lower balance-of-payments deficits from capital outflows and lower in-
        terest rates for economic expansion
    (d) between lower balance-of-payments deficits and freer world trade and travel
    (e) at one time or another, all of the above and more

11. West Germany has been piling up surpluses in its balance of payments for years
    while the United States has been suffering deficits. If we take the position that
    part of the adjustment of international disequilibrium should be made by the
    surplus countries as well as by the deficit ones, which measure would be appro-
    priate for West Germany to take?
    (a) a large budget surplus
    (b) an upward revaluation of its currency
    (c) an increase in interest rates
    (d) all of the above

12. The Phillips curve shows
    (a) the tradeoff between unemployment and inflation
    (b) that there is little conflict between the two policy goals
    (c) that prices rise before full employment is reached but do not fall even when
        unemployment becomes quite high
    (d) how much of an increase in aggregate expenditure is needed to achieve full
        employment

13. The L-shaped supply curve implies
    (a) micro assumptions that seem to contradict observed behavior
    (b) that prices fall as recession gets worse
    (c) that all markets are always in equilibrium
    (d) that changes in aggregate demand do not affect the level of employment

14. Large amounts of investment in Canada made by U.S. firms will
    (a) reduce the standard of living in Canada
    (b) add to the U.S. balance-of-payments deficit ˈⁱᵐᵖᵗ
    (c) be accepted by the N.D.P. Waffle group
    (d) add to Canada's immediate balance-of-payments deficit

15. Technological unemployment, according to the text,
    (a) seems to be becoming more of a problem than it used to be
    (b) is now affecting skilled workers more than unskilled workers
    (c) may occur if productivity of labour rises faster than demand in an industry
    (d) is a problem unrelated to the ease with which resources can move

EXERCISES

1. In 1974, the Fuddy Dud Corporation was producing under the conditions indicated below. At the time, early 1975, that the union negotiated a wage increase (as shown), labour productivity rose by 5 percent through some plant changes. Fill in the blanks below.

Year	Number of Employees	Hourly Wage	Hourly Pay-roll	Output of Duds per Man-hour	Unit Labour Cost	Total Hourly Output	Market Price per Dud	Total Hourly Revenue
1970	100	$2.00	_____	10	$.20	_____	$1	_____
1971	100	2.06	_____	10.5		_____	1	_____

(a) Compare the increase in the hourly payroll with the increase in total hourly revenue. Assuming that all output is sold and that there are no other changes, does this company seem more or less profitable than before? _____

(b) Should this wage increase in 1971 justify a price increase? _____

(c) If this were a competitive industry, what does theory predict would happen to the price of this product, *ceteris paribus?*

(d) Assume that labour productivity has increased by only 3 percent and that the company has increased its investment by 3 percent (maintaining the same capital/output ratio). Would labour's share in company revenue be the same in 1971 as in 1970? _____ Would the return per unit of capital have been the same?

2. The data in the table below pertain to the Canadian economy over the postwar period.

Year	Percentage Change in Consumer Price Index ($\dot{P}$)	Average Annual Rate of Unemployment (U)
1949	3.1	2.6
1950	2.8	3.2
1951	10.6	2.0
1952	2.5	2.4
1953	-0.9	2.5
1954	0.6	4.3
1955	0.2	4.1
1956	1.4	3.1
1957	3.2	4.3
1958	2.7	6.6
1959	1.1	5.6
1960	1.2	7.0
1961	0.9	7.1
1962	1.2	5.9
1963	1.7	5.5
1964	1.8	4.7
1965	2.5	3.9
1966	3.7	3.6
1967	3.6	4.1
1968	4.1	4.8
1969	4.5	4.7
1970	3.3	5.9
1971	2.9	6.4
1972	4.8	6.3
1973	7.6	5.6
1974	10.9	5.4

Source: Statistics Canada.

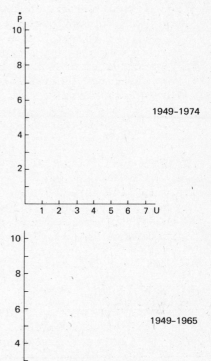

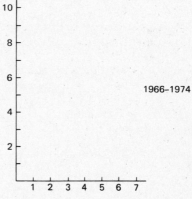

(a) On the three graphs to the right of the table, plot P and U for the three periods indicated.

(b) What can you say about a tradeoff between prices and unemployment in each case? (Try to fit a curve to the data you have plotted.)

(c) Do you think the graphs alone validate or deny the existence of a Phillips curve for Canada?

(d) Is there anything especially different about the two sub-periods, 1949-1965 and 1966-1974?

3. Canada, as an open economy, is continually confronted with the problem of maintaining internal balance (relative price stability and full employment) and external balance (an overall balance on the balance of payments). At times, policies to promote internal balance objectives may conflict with external balance and vice versa.

   (a) In a period of unemployment, price stability, and external balance, in what way would a reduction in taxation to stimulate employment affect (initially, at least) the country's external position?

   (b) Given the same conditions above, in what way would an expansion of the money supply, to encourage domestic spending, affect the external position?

   (c) If there was internal stability but a chronic balance-of-payments deficit, in what way would raising interest rates in Canada, to encourage an inflow of foreign capital, affect internal balance?

   (d) Given the same conditions as in (c) above, how would a devaluation of the Canadian dollar affect the country's internal balance?

PROBLEMS

1. *CANADIAN PRODUCTIVITY AND WAGES*

The following information pertains to Canada for the 1962-1970 period.

Year	PRODUCTIVITY Index of Output per Man-hour in Manufacturing	WAGES Percentage Increase in Average Weekly Wage	PRICES Percentage Change in Consumer Price Index
1961	100.0		
1962	105	3.0	1.2
1963	109	3.4	1.7
1964	114	4.0	1.8
1965	118	4.8	2.5
1966	122	5.7	3.7
1967	126	7.4	3.6
1968	135	7.4	4.1
1969	142	7.5	4.5
1970	145	8.0	3.3
1971	153	8.5	2.9
1972	160	8.4	4.8

Source: Statistics Canada.

Questions

1. Is there any relation between productivity and wage changes that would explain the price stability in the 1961-1964 period?

2. Could the price changes in 1965-1969 reflect any particular relation between productivity and wage changes in that period?

3. Let us suppose that price controls had been imposed on the Canadian economy in the 1962-1972 period such that price increases could not exceed 1.5 percent per annum. What impact would such a move have on the corporate sector?

2. *POLICIES FOR PRICE STABILITY*

Early in 1969, the Government of Canada published its White Paper entitled *Policies for Price Stability*, which led to the establishment of the Prices and Incomes Commission. The White Paper was designed to ". . . examine the problem of rising costs and prices . . . and outline some of the possible causes of this upward price pressure . . ." (p. 3). Canada's price problems stemmed from the possibility of structural unemployment, the impact of the U.S. economy, and "market power" which, when organized by "powerful businessmen, strong trade unions . . . makes it difficult to restore price stability" (p. 7).

The Prices and Incomes Commission was established in late 1969. Its first objective was to plan a conference of business and union leaders to try and reach an agreement on voluntary wage and price guidelines. The conference failed to materialize, and shortly thereafter the steel workers' union settled for a 28-percent wage increase over 3 years with a 13-percent increase the first year. Six days later the Steel Company of Canada raised its product prices by 6 percent. This affair brought a warning from the Prime Minister, who stated that unless these kinds of wage and price increases could be avoided by voluntary agreement, harsh, restrictive monetary and fiscal policies would be imposed upon the economy.

Throughout 1970, there was a lively debate about the role of the Commission and the problem of inflation in general. Some of the views expressed are as follows.

1. Three years (1965-1968) of inflation had led to ". . . strong expectations of continuing inflation." (L. Rasminsky, Governor, The Bank of Canada)
2. The idea of voluntary restraints was ". . . the slickest, most sophisticated con job any government had tried to put over the people. . . ." (M. Rygus, International Association of Machinists, Vice President, as reported in *The Globe and Mail*)
3. ". . . it is difficult to maintain that the current inflation is a reflection of excessive demand pressures . . ." (Economic Council of Canada, *Annual Review,* 1970)
4. "I don't accept the trade-off theory—it doesn't apply to Canada anymore." (E. Benson, Minister of Finance)
5. "When the economy starts to cool off, workers will be realistic enough to take that into account in their bargaining." (J. Morris, Canadian Labour Congress, as reported in *The Globe and Mail*)

Questions

1. Would a Prices and Incomes Commission which had only powers of inquiry, research, and publication be able to deal with the expectation problem noted by Mr. Rasminsky?

2. Mr. Trudeau's threat of harsh monetary and fiscal policies might imply a type of inflation that is not implied by the Economic Council of Canada. Who do you think is correct?

3. Was Mr. Benson's statement correct? Why?

4. Can traditional monetary and fiscal policies deal with inflation caused by market power that is excessive? Explain your answer.

5. Why would a union official charge that an attempt by the Commission to get a voluntary agreement was a "con job"?

Chapter Forty-three
Growth in Developed Economies

CHECKLIST	Make certain that you understand the following concepts: output/capital ratio; embodied technical change; disembodied technical change; optimal population.

REVIEW QUESTIONS

1. For economic growth to occur there must be an increase in the _____ of a nation. The quantity of total output that a nation can produce at full employment is called its _____ GNP or national income.

2. For economic growth to result in an increase in the standard of living, total output must increase faster than _____. Thus to measure relative standards of living we divided _____ by _____.

3. The concept of the "growth rate" should be kept separate from the change in the percentage of _____ of capacity.

4. In order to measure changes in real potential income, it is necessary to use (constant/current) dollar figures.

5. To measure labor productivity we use output per _____. With more capital per worker and better trained workers, productivity will _____.

6. By the "rule of 72," a growth rate of 4 percent means that output will double itself in _____ years, if that rate continues.

7. Because investment is necessary for economic growth, an increased rate of economic growth will usually require an increased rate of _____; a reduction of current _____ will therefore be needed.

8. Economic growth is desirable even for a developed country such as Canada, because it makes possible an easier _____ of income to the poor. However, growth has costs in using up scarce _____ more rapidly and in causing more damage to the _____.

9. Without any increase in knowledge or technology, the marginal efficiency of capital will _____ as the capital stock increases, and the ratio of capital to output will _____. New profit opportunities from new knowledge or

technology will cause the MEC schedule to shift to the _____, in which case the ratio of capital to output may _____.

10. Nineteenth-century classical economists thought that investment opportunities would (expand/be used up) and therefore predicted (low/high) rates of return on capital and a (high/low) capital/output ratio.

11. In North America, with enormous growth in the amount of capital, the capital/output ratio over many decades has (risen/fallen/remained about constant). It is clear that not just the quantity but the _____ of productive resources has been important in economic growth.

12. The theoretical optimal population of a country would be where income per _____ is _____.

13. A land tenure system of absentee landowners or very small individual plots may prevent agricultural growth and require land _____ or even political _____ for growth to be possible.

14. The major threat to future standards of living in the world is from increases in _____ and _____, and from the exhaustion of _____.

15. The model that predicts approximate doomsday from these effects in three generations if growth is not sharply limited does not allow for changes in _____, _____, and _____.

_____

If you have not answered all questions correctly, review the text in order to be sure that you have all of the important concepts clearly in mind before going on to the next chapter.

1. productive capacity; potential 2. population; output or income, population 3. utilization 4. constant 5. man-hour; rise 6. 18 7. investment; consumption 8. redistribution; resources, environment 9. fall, rise; right, fall 10. be used up, low, high 11. remained about constant; quality 12. capita, at a maximum 13. reform, revolution 14. population, pollution, resources 15. technology, supply of resources, prices and substitution

_____

MULTIPLE-CHOICE QUESTIONS

1. Economic growth can best be defined as
   (a) a rise in the GNP as unemployment is reduced
   (b) an increase in real income
   (c) a rise in potential GNP per capita
   (d) an increase in investment and capital stock

2. An increase in the rate of economic growth
   (a) will usually require a reduction in consumption
   (b) will usually be encouraged by an increase in consumption
   (c) seems to be the result of increased investment alone
   (d) will be aided by high interest rates

3. Without technical change or new knowledge,
   (a) diminishing returns to additions to the capital stock will cause the capital/output ratio to rise
   (b) the marginal-efficiency-of-capital schedule will become horizontal
   (c) the shortage of investment will cause interest rates to rise
   (d) the marginal-efficiency-of-capital schedule will shift to the left

4. If, for a given state of technology and resource supplies, an increase in population causes a reduction in per capita income,
   (a) investment must have been decreasing
   (b) the optimal population has apparently been exceeded
   (c) labour productivity must have fallen
   (d) inflation is inevitable and will discourage further growth

5. Output per man-hour increases as a result of
   (a) a rise in the labour force
   (b) a rise in total output
   (c) better machinery and training supplied to workers

6. Economic growth
   (a) has characterized most of mankind's history
   (b) has recently been most rapid in countries with the most rapidly increasing populations
   (c) has been largely independent of social and legal patterns
   (d) has been particularly characteristic of Western countries in the last two centuries

7. Classical theories of growth
   (a) predicted a declining return on capital
   (b) predicted an increasing return on capital
   (c) predicted a constant return on capital
   (d) had no prediction for the rate of return on capital

8. An embodied technical change is one that
   (a) improves the quality of labour
   (b) inheres in the form of capital in use
   (c) is concerned with techniques of managerial control
   (d) is exogenous to the economic system

9. Predictions of future trends based on present rates indicate eventual
   (a) rapidly rising worldwide per capita income
   (b) serious resource shortages from growing population and industrialization
   (c) reversal of damage to the environment with successful and increasing efforts
   (d) leveling off of world population at about 5 billion people

EXERCISE

Assume that the productivity of labour increases by 2.5 percent a year, the labour force increases by 1.75 percent a year, hours worked per member of the work force decline by .25 a year, and population increases by 1 percent a year. Predict:

(a) the annual increase in real GNP

(b) the annual increase in output per capita

(c) the number of years to double real GNP

(d) the number of years to double output per capita

PROBLEM

POT EQUALS POLLUTION

The title for this problem suggests a simple framework for considering aspects of the growth controversy. P is taken as population, O as output per capita, and T as a technological variable to express how polluting are the methods used to produce or consume output. Pollution can be thought of as that of a particular type (such as sulfur dioxide in air, oxygen-consuming waste in water, solid waste) or more generally as a weighted index of all types of pollution, which of course would constitute a formidable measurement problem.

P, O, and T could all be expressed as having values of 1 in some base year plus a percentage addition to represent the annual growth rate. Thus pollution at the end of n years could be expressed as follows, for an economy in which the annual population growth was 1 percent, output per capita increased by 3 percent, and technology in respect to pollution was unchanging:

$$\text{pollution} = (1.01)^n (1.03)^n (1.00)^n$$

This formulation implies that pollution increases proportionally with the increase in total output (P x O) if technology is unchanging. This is not necessarily true. For example, much of the particulate matter in the air comes from volcanic discharges, so that a doubling of man-made output would less than double this form of pollution. On the other hand, because rivers have some natural cleansing powers, a doubling of output could more than double the level of oxygen-consuming discharges into rivers. A simple way out of this problem is to think of T as including the effect of these nonproportionalities.

In the formulation above, pollution would increase 16-fold in 72 years. (You should use the "rule of 72," which states that the doubling time is equal to 72 divided by the annual rate of growth.)

Questions

1. The annual population growth of 1 percent and per capita output increase of 3 percent are assumptions betters suited to developed countries. Assume that 2-percent increases in each are appropriate for the world as a whole. Does this change the projection for pollution over 72 years as made above?

2. What assumption in either of these formulations of the model puts it in the "doomsday" class? What value would the T term have to have to prevent an increase in pollution?

3. Consider how these following interrelationships or developments would influence the variables above and thus the eventual projections for pollution:

(a) A switch back to the use of returnable bottles, with significant savings in the energy now used to make nonreturnable bottles, steel cans, and (in particular) aluminum cans.

(b) An increased death rate from respiratory diseases in infants and the elderly, associated with increased air pollution.

(c) The commitment of a $100 billion investment to complete the achievement of purer water standards (assume that this also decreases investment funds available for increasing output).

(d) The reduced death rate following initial increases in output for a very poor country.

(e) The reduced birth rate in a country well on its way to development.

4. The POT formulation does not incorporate prospective or actual famine. How might economics attempt to adjust to these threats in ways that might reduce the pollution threat? In ways that might increase it?

Chapter Forty-four
Growth and the
Underdeveloped
Economies

CHECKLIST   Make certain that you understand the following concepts: allocative inef-
             ficiency; X-inefficiency; balanced growth; unbalanced growth.

REVIEW QUESTIONS

1. The typical although not completely adequate figure used to compare relative living standards among countries is _____.

2. If a country's national output grows by 2 percent per year and its population grows by 3 percent per year, per capita income (rises/falls/is not affected).

3. The population explosion in the underdeveloped countries, as in developed ones, has been caused by a (rise/fall) in (birth/death) rates.

4. To raise the level of incomes, it is necessary to increase productive capacity, which requires increased _____.

5. In order to raise per capita income by $100, a country with a population of 10 million people and a capital/output ratio of 3:1 will need an investment of $_____.

6. Savings of the public in underdeveloped countries are often not made available for investment because of an inadequate _____ system.

7. Roads and transportation and communications systems are vital to development and often referred to as _____ capital.

8. Human capital in underdeveloped countries may be inadequate in several ways for successful economic growth. List three: _____
   _____
   This can be a source of what the text calls _____-inefficiency in production.

9. Using resources for a high-cost steel plant instead of buying cheaper steel abroad is an example of _____ efficiency.

10. Underdeveloped countries using the same technology as developed countries have been shown to achieve (lower/higher) levels of productivity, due to cultural differences; this effect is called the _____ gap.

11. A country that wants more rapid economic growth and in a certain direction will probably need to use (market forces/centralized planning). The governments of the Soviet Union and China forced their people to consume less and thus achieved increased _____ and _____.

12. In putting greater effort into education for economic development, a country has to choose between two general approaches: _____ and _____ _____.

13. An underdeveloped country is typically short of investment capital because of insufficient domestic _____. Another source of capital is _____. This source requires (less/greater) immediate sacrifice than does accumulation through domestic saving, but costs (more/less) later.

14. A country that imports capital must sooner or later increase its _____ to pay for it.

15. An underdeveloped country with few resources and too much population will have trouble borrowing from private sources abroad because of _____ _____.

16. The theory of international trade leads to the prediction that the developed countries should (gain/lose) from the economic growth of the poor countries. However, it means that wages and prices in poor countries would probably (rise/fall), so that raw materials costs would (rise/fall) for the richer countries. Also, higher wages could mean (lower/higher) profits for American and European firms operating in such countries.

17. Much of U.S. grants and loans to underdeveloped countries has been used to buy U.S. products; thus, U.S. employment (has/has not) been affected and the U.S. balance-of-payments deficit (has/has not) been made much worse by foreign aid.

18. A country following the principle of comparative advantage in its development will tend to follow a path of (balanced/unbalanced) growth. But too much specialization may be risky for a country if what occurs? _____ _____.

19. A developing country has a choice of three alternative strategies, or a combination of them: (a) agricultural development, (b) _____, and (c) industrialization for export.

20. Although the food needs of the rapidly expanding populations of the underdeveloped countries will require them to improve their agricultural output, there are two major difficulties with this approach: (a) if all countries do it, prices will _____, in the short run at least, so that the value of their exports will _____; and (b) mechanized modern farming methods result in (greater/less) unemployment.

21. In countries with much underemployment, production techniques of a (labour-saving/labour-intensive) type are apt to be more economically efficient.

22. The strategy of import substitution usually means (higher/lower) costs of production of goods at home, and necessitates keeping out imports by means of _____.

23. The most serious single obstacle in the long run to higher standards of living in the underdeveloped countries is probably _____. Many social scientists feel that programs of _____ are therefore of greatest urgency.

If you have not answered all of the questions correctly, review the text in order to be sure that you have all of the important concepts clearly in mind before going on to the next chapter.

1. GNP per capita 2. falls 3. fall; death 4. investment 5. $3 billion 6. banking 7. social overhead 8. no entrepreneurship, poor health, low educational levels, traditional attitudes; X 9. allocative 10. lower, technology 11. centralized planning; savings, investment, *or* investment, growth 12. education for the masses, higher education for a few 13. savings; foreign borrowing; less, more 14. exports 15. low profit possibilities, risk 16. savings; foreign borrowing; less, more 17. has; has not 18. unbalanced; changes in tastes or technology, fall in demand 19. import substitution 20. fall, fall, greater 21. labor-intensive 22. higher; tariffs and quotas 23. too rapid population growth; birth control

---

MULTIPLE-CHOICE QUESTIONS

1. We might define an underdeveloped country as
   (a) one with a per capita national income of less than $500
   (b) one with substantial quantities of undeveloped resources
   (c) one with a low amount of capital per head
   (d) any of the above

2. In choosing between building a steel industry and investing more in education, an underdeveloped country
   (a) will be better off with the industry so that it can get cheaper steel
   (b) will probably get greater returns in the long run from more education
   (c) will get immediate short-run returns from education
   (d) finds all of the above true

3. When deciding whether growth should be financed by imported capital or domestic savings, an underdeveloped country's leaders
   (a) should realize that finance by savings will yield a greater return later on
   (b) should realize that finance by imported borrowed capital will requires less financial sacrifice now but more later
   (c) might want to consider noneconomic consequences of each method
   (d) find all of the above true

4. Medical advances in an underdeveloped country
   (a) increase per capita income
   (b) increase the rate of population growth
   (c) are very expensive to bring about
   (d) have been self-defeating because the death rate from famine has risen equivalently

5. Among the arguments for unbalanced growth are that
   (a) it will insulate the economy from the vagaries of foreign trade
   (b) it will enable the citizens of that country to exercise a wide variety of talents in their work
   (c) it will lead to more rapid growth
   (d) diversification is always more expensive in the long run

6. Developing countries often have balance-of-payments problems because
   (a) as income rises, imports often rise even more rapidly
   (b) most of their exports are primary commodities with low elasticities of demand
   (c) most of their machinery must be imported
   (d) all of the above

7. It is usually important that developing countries improve their agricultural output because
   (a) agricultural surpluses will be needed to feed a growing industrial population
   (b) population is apt to be growing rapidly
   (c) agricultural products may be exported to help pay for needed imports
   (d) all of the above

8. A possible obstacle to scientific agriculture in the underdeveloped countries is likely to be
   (a) too-small peasant plots or large feudal-type estates
   (b) inadequate capital
   (c) a preference for traditional ways
   (d) all of the above

9. The GNP is a measure not only of total production but also of resources used. Judging from the per capita GNP, the average American uses about how many times more resources than the average Indian annually?
   (a) 5 times
   (b) 10 times
   (c) 20 times
   (d) 30 times

EXERCISES

1. Why may the gap between the rich and poor countries grow larger, even if both have the same rate of growth? Consider the following example.

	Country A	Country B	Difference
Year X, GNP per capita	$2,000	$100	_____
Annual rate of per capita grpwth	3%	3%	_____
Year X + 1, real GNP per capita	_____	_____	_____
Year X + 23, real GNP per capita	_____	_____	_____

   (Use the "rule of 72," recognizing that, for continuous compounding, as in population growth, the doubling time is more nearly the number 69 divided by the annual rate.)

2. Use the "rule of 72" for the following (assume annual compounding):
   (a) If real GNP is rising at a steady rate of 4 percent, it will be doubled in how many years? _____ If the population is rising steadily at 3 percent per year, it will double itself in how many years? _____ In how many years, then, will real GNP per capita be doubled in this example? _____

   (b) It is predicted that at current rates of increase the population of the underdeveloped countries (the "third world") will double itself by the year 1996. What must be the approximate annual rate of increase in population in these countries? _____ (The prediction was made in 1971.)

PROBLEM

PRODUCTION POSSIBILITIES, EFFICIENCY, AND GROWTH

You are told that a country has a resource endowment of x units of labour and y units of capital and that only two goods are produced and consumed: wheat and housing. Assuming that all resources are fully utilized, the production possibilities are given in the schedule below.

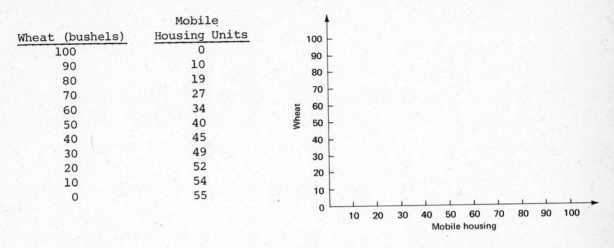

Wheat (bushels)	Mobile Housing Units
100	0
90	10
80	19
70	27
60	34
50	40
40	45
30	49
20	52
10	54
0	55

Questions

1. Plot this curve on the graph. To obtain successive increases in wheat production, what is happening to the rate of loss in housing production? Therefore, what can be said about the change in opportunity costs? (See Chapter 1 for a reference.)

2. Suppose that prices between the two goods are such that 50 units of wheat and 40 units of housing were demanded. Can this economy provide for this demand?

3. A production of 52 housing units and 20 wheat units represents (allocative/X-) inefficiency, whereas a production combination of 32 housing units and 40 wheat units represents (allocative/X-) inefficiency. Locate these combinations on your graph.

4. If this economy decided to produce housing exclusively in the current time period, how could it obtain wheat for consumption? How would it pay for the wheat?

5. Suppose that a technological innovation were adopted which increased production 10 percent in housing. Wheat production is unaffected. Calculate the new production-possibility schedule and plot it on the diagram.

6. Suppose that this country receives a generous gift of capital equipment from a more developed and wealthier country. How would this affect the production-possibilities curve?

Chapter Forty-five
Comparative Economic
Systems

| CHECKLIST | Make certain that you understand the following concepts: socialism; turnover tax. |

REVIEW QUESTIONS

1. All economic systems face the basic problem of _____ and the questions of how and what to _____.

2. An economic system where the natural resources and means of production are mostly privately owned is known as a _____ system. An economic system where productive assets are predominantly publicly owned is known as a _____ system.

3. We distinguish between an economic system of the market type and one of the _____ type, in which decision making is (centralized/decentralized).

4. For predicting market behavior, not only the question of ownership of means of production but also that of motives behind decisions is important to an economist. Publicly owned firms (may/will not) have profit motives to guide them—they (may/will not) respond to consumer preferences as do private firms.

5. Incentives for work and production are important (only in capitalist/in all types of) systems.

6. The people of underdeveloped countries are apt to be (more/less) concerned about political and economic freedom than about raising their standards of living.

7. Agriculture in the Soviet Union uses about _____ percent of the labour force. State-owned and collective farms produce (all/about two-thirds) of the agricultural output of the Soviet Union; the rest is from private plots. Soviet farm prices and wages have been set at (high/low) levels; compulsion in this sector (has/has not) results in high agricultural activity.

8. Managers of firms in the Soviet Union are given (orders/much latitude) about what and how much to produce. In trying to fulfill assigned quotas of output, emphasis is apt to be on (quantity/quality). Wage rates are determined by the (firm/worker/central authorities). Prices are set by the (firm/government/consumer). Centralized direction of output, prices, and wages seems to be economically (more/less) efficient than in a decentralized system; surpluses, shortages, and low quality seem (more/less) common under the former.

9. Russian consumers have (a choice/no choice) of what they buy; however, in the past their demands (determined/did not much affect) prices or what was produced. Soviet planners (are/are not) now becoming more interested in satisfying consumers, partly because it is (now possible/not possible) to produce greater quantities of consumer goods. These subsidized services and the fact that incomes from property are limited contribute to a (more equal/less equal) distribution of income in Russia compared with the United States.

10. Wage and salary differentials in Russia are (not large/much larger than in North America). Medical care and higher education are (free/very expensive) in Russia. Rents for housing are (low/high) and housing is (scarce/plentiful).

11. Successive five-year plans in Russia emphasized (welfare/growth) and therefore concentrated on (consumer/capital) goods. Until recently, scarce capital was used inefficiently because it had (no cost/high cost) in terms of an interest rate.

12. The detailed individual program for production and production requirements of each industry is contained in the (five-year/one-year) plan.

13. The Soviet Union (uses/does not use) a price mechanism to influence consumption. A tax called a _____ tax is imposed on goods; it is frequently (high/low) on luxuries and (high/low) on necessities. Turnover taxes are a way of forcing the people to save and thus provide funds to the state for _____.

14. It is estimated that Soviet real purchasing power per capita is (about equal to/about half of) that of the United States at present. In the postwar period, Soviet rate of growth has been (about equal to/about double) that of the United States.

15. Unemployment in the Soviet Union has been caused by (deficient demand/structural changes). The government has (prevented/not been able to prevent) surplus farm labor from moving to the cities.

16. The Soviet central authorities have (total/partial) control over the supply of money through the central bank, called the _____. The commercial banks are (separate from/branches of) the central bank.

17. The Soviet government handled the problem of postwar excess demand by (allowing inflation/confiscating money balances).

18. Two major drawbacks to the Soviet system, as outlined in the text, have been microeconomic _____ and excessive absorption of manpower in the _____ function.

19. The text describes Yugoslavia as a _____ economy. The means of production are owned by _____. The amounts of production and employment in each firm are decided by _____. Marginal cost concepts and certain microeconomic principles are (observed/ignored); resource allocation is probably (more/less) efficient than in the Soviet Union.

20. Management of Yugoslavian firms is (appointed by the state/elected by the workers). Profits go to (the state/the workers) or are reinvested. Incentives for efficient production are thus (high/low).

21. Tendencies toward monopolistic practices by firms in Yugoslavia are (very common/very rare) because of the (ease/difficulty) of organizing new firms.

22. Yugoslavia has been (reducing/increasing) the collectivization of agriculture. Individual farmers produce what they (want/are told).

23. Planning and five-year plans are (sometimes/never/always) used by nonsocialist countries. Implementation of five-year plans is made more effective in Yugoslavia than in nonsocialist countries by the fact that two-thirds of all investment is undertaken by _____.

24. It is (possible/not possible) to claim that one type of economic system is better than all others.

   If you have not answered all questions correctly, review the text in order to be sure that you have all of the important concepts clearly in mind before going on to the next chapter.

1. scarcity, produce 2. capitalist; socialist 3. command; centralized 4. may, may 5. in all types of 6. less 7. 40; about two-thirds; low, has not 8. orders; quantity; central authorities; government; less, more 9. a choice, did not much affect; are, now possible; more equal 10. much larger than in North America; free; low, scarce 11. growth, capital; no cost 12. one-year 13. uses; turnover, high, low- investment capital 14. about half of; about double; rapidly 15. structural changes; prevented 16. total, Gosbank, branches of 17. confiscating money balances 18. inefficiencies, planning 19. socialist-market; the state; the state; the firm; observed, more 20. elected by the workers; the workers; high 21. very common, difficulty 22. reducing; want 23. sometimes; the state 24. not possible

---

MULTIPLE-CHOICE QUESTIONS

1. All types of economic systems can be said to
   (a) operate for private profit primarily
   (b) operate to favor a wealthy few
   (c) reward only the hard worker
   (d) face the basic problem of scarcity relative to wants

2. All types of economic systems must
   (a) have a mechanism for making choices about production
   (b) have a price system that is flexible and responsive to demand
   (c) do away with large fortunes and inherited wealth if economic growth is desired
   (d) have centralized planning or nothing gets done

3. The ownership and operation by Canada of a major railroad network
   (a) means that Canada is a socialist country
   (b) guarantees better service than if the railroad were privately owned
   (c) is an example of the mixed type of economy so common in the world
   (d) is very unusual among Western capitalist countries

4. The Soviet Union achieved rapid growth since 1928 primarily by
   (a) borrowing capital from other countries
   (b) putting everybody to work efficiently
   (c) investing heavily from tax receipts
   (d) centralized, efficient planning that eliminated surpluses and shortages

5. By definition, socialism means
   (a) centralized planning and control of all production
   (b) state ownership of most of the means of production
   (c) no freedom of choice of occupation
   (d) to each according to his need, from each according to his ability

6. It is probably fair to say of the standard of living in the Soviet Union that
   (a) it is much higher than it used to be
   (b) it is as high as that of the United States, but different
   (c) it is about 25 percent of that of the United States
   (d) it has been increased by the large amounts of expenditures on armaments and space exploration

7. The five-year plan is used in the Soviet Union
   (a) to indicate what and how much each firm will produce
   (b) to establish general guidelines for growth and priorities
   (c) to enforce rigid quotas and targets for each industry
   (d) only as window-dressing to be ignored in practice

8. Which of the following is *not* true of the price system in the Soviet Union?
   (a) Some prices of agricultural produce from private plots are set by supply and demand.
   (b) Wage rates recognize the need for incentives to induce greater output.
   (c) Prices contain high or low taxes deliberately to influence consumption.
   (d) Prices fluctuate frequently to reflect market conditions.

9. Turnover taxes in the Soviet Union are
   (a) used contracyclically to affect aggregate demand
   (b) used as direct anti-inflationary measures
   (c) the source of much of the investment capital for the economy
   (d) more regressive than a general sales tax

10. It is believed that at least in the past capital was used inefficiently in the Soviet Union because
    (a) it was so scarce
    (b) their engineers were so poorly trained
    (c) interest rates were set too high
    (d) the cost of capital was not recognized

11. Profits—that is, revenue exceeding cost—in the Soviet Union
    (a) are divided up by the workers
    (b) are partly used for investment by the firm and partly turned over to the State
    (c) are forbidden by law
    (d) cannot exist, since production is not for profit

12. The Yugoslav economic system differs from that of the Soviet Union in that
    (a) most workers can choose their occupation
    (b) profits are permitted
    (c) the workers choose their plant management, and the plant determines its own otuput
    (d) prices are generally determined in free markets

13. The least serious of the following problems for a socialist, command type of system is probably
    (a) economic depression
    (b) economic growth
    (c) inflation
    (d) efficient production and distribution

PROBLEM

COMPARISON OF THE UNITED STATES AND THE SOVIET UNION

    The Joint Economic Committee of the Congress of the United States had studies prepared on "Economic Indicators in the U.S.S.R." (1964) and "New Directions in the Soviet Economy" (1966). Many of the figures are estimates and may not directly be counterparts of those for the United States, but the quality is good enough for making hypotheses about the differences in the economy they reveal.

    You are asked, for each pair of figures below, to hypothesize whether the comparison simply indicates that the United States is more economically advanced than Russia, whether it indicates some difference in the priorities of the two countries, or whether it reflects the differences in operations of a primarily private enterprise versus a centralized economy with most industry nationalized. More than one of these categories may be involved.

	U.S.S.R.	U.S.	Hypothesis
1. Consumption of electricity per production worker (kwh, 1962)	11,492	28,771	
2. Hydro capacity as a percentage of total electric generating capacity			
1940	14	24	
1962	20	18	
3. Percentage of intercity passenger traffic that travels			
by rail	79.3	2.5	
by air	8.5	4.7	
4. Number of tractors per 1,000 acres of harvested cropland			
1940	1.43	4.37	
1962	2.49	15.90	
5. GNP per unit of fixed capital stock (index). For United States second figure is for potential GNP.			
1940	100	100	
1962	61	137, 125	
6. Estimated automobile stock (millions—1964)	1	70	
7. Industrial output per employee (1962)	$3,531	$10,100	
8. Per capita figures, 1962 (1961 dollars)			
Investment	$ 486	$ 480	
Defense	192	300	
Consumption	372	1,889	
GNP	1,158	3,004	
9. Annual growth in GNP per capita (1950–1962)	≈4.3%	≈1.7%	

Answers to Multiple-Choice Questions and Exercises

CHAPTER 1
Multiple-Choice Questions

1. (c) 2. (b) 3. (c) 4. (a) 5. (c) 6. (a) 7. (c) 8. (b) 9. (d) 10. (a)
11. (b) 12. (b)

Exercises

1. (1) What goods and services are being produced and in what quantities?
   (2) By what methods are these goods produced?
   (3) How is the supply of goods allocated among the members of the society?
   (4) Are the country's resources being fully utilized, or are some of them lying idle and thus going to waste?
   (5) Is the purchasing power of people's money and savings constant, or is it being eroded by inflation?
   (6) Is the economy's capacity to produce goods growing or remaining the same over time?

   (a) 1 (b) 2 (c) 4 (d) 3 (e) 6 (f) 5 (g) 1 (h) 2

2. (b) yes (c) no (d) approximately 3300 bushels of corn (e) underutilized
   (f) increase in the productivity of land or the reclaim of presently nonarable land

CHAPTER 2
Multiple-Choice Questions

1. (d) 2. (d) 3. (b) 4. (c) 5. (d) 6. (a) 7. (b)

Exercise

(a) There is an inverse relationship between the percentage change in housing starts and the change in the mortgage rate of interest.
(b) Yes; using the data to plot a scatter diagram, you could examine changes in the two variables to see if they support the hypothesis.

CHAPTER 3
Multiple-Choice Questions

1. (b) 2. (c) 3. (b) 4. (d) 5. (c) 6. (a) 7. (b) 8. (d) 9. (c) 10. (b) 11. (a)

Exercises

1. (b) 1.5 (c) Y is the variable that *determines* the value of X.
2. S = $100; -50; 0; 50; 100
3. (a) $S = .07Y$ (b) $C = 1,000 + .95Y$ (c) $c = C/Q$ (d) $R = PQ$ (e) $\Pi = R - C$
4. (a) directly (b) inversely (c) directly (d) directly (e) directly
5. (a) $TC = 500 + 0.10N$.
   (b) The fixed-cost graph is a horizontal line at 500, whereas the cleanup-cost line
       would start at the origin and slope upward to the right with a slope of .10.

CHAPTER 4
Multiple-Choice Questions

1. (b) 2. (d) 3. (c) 4. (d) 5. (b)

Exercises

1. (a) extreme right blank (b) extreme left blank (c) third blank from left
   (d) same as (c) (e) second blank from left

2.

	Price	Profit	Employment
1	down	down	down
2	up	up	up
3	down	down	down
4	up	?	down

CHAPTER 5
Multiple-Choice Questions

1. (a) 2. (b) 3. (d) 4. (d) 5. (d) 6. (d) 7. (a) 8. (c)

Exercises

1. (a) equilibrium price = $0.60
       equilibrium quantity = 12 units

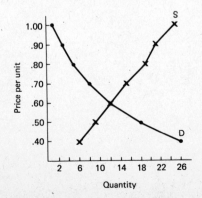

(b) column (4): -24, -18, -7, 0, +9, +20

At equilibrium, excess demand = 0 = excess supply.

(c) Excess demand: Price will rise because of the competition (demand) for a limited number of goods.

Excess supply: Price will fall as producers attempt to sell accumulated inventories.

2.

	D	S	P	Q
1	0	-	+	-
2	+	0	+	+
3	+	0	+	+
4	+	+	U	+
5	-	0	-	-
6	0	-	+	-

CHAPTER 6
Multiple-Choice Questions

1. (d)   2. (a)   3. (b)   4. (c)   5. (d)   6. (a)   7. (a)   8. (d)   9. (c)   10. (c)
11. (d)   12. (d)   13. (c)   14. (b)   15. (d)   16. (b)

Exercises

1. (a) down   (b) none   (c) 1   (d) down   (e) up
2. (a)

		Elasticities		
P	Q	Arc	Point	TR
$11	1		11	$11
9	3	5	3	27
7	5	2.0	1.4	35
5	7	1.0	.7	35
3	9	.5	.3	27
1	11	.2	.1	11

(b) Demand is elastic when TR rises with falling price, is unitary at peak of TR, and is inelastic when TR falls with decreasing price.

(c) It is less elastic. Point elasticity at $11 is now 3.7 and at $9 is now 1.8.

3. $Q = 1,840,000, 4,270,000$; elasticity = 1.52

4. (a) that it was elastic

(b) If TR went up with a fall in P, it would be elastic.

(c) They would be cheaper as demand falls.

CHAPTER 7
Multiple-Choice Questions

1. (d)   2. (a)   3. (a)   4. (c)   5. (a)   6. (a)   7. (b)   8. (c)   9. (a)   10. (c)
11. (d)   12. (c)   13. (b)   14. (b)

Exercises

1. (a) $8,000,000   (b) 2,000,000   (c) 2,000,000; $4,000,000   (d) 3,000,000; $1.50 or a little less

2. (a) Revenue would decrease substantially with rightward shift of supply.

(b) Revenue would increase substantially with rightward shift of demand; this shift, if it occurs more rapidly than the supply shift, threatens mass famine.

3. I. (a) oc, oi
    (b) oe; ok; less than; inelastic
  II. (a) It would be too hard to enforce—pressure on farmers with surpluses to sell below the minimum price would be too great.
    (b) purchase; ik
    (c) sell; gi
 III. (a) od; purchase; jk
    (b) ob; sell; gh
    (c) It would be buying at a lower price than it would be selling at. Under III, it is buying, storing, and selling smaller amounts.
  IV. This is a discussion question. With long-run steady increases in supply, growing government-held surpluses and storage costs would become politically unacceptable. Stringent crop controls, reductions in support levels, limits on total payments to any one farmer, and efforts to move marginal farmers out of farming all are modifications that Canada and the United States have either adopted or considered. In the very long run, of course, population pressures will very probably reverse the problem.

CHAPTER 8
Multiple-Choice Questions

1. (a) 2. (d) 3. (c) 4. (c) 5. (c) 6. (d) 7. (b) 8. (b) 9. (c) 10. (a)
11. (d) 12. (b)

Exercises

1. (a)

	Food Intercepts	"Other" Intercepts
1920	3,150	3,150
1940	5,000	3,850
1970	7,400	7,400

  (b) Yes, because in 1940, despite decline in money income, purchasing power for both food and other items has risen. Budget line has shifted outward.
  (c) 1940; with food prices relatively low, family budget could buy more food relative to all other items than 1920 or 1970.

2. (a) Indifference curves should be tangent where price-consumption lines intersect budget lines.
  (b)

P	Q_A	Q_B	Total Exp. on Beef A	B
1.50	400	600	$600	$ 900
1.00	600	1,000	600	1,000
.75	800	1,300	600	975
.60	1,000	1,500	600	900
.50	1,200	600		800

  (c) 1. elasticity = 1
    2. at approximately $1.00, where TR is at a maximum

CHAPTER 9
Multiple-Choice Questions

1. (c) 2. (b) 3. (d) 4. (a) 5. (b) 6. (a)

Exercises

1. (a) Nothing; both demand and supply curves probably have shifted.
   (b) Show probably rightward from 1900 to 1915 and leftward shift from then on. Because razor strops are technical complements to straight razors in furnishing shaving services, these events help to explain the pattern of shifting.

2. (a)

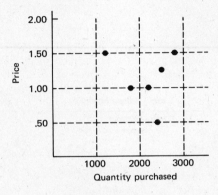

   (b) No; there is no clearly defined demand schedule. It could be calculated for each annual change in quantity and price.

CHAPTER 10
Multiple-Choice Questions

1. (b) 2. (c) 3. (b) 4. (c) 5. (c) 6. (c) 7. (a) 8. (c) 9. (b) 10. (a)
11. (c) 12. (c)

Exercises

1. at approximately 500 square feet
2. Yes; the power-tool production of food would not be economical until a garden size somewhat greater than 500 square feet.

CHAPTER 11
Multiple-Choice Questions

1. (d) 2. (b) 3. (c) 4. (a) 5. (b) 6. (a) 7. (d) 8. (b) 9. (c) 10. (c)

Exercises

1. (a)

Variable Input	Total Output	Average Product	Marginal Product	Average Cost	Marginal Cost
0	0				
			3		1
10	30	3		1	
			3		.3
20	60	3		.67	
			2		.5
30	80	2.7		.62	
			1		1
40	90	2.25		.67	
			0		
50	90	1.80		.78	
			0		
60	90	1.50		.89	

2. (a) The most appropriate way to deal with this question is to set up a table as shown below.

Output	Fixed Cost	Marginal Cost	Total Cost	Average Cost	Total Variable Cost	Average Variable Cost
0	2					
1	2	4.00	6.00	6.00	4.00	4.00
2	2	1.50	7.50	3.75	5.50	2.75
3	2	1.00	8.50	2.83	6.50	2.16
4	2	1.25	9.75	2.43	7.75	1.95
5	2	1.75	11.50	2.30	9.50	1.90
6	2	2.50	14.00	2.33	12.00	2.00
7	2	3.50	17.50	2.50	15.50	2.21

(b) Columns 2 and 3 are given. The total cost for the first unit is the increased cost of going from zero production to one unit (4.00) plus the total cost of zero production, the 2.00 fixed cost. The rest of the total cost column is similarly calculated, building on the cost of the previous units of production. Total variable cost is the total cost less the fixed cost. The relevant schedules are then graphed.

(c) That will depend on price. The firm must cover its average cost normally but may be able to produce for a short while at a price that covers average variable cost.

(d) Precisely, the firm would produce 5½ units of output. Here price equals marginal cost and the price more than covers the firm's average total cost.

3. (a) AFC = $93.89; AVC = 0
   (b) $187.78
   (c) zero
   (d) No; even if the airline could fill the remaining 40 seats at the "normal" price, the total cost of the flight would not be covered.

4. (a)

Q	FC	VC	TC	MC	AFC	AVC	ATC
0	50	0	50				
1	50	4	54	4	50	4	54
2	50	10	60	6	25	5	30
3	50	18	68	8	16.66	6	22.66
4	50	28	78	10	12.50	7	19.50
5	50	40	90	12	10	8	18
6	50	54	104	14	8.30	9	17.30
7	50	70	120	15	7.14	10	17.14
8	50	88	138	18	6.25	11	17.25
9	50	108	158	20	5.55	12	17.55
10	50	130	180	22	5	13	18
.	.	.	.		.	.	.
.	.	.	.		.	.	.
.	.	.	.		.	.	.
20	50	460	510		2.50	23	25.50

(b) 7
(c) 16
(d) no
(e) Although average fixed costs are declining because of the 50 being spread over more and more units of output, average variable costs are rising and at some point (output level of 8) they offset the falling average fixed costs.

CHAPTER 12
Multiple-Choice Questions

1. (c) 2. (d) 3. (d) 4. (c) 5. (d) 6. (b) 7. (b) 8. (c) 9. (c) 10. (c)
11. (b) 12. (b)

Exercises

1. (a) At the output levels shown in the first column of the problem, the corresponding average total cost figures are 0.46, 0.39, 0.35, 0.46, and 0.52.
   (b) 60,000
   (c) It increases up to an output level of 80,000, then decreases to an output level of 60,000, and then increases up to the output level of 100,000.
   (d) If the firm could substitute capital for labour in its production processes, a rise in the relative price of labour would lead to more capital being used relative to the amount of labour being used.
2. (a) $2.00, $1.85, $1.80, $1.78, $1.82
   (b) 400,000
   (c) No—proportions of labour and capital are constant.
   (d) Build two plants to produce 400,000 each.
   (e) if factor prices rose as industry output expanded
3. (a) one of capital and two of labour
   (b) two units of each

4. (a)

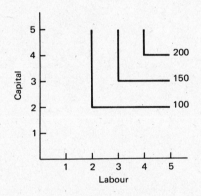

   (b) Very little (likely), because the firm cannot readily substitute one factor for another, according to the isoquant map above.

CHAPTER 13
Multiple-Choice Questions

1. (c) 2. (d) 3. (d) 4. (c) 5. (d) 6. (b) 7. (b) 8. (c)

Exercises

1. (a) crop production (output) per acre (input)
   (b) Because overall production has doubled and the acre productivity has doubled, the number of acres should be about the same. (Actually you will find the number of acres for harvestable crops has declined somewhat; this discrepancy reflects weighting problems in index number.)
   (c) Fertilizer; over all the whole period fertilizer input increased more than 10 times for a doubling of output; between 1960 and 1970, it doubled, whereas output rose only 15 percent.
   (d) six

(e) The great increase in machinery inputs suggests the tractors, cornpickers, etc., that would enable labour input to be reduced.

(f) Land productivity only doubled and many other resources such as fertilizer and machinery were used as inputs. The total *productivity* index rose only from about 60 (89/53) to 99 (104/103). Technological change permitted a substitution of capital for labour; of fertilizer, etc., for the additional land that would have been required.

(g) 1930 *17*; 1940 *21*; 1950 *35*; 1960 *67*; 1970 *112*

(h) Either 1940-1970, 1950-1970, or 1950-1960, depending on how rapid a change constitutes a "revolution." Some of the increase from 1940 to 1950 was attributable to eliminating redundant workers in agriculture because of the higher employment needs elsewhere associated with World War II.

2. (a)

APC	MPC	ASC	MSC
	500		600
500	50	600	175
275	70	387.59	210
206	90	327.60	240
177.50	110	306.25	270
164	230	299	460
175	300	315.83	480
192.85		339.28	

(b) $177.50 and $306.25, respectively

(c) greater

CHAPTER 14
Multiple-Choice Questions

1. (d) 2. (d) 3. (d) 4. (a) 5. (c) 6. (a) 7. (c) 8. (b) 9. (a)

Exercises

1. (a) No; MC exceeds price. (b) It should produce less.
2. (a) 100; 80; 60 (b) $1,000; $600; $330 (c) $800; $600; $480 (d) $200; 0; -$150
   (e) $10; $7.50; $5.50 (f) $10; $7.50; $5.50 (g) $8; $7.50; $8 (h) $2; 0; -$2.50
   (i) At $10, profits will induce entry; at $5.50, losses will induce exit of firms, so industry supply curve shifts.
3. (a) $7.50 (b) yes (c) no (d) Yes, it should increase output to 100.
4. (a) above-normal profits
   (b) No, not in a perfectly competitive industry, because the abnormal profits will attract firms into the industry and the expanded market size will drive the price back to a level where all firms make only normal profits.
5. (a) Yes. Briefly, there are no excess profits for the firms; they are price takers; any individual firm has a very small share of the total market.
   (b) Price and output will rise and firms will be enjoying above-normal profits, e.g., revenue over and above that sufficient to cover average total costs.
   (c) The market-supply schedule would shift to the right because of the entry of new firms until it intersects the D' schedule at such a point so as to produce a price (equilibrium) the same as the initial price in the market.

CHAPTER 15
Multiple-Choice Questions

1. (d) 2. (c) 3. (b) 4. (c) 5. (c) 6. (a) 7. (d) 8. (b) 9. (c) 10. (a)

Exercises

1. (a) 60 (b) $11 (c) $660 (d) $480 (e) $180 (f) output; about 25 to 90 units; price: about $14.75 to $7.50 (g) $7.50
2. (a) the marginal-cost and marginal-revenue schedules

   (b)

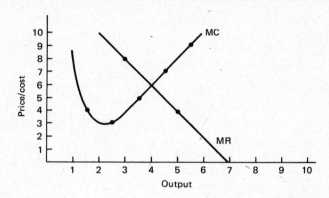

   (c) four units
   (d) $10.00
   (e) the average-cost schedule
   (f) The average cost of producing an output of four is $9.75 and hence the monopolists' profits are $10.00 - $9.75 times the output.

CHAPTER 16
Multiple-Choice Questions

1. (c) 2. (d) 3. (b) 4. (b) 5. (c) 6. (c) 7. (d) 8. (a) 9. (b) 10. (c)
11. (a) 12. (d) 13. (b)

Exercises

1. (a) output, $0q_1$; price, $0p_4$ (b) $p_3 df p_4$, or $df \times 0q_1$
   (c) Profits are being made, and firms will enter.
   (d) ATC curve will rise; D curve will shift to right; MR curve will shift according to shift in D; MC curve will not be affected because in this case advertising is a fixed, not a variable, cost.
   (e) D curve should be shifted to left, tangent to ATC curve.
2. These answers may be approximate, depending on how students read off the values on the horizontal axis.
   (a) from 5,000 to 7,000, from $10,000 to $10,500
   (b) from 5,000 to 5,500, from $10,000 to $8,250
   (c) from 5,000 to 3,000, from $10,000 to $7,500
   (d) from $10,000 to $11,050
   (e) He would raise his price only if everyone else did; he would not lower it even without retaliation because additional revenue would be less than additional costs. For instance, at 6,000 units MC would equal 75 cents but MR would be only 50 cents.
   (f) yes, no

CHAPTER 17
Multiple-Choice Questions

1. (b)   2. (b)   3. (b)   4. (d)   5. (c)   6. (d)

Exercise

   (a) There is a profit incentive for both firms to move away from the present price, because neither firm is producing at the profit-maximizing position where marginal cost equals marginal revenue.
   (b) Neither firm knows what the other might do in the case where there is a decision by one firm to alter price. To avoid the possibility of a "price war," they may remain where they are.

CHAPTER 18
Multiple-Choice Questions

1. (c)   2. (b)   3. (b)   4. (c)   5. (b)   6. (a)   7. (d)   8. (c)   9. (b)   10. (d)
11. (a)

CHAPTER 19
Multiple-Choice Questions

1. (c)   2. (c)   3. (a)   4. (d)   5. (d)   6. (c)   7. (d)   8. (d)   9. (c)

Exercise

   (a) p_2, q_1 (b) from p_3, q to p_1, q_2 (c) p, q_3

CHAPTER 20
Multiple-Choice Questions

1. (b)   2. (b)   3. (d)   4. (a)   5. (b)   6. (c)   7. (c)   8. (c)   9. (c)   10. (c)
11. (c)   12. (c)   13. (d)

Exercises

1. MPP: 0, 20, 20, 18, 16, 14, 12, 10, 8, 6, 4
   MRP (a): 0, $40, $40, $36, $32, $28, $24, $20, $16, $12, $8
   MRP (b): 0, $38, $36, $31.50, $27.20, $23.10, $19.20, $15.50, $12.00, $8.70, $5.60
   (a) 7; about 5   (b) 5; about 3   (c) 7   (d) because of diminishing returns
   (e) Case (b) is evidently monopolistic with a downward-sloping marginal-revenue curve.
2. Table MRS: 40, 15, 10, 8, 7, 6, 5, 4, 3, 1; MRP: $1,000 multiplied by MRS
   (a) 4, 27   (b) 3   (c) right, 5
3. (a) The total number of hours supplied will be the sum of the hours from individuals B and C.
   (b) Hours offered by individuals B and C increase and now individual A offers hours for the first time. The participation rate has increased from 2 out of 3 to 3 out of 3 adults.
   (c) It appears that only individual B will offer hours (a small amount) to the market. Therefore, the participation rate is .333 (1 out of 3).

CHAPTER 21
Multiple-Choice Questions

1. (a)   2. (c)   3. (b)   4. (c)   5. (d)   6. (a)   7. (d)

Exercise

(a) Ow_3, Oq_4
(b) Oq, Oq_5 - Oq; horizontal at w_6 to q_5
(c) Ow, Ow_2; Ow_5, Oq_2, Ow_1, Ow_4, Ow_4. Wage is lower; employment is less than in (a).
(d) Oq_4; wage between Ow_1 and Ow_4; employment between Oq_2 and Oq_4
(e) Supply curve shifts leftward halfway to origin. All wage predictions are raised.

CHAPTER 22
Multiple-Choice Questions

1. (b)   2. (a)   3. (a)   4. (c)   5. (b)   6. (a)   7. (b)   8. (c)   9. (c)   10. (c)
11. (d)

Exercises

1. (a) $7.47   (b) 1 percent   (c) 50   (d) 10
2. (a) $42.12   (b) 1 percent   (c) 50   (d) 10
3. (a) Just barely; it would bring him $13,590 per year.
   (b) Yes, but it just meets the 14-percent requirement.
       The annual savings would have PV of $14,000 x 5.216 = $73,024
       The $10,000 salvage value has PV of   2,700
                                                            $75,724
   (c) At 6% the PV of the cost of the medical education is (6.802)($10,000) or
       $68,000. The worth of the extra medical earnings is (15.046 - 6.802)($10,000) or
       approximately $82,440. The return is over 6%. At 8% the cost is $62,470 and the
       estimated worth is $56,780, i.e., (11.925 - 6.247)($10,000). The return is
       therefore slightly less than 8 percent, enough for Mr. Schmidt to give his
       blessing to Hermann's medical career.
   (d) There are 5 years to maturity (assuming the current period is 1974). Take 10%
       in the tables. Total capitalized value is $99.07.

CHAPTER 23
Multiple-Choice Questions

1. (d)   2. (a)   3. (b)   4. (a)

CHAPTER 24
Multiple-Choice Questions

1. (d)   2. (d)   3. (c)   4. (d)   5. (b)   6. (a)

Exercises

1. (a) rise by \$10 (b) rise by \$10 (c) shift to left (d) rise, less than \$10
   (e) decline
2. (a) be unaffected (b) rise (c) be unaffected (d) be unaffected (e) be unaffected
   (f) rise
3. (a) trucking down; railroads up
   (b) private gasoline consumption down; trucking unaffected; public transportation up
   (c) airlines down; railroads up
   (d) foreign publishers down; Canadian publishers up

CHAPTER 25
Multiple-Choice Questions

1. (a) 2. (a) 3. (d) 4. (b) 5. (c) 6. (d) 7. (c) 8. (b) 9. (b) 10. (c)

Exercises

1. (a) c, d, f (b) e (c) a, because the supply elasticity is greater with the same
   demand (d) d, because the demand elasticity is less with the same supply
2. A, progressive; B, proportional; C, progressive; D, regressive; E, proportional to
   \$5,000, regressive above \$5,000
3. Dimeland would prefer policy (1) as it can spend the money where its preferences
   dictate. The federal government should follow (2) because it reduces the cost of
   additional educations expenditure to Dimeland by 50 percent, a substantial incentive.

CHAPTER 26
Multiple-Choice Questions

1. (b) 2. (d) 3. (a) 4. (a) 5. (c) 6. (a) 7. (a) 8. (c) 9. (b) 10. (b)
11. (b)

Exercises

1. GNE = (277.1 + 3.6 + 201.5 + 805.0) = 1286
   GNP = (785.3 + 84.3 + 117.8 + 109.6 + 126.4 + 75.5 - 10.7) = 1286
2. 1929 GNP in 1961 dollars = 12.24; implicit price deflator 1970 = 133.9
   (a) 116 percent (b) 34 percent (c) 61 percent (d) 24 percent
3. real per-capita disposable income 1950 = 925.60; 1970 = 1760.60; percent
   increase = 90
4. (a) (1) C and F (2) I (if clippers are considered investment) (3) S_b or S_p (4) N
   (5) I (6) T (7) F and S_b (8) (a) T (b) F (c) S_b (9) C, M (10) X_p (11) I
   (12) G
   (b) 2, 5, 9, 10, 11, 12

CHAPTER 27
Multiple-Choice Questions

1. (d) 2. (b) 3. (c) 4. (a) 5. (d) 6. (b) 7. (a) 8. (d)

Exercises

1. (b) 500   (c) .8; yes   (d) It declines.   (e) Savings values are -100, -80, -60, -40, -20, 0, 20, 40, 60.   (f) $C = Y$ at the break-even level of national income. Therefore, $S = 0$.

2.

Y	Aggregate Expenditure	J	Y - C = W
0	140	50	-90
50	170	50	-70
100	200	50	-50
150	230	50	-30
200	260	50	-10
250	290	50	10
300	320	50	30
350	350	50	50
400	380	50	70
450	410	50	90
500	440	50	110

(a) 350; 350; $W = 50$; $J = 50$ (b) $C = 90 + .6Y$; $W = -90 + .4Y$ (c) $C + W = Y$
(d) MPC = .6 for all changes in income

3. (a) This is an overproduction situation, because actual output (Y) is 100, whereas intended aggregate expenditure is 97. Inventory investment is 3 and in unintended.
(b) Businessmen would cut production.
(c) Income would fall, because resource demand has declined. Factor payments are therefore reduced.
(d) Consumption would fall. This is shown diagrammatically by a movement down the E curve.
(e) output or GNP

CHAPTER 28
Multiple-Choice Questions

1. (a)   2. (a)   3. (c)   4. (c)   5. (c)   6. (d)   7. (a)   8. (c)   9. (c)   10. (b)
11. (c)   12. (c)

Exercises

1.

	C	ΔC	ΔI	Income	ΔY
0	80	0	0	100	0
1	80	0	10	110	10
2	88	8	0	118	8
3	94.4	6.4	0	124.4	6.4
4	99.5	5.1	0	129.5	5.1
5	103.6	4.1	0	133.6	4.1
6	106.9	3.3	0	136.9	3.3
7	111.6	1.9	0	141.4	1.9
Total	120.0	0	0	150.0	0

(a) At each and every round of spending, withdrawals are occurring.
(b) Yes; a new level of 150. Injections have increased, causing income to rise.
(c) $1/(1 - MPC) = 5$
(d) The total change in savings will be 10, which is equal to the change in injections. Savings originally were 20, and hence the new level after the multiplier process will be 30.

2.

	ΔC	ΔW	ΔY
0	—	—	-5.0
1	-3.0	-2.0	-3.0
2	-1.8	-1.2	-1.8
3	-1.1	- .7	-1.1
4	- .7	- .3	- .7
5	- .4	- .3	- .4
6	- .2	- .2	- .2
Total	-7.5	-5.0	-12.5

multiplier = -12.5/-5.0 = 2.5 or 1/.4 = 2.5 or 1/5.0/12.5

3. (a)

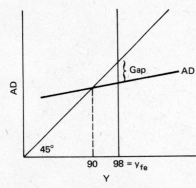

(b) multiplier = 1/.5 = 2
(c) deflationary aap = 4
(d) No; an increase in investment of 3.5 generates an increase in national income of only 7.
(e) yes (2 times $4 = $8)

CHAPTER 29
Multiple-Choice Questions

1. (c) 2. (c) 3. (c) 4. (a) 5. (b) 6. (b) 7. (c) 8. (c)

Exercises

1. (a) OH;LH/OH (b) KJ/OJ; OK; less (c) FG/OG; greater (d) C; constant; falling
   (e) KM; -EF
2. (a) 0.9 (b) 300 (c) falling (d) 3,000
3. (a) 0.54 (b) 0.46 (c) 2 (specifically 1/.46, or 2.17)

CHAPTER 30
Multiple-Choice Questions

1. (c) 2. (c) 3. (b) 4. (b) 5. (c) 6. (a) 7. (c) 8. (c) 9. (a) 10. (c)
11. (b) 12. (b)

Exercises

1.

Year	Units of Capital Needed	New Machines Required	Replacement Machines	Total Machines to Be Purchased
1	10	0	1	1
2	10	0	1	1
3	11	1	1	2
4	12	1	1	2
5	15	3	1	4
6	17	2	1	3
7	18	1	1	2
8	18	0	1	1

(a) 50 percent   (b) 300 percent

2.

Week	End of Week	Inventory/ Sales Ratio	Desired Inventory	Desired Inventory plus Expected Sales	Weekly Orders for Next Week
1	200	2	200	300	100
2	200	2	200	300	100
3	190	1.7	220	330	140
4	220	2	220	330	110
5	210	1.8	240	360	150
6	240	2	240	360	120
7	250	2.3	220	330	80
8	220	2	220	330	110
9	230	2.3	200	300	70

(a) 100; 120   (b) 70; 150

3. (a) At an interest of 14%, desired capital stock is 300. Because the economy has reached its desired level, investment is 0.
   (b) Desired capital stock is 400; therefore, desired investment is 400 - 300 = 100.
   (c) Only 60 units are possible.

CHAPTER 31
Multiple-Choice Questions

1. (c)   2. (a)   3. (d)   4. (b)   5. (a)   6. (d)   7. (c)   8. (c)   9. (d)

Exercises

1. (a) 400   (b) deficit; 50   (c) surplus; 25   (d) no
   (e) Shift T_n down (to $T_n = .2Y$ or to $T_n = -25 + .25Y$); raise G to 125, or a combination of two. (This implies the assumption that $X = M$ and $S = I$ continually so that equilibrium will require that $G = T_n$.)
2. (a) 300   (b) 100   (c) 50
   (d) The injection is multiplied by 2 by subsequent rounds of respending.
   (e) tax cut or increased government spending, or both
   (f) new AD = 200 + .5Y
3. (a) 25   (b) 15   (c) 10
4. (a) $55B   (b) A tax *reduction* of 2½B is required.   (c) A deficit will occur.

CHAPTER 32
Multiple-Choice Questions

1. (b) 2. (b) 3. (b) 4. (a) 5. (b)

CHAPTER 33
Multiple-Choice Questions

1. (b) 2. (c) 3. (d) 4. (a) 5. (c) 6. (c) 7. (a) 8. (d) 9. (b)

Exercises

1. 1. (b) 2. (c) 3. (a) 4. (d) or perhaps (c) 5. (a); and the rug serves the function (b)
2. $M_1 = 581 + 4,559 + 9,308$ $M_2 = 581 + 4,559 + 9,308 + 24,278 + 9,686$

CHAPTER 34
Multiple-Choice Questions

1. (d) 2. (a) 3. (b) 4. (d) 5. (d) 6. (b) 7. (a) 8. (d) 9. (a)

Exercises

1. $20; 5
   (b) Quantity theory: Extra cash balances will be spent on goods and services, and prices will rise until large cash balances are needed to handle the higher value to transactions. Modern theory: Extra cash will be spent on securities, raising their prices and lowering the rate of interest; the lower interest rate will stimulate investment spending and increase incomes, and also prices if at full employment.
2. (a) a (b) c (c) c (d) a; income (e) b
   (f) c; All increases in money supply are kept in cash balances rather than being made available to be borrowed, thus preventing interest rates from dropping to 2 percent.
3. (a) I_1 (b) I_2

CHAPTER 35
Multiple-Choice Questions

1. (c) 2. (b) 3. (d) 4. (a) 5. (b) 6. (b) 7. (d) 8. (b) 9. (b)

Exercises

1.

Currency in vaults	$ 60,000	Demand deposits	$5,000,000
Deposits in B of C	1,000,000	Notice deposits	1,000,000
Loans to public	4,000,000		
Security holdings	1,500,000		
Banking building and fixtures	360,000	Capital and surplus	920,000

2. (a) reserves +100; deposits +100 (b) reserves +10,000; securities -10,000
   (c) loans +5,000; deposits +5,000 (d) reserves +50,000; securities -50,000
   (e) loans -5,000; deposits -5,000 (f) total reserves unchanged; currency +5,000
   and reserve deposits with the Bank of Canada, -5,000
3. (a) Required reserves = $10,000. Bank A was loaned up.
   (b) deposits -1,000 to 99,000 and reserves -1,000 to -9,000
   (c) Required reserves = 9,900; actual reserves = 900; hence reserve deficiency = 900.
   (d) Bank A: reserves +900; loans -900. Bank B: reserves -900; deposits -900.
   (e) Bank A is loaned up, but Bank B has a deficiency of 810.
   (f) Bank B: reserves +810; loans -810. Bank C: reserves -810; deposits -810.
   (g) Bank B is loaned up, but Bank C has a deficiency of 729.
   (h) (-900 + -810 + -729) = -2439. Loans down by 1710.
   (i) 10,000; 9,000

CHAPTER 36
Multiple-Choice Questions

1. (c) 2. (c) 3. (d) 4. (a) 5. (d) 6. (b) 7. (d) 8. (b) 9. (a) 10. (a)

Exercises

1. Assets: (d), (e), (f) Liabilities: (a), (b), (c)

2. (a)

Bank of Canada		Banks	
Securities: +100	Bank reserves: +100	Reserves: +100	Deposits: +100

(b) $500 million

3. (a)

Banks		Bank of Canada	
Reserves:	Deposits: -5		
Securities: -5		no	change

(b)

Banks		Bank of Canada	
Reserves: +5	Deposits:	Securities: +5	Bank reserves: +5
Securities: -5			

(c) (b) is more expansionary, because reserves and deposits increase, permitting a further increase in loans and deposits if there are now excess reserves.

4. (a) Demand for cash directly reduces bank reserves.

All Banks		Bank of Canada	
Reserves: -50	Deposits: -50		Bank reserves: -50
			Bank of Canada notes outstanding: +50

(b) by open-market purchases of securities
(c) Cash will flow bank to banks, and the process will be reversed.
5. (a) $2.4 million (b) $4.8 million (c) 0
6. Sell bonds at a $93.46 price.
   (b) 8%
   (c) All interest rates would tend to increase to 8%, because individuals holding securities that people dump would fall, and hence their yield would increase.

CHAPTER 37
Multiple-Choice Questions

1. (b)   2. (d)   3. (c)   4. (d)   5. (b)   6. (a)   7. (d)   8. (d)   9. (c)   10. (c)

Exercises

1. buy; £255 million
2. (a) Exports could be subsidized.
   (b) Imports could be subject to new quotas or tariffs.
   (c) Tourist expenditures might be controlled by restricting pounds that could be
       taken abroad.
   (d) Interest rates could be raised to encourage dollar inflow.
   (e) Government expenditures could be reduced. If employment and income were reduced,
       imports would decline.
   (f) Taxes on investment in England could be reduced, on investment abroad increased.
3. current account: (b), (c), (d), (g), (j), (k), (l), (m)
   capital account: (a), (e), (h), (i)
   official reserve: (f)   balance-of-payments surplus of 777
4. (a) D curve shifts to right and up (because Canadian exports are up).
   (b) D curve shifts to left and down and possibly S curve shifts to right. Less capital
       coming into Canada and more capital leaving Canada.
   (c) D curve shifts to right (because Canadian exports increase).
   (d) D curve shifts to left and S curve shifts to right (fewer exports and more im-
       ports).
   (e) S curve shifts to left (fewer imports into Canada).
   price effect: (a) +   (b) -   (c) +   (d) -   (e) +

CHAPTER 38
Multiple-Choice Questions

1. (d)   2. (a)   3. (b)   4. (a)   5. (d)   6. (d)   7. (c)   8. (a)

Exercises

1. (a) If L specialized in grapes and A in wool, 100,000 kilos of wool and 100,000 kilos
       of grapes would be available for consumption, greater than the present total of
       100,000 wool and 75,000 grapes. A possible exchange would be 50,000 of A's wool
       for 35,000 or L's grapes. Both countries would have more grapes to consume.
   (b) A, wool; L, grapes   (c) A, 2; L, 1; terms—1:1 to 2:1
2. (a) A   (b) B   (c) dairy products, watches   (d) 100, 200
3. (a) 99.1; 1970   (b) more; 99.1; 104.1

CHAPTER 39
Multiple-Choice Questions

1. (a)   2. (d)   3. (c)   4. (d)   5. (c)   6. (c)   7. (d)   8. (c)   9. (d)   10. (b)

Exercise

   (a) When opportunity cost ratios differ, both partners can have more goods by trade.
   (b) Dollars abroad represent purchasing power for Canadian goods just as dollars at
       home do.

(c) Cheaper imports mean more goods for Canadian workers.
(d) Whether tariffs remain or not, the real costs of production and thus resources required have been reduced as the infant industry developed.
(e) Imports are the only way in which resources used for exports can be recovered.

CHAPTER 40
Multiple-Choice Questions

1. (b)   2. (d)   3. (b)   4. (c)   5. (d)   6. (d)   7. (c)   8. (c)   9. (d)

Exercise

(a) A chronic deficit, and one that is worsening, raises the spectre that the Canadian government may have to devalue the Canadian dollar. This would raise the price of imports, and hence an importer, anticipating this, may try to arrange future purchases at present fixed prices regardless of the change in the exchange rate.
(b) Purchase U.S. dollars in the foreign-exchange market. If the speculator anticipates a devaluation of the Canadian dollar, it means that, if he is holding U.S. dollars, he will, after the devaluation, be able to sell them for more Canadian dollars than he paid to acquire them.
(c) Worsen conditions. The selling of Canadian dollars to acquire U.S. dollars would bring further downward pressure on the Canadian dollar.

CHAPTER 41
Multiple-Choice Questions

1. (d)   2. (b)   3. (a)   4. (a)   5. (c)   6. (d)   7. (a)

Exercise

1. K   2. M   3. M   4. K   5. K   6. M   7. M   8. K

CHAPTER 42
Multiple-Choice Questions

1. (d)   2. (d)   3. (b)   4. (a)   5. (b)   6. (c)   7. (d)   8. (d)   9. (b)   10. (b)
11. (d)   12. (a)   13. (a)   14. (b)   15. (c)

Exercises

1.

Hourly Payroll	Unit Labour Cost	Total Hourly Output	Total Hourly Revenue
$200	$.20	1,000	1,000
206	.196	1,050	1,050

(a) more; profits increased by $44
(b) no apparent reason that it should
(c) The price would fall.
(d) yes; yes

2. (a)

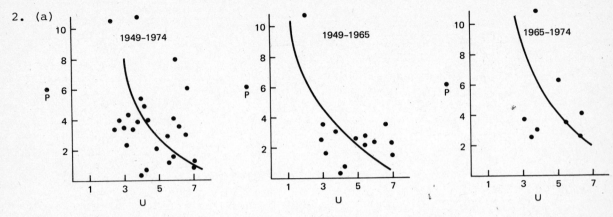

(b) In all three cases, it is impossible to draw a smooth line through all the points. In fact, you will see that whatever reasonable attempt you make, there will be points above and below the line. The one main difference that is visible is that a hand-fitted line for 1965-1974 lies above those drawn for 1949-1974 and below that for 1949-1965.

(c) In simple plotting like this, using annual data can be deceiving. First, price and unemployment relationships may involve lags measured in quarterly year periods. Second, structural changes in the economy and the impact of external forces may change the position of the gradeoff (if it exists) over time. Hence, long-term observations on annual data may not be very reliable in terms of establishing a short-run tradeoff.

(d) The data would suggest that the tradeoff has "shifted" over the postwar period such that a higher rate of inflation has in recent years been associated with a given rate of unemployment.

3. (a) cause a deficit on current account as higher incomes stimulate imports
   (b) cause a deficit as the lower interest rate would reduce the inflow of foreign capital
   (c) reduce investment and employment
   (d) encourage exports and possibly lead to demand inflation

CHAPTER 43
Multiple-Choice Questions

1. (c)   2. (a)   3. (a)   4. (b)   5. (c)   6. (d)   7. (a)   8. (b)   9. (b)

Exercise

(a) 4 percent   (b) 3 percent   (c) 18   (d) 24

CHAPTER 44
Multiple-Choice Questions

1. (d)   2. (b)   3. (d)   4. (b)   5. (c)   6. (d)   7. (d)   8. (d)   9. (d)

Exercises

1.

	Country A	Country B	Difference
Year X	$2,000	$100	$1,900
Year X + 1	2,060	103	1,957
Year X + 23	4,000	200	3,800

2. (a) 18; 24; 72 (b) 3 percent

CHAPTER 45
Multiple-Choice Questions

1. (d) 2. (a) 3. (c) 4. (c) 5. (b) 6. (a) 7. (b) 8. (d) 9. (c) 10. (d)
11. (b) 12. (c) 13. (a)